Washing

A SMITHSONIAN BOOK OF THE NATION'S CAPITAL

ton, D.C.

Smithsonian Books
Washington, D.C., MCMXCII

©1992 Smithsonian Institution
All rights reserved. No part of this book may be reproduced or utilized in any form or by any means, electronic or mechanical, including photocopying, recording, or by any information storage and retrieval system, without permission in writing from the publisher.

LIBRARY OF CONGRESS
CATALOGING-IN-PUBLICATION DATA
Washington, D.C. : a Smithsonian book of the nation's capital.
         p.   cm.
         Includes index.
         ISBN 0-89599-032-6
         1. Washington (D.C.)—History. 2. Washington (D.C.)—Buildings, structures, etc.   I. Smithsonian Institution.
F194.W35   1992
975.3—dc20   92-17647
                         CIP
Manufactured in the United States of America
First Edition
10 9 8 7 6 5 4 3 2 1

Page One: Peering between pillars of the Lincoln Memorial, one sees the Washington Monument and the United States Capitol along the axis of the National Mall; *opposite:* a mural by Betty Calomiris captures the ebb and flow of everyday life in the District of Columbia; *pages 8-9:* Francis Scott Key Bridge at Georgetown and the Washington Monument on the Mall punctuate a sylvan vista along the Potomac River's approach to the District of Columbia; *pages 64-65:* tulips glow in early springtime near the Jefferson Memorial and the flowering-cherry trees at the Potomac's Tidal Basin; *pages 118-119:* the East Building of the National Gallery of Art soars on the Mall at the base of Capitol Hill; *pages 190-191:* turrets of the Smithsonian's Arts and Industries Building grace the south side of the Mall. The clock tower of the "Castle" rises at far left.

Contents

A Sleepy Southern Town

A Tale of Two Rivers

JOHN F. ROSS

FLY EAST FROM CHICAGO FOR A LANDING AT NATIONAL AIRPORT, WASHINGTON'S

CLOSE-IN GATEWAY. DURING ITS DESCENT, YOUR JET WILL SHADOW THE POTOMAC

RIVER FOR SEVERAL MILES, GLINTING HIGH ABOVE THE WHITE WATER OF LITTLE

FALLS, THEN THE BUSTLING CROWDS OF

GEORGETOWN, AND FINALLY THE TRANQUIL,

GREEN COVER OF THEODORE ROOSEVELT

ISLAND. AS YOU TURN ONTO FINAL APPROACH,

THE CONFLUENCE OF TWO RIVERS BECOMES

CLEARLY VISIBLE. THE POTOMAC AND THE ANACOSTIA SEEM TO HOLD THE CITY

IN THEIR GENTLE GRASP, LIKE A KITE RESTING IN THE CROOK OF A TREE.

★ ★ ★ ★

Geology and history con-
spired to fashion a site for
Washington, the District of
Columbia; here Southern
states meet Northern, here
the Atlantic coastal plain
meets Appalachian uplands,
all at the junction of the
wide Potomac estuary with
the short Anacostia River.
Above right, Great Falls
cascades just west of
Washington.

Dinosaurs once roamed where the nation's capital now rises. These, *Pleurocoelus*, ranged the Cretaceous forest of 110 million years ago.

From such a vantage, it's easy to see how much these two rivers dominate the capital city. Yet such a glance only hints at the whole story. Across the ages, these rivers and their tributaries have formed the topography of this hallowed site: swelled by glacial melt, then drained, then swelled again during the Ice Ages, these waters dropped gravel and other sediments to form the natural terraces upon which our city is built. Yet in the past few centuries, they have received not only our reverence, but our scorn; our admiration, and also our neglect. But that is the white man's story; the Native Americans posed little threat to land and waters.

Indian traces reach back at least 6,000 years. When the first Europeans arrived, these crystal waters, chockfull of schooling shad and herring and 10-foot-long sturgeon, supported populous villages of woodland tribes. To George Washington, the surveyor-turned-first-President, the two rivers were central to a strategy for making the

District a major port and center of commerce, perhaps even the nation's greatest metropolis, a political and economic wedding ring to bind the divergent states into a more perfect Union. In fact, the brisk international commerce in tobacco, trafficked along the water highways of the Potomac and Anacostia, jumpstarted the early economies of Georgetown and Bladensburg.

Today, commerce in Washington no longer depends on agriculture and bumper crops of tobacco; instead it revolves around the less tangible but no less real commodities of power and influence. The importance of the rivers appears now to lie in their enduring worth, rather than in their value for economic extraction. The rivers are seen as ecological treasures that must be safeguarded, yet are accessible to all.

Weekend warriors of the late-20th century head to Mather Gorge on the Potomac to battle waves in impossibly tiny boats of Fiberglas and Kevlar. Fishermen angle for sunnies on the

Anacostia, whiling away the dog days of summer. And, in the evenings, tuxedoed theater-goers savor an intermission break on the terrace of the John F. Kennedy Center for the Performing Arts by basking in the moonlight as it dances on the wave tips of the Potomac.

The Potomac and Anacostia rivers couldn't be more different if they were characters in a novel by Charles Dickens. If he had included them in one of his stories, the Potomac would be a thin and wiry gentleman

provinces—the piedmont plateau and the Atlantic coastal plain—meet with significant results for the history of the area. The Potomac is born from the Appalachian Mountains, its waters flowing southeast over the rolling hills that separate the mountains from the sea. Geologists call this area the piedmont, literally the "foot of the mountain." Along the Potomac's shores above Washington are rocky outcrops of granite, gneiss, and schist that underlie the piedmont plateau. These are 400- to 600- million-year-old metamorphic rocks created deep within the Earth by the searing heat and millions of tons of pressure that were brought to bear when the continents were emerging. They form a hard and solid bedrock that runs near the surface in Northwest Washington. Several years ago, when engineers were building the red line of Metrorail, the area's subway system, between Dupont Circle and Woodley Park, they needed high explosives to blast holes in the bedrock and form the tunnel that would later shuttle commuters and tourists.

with a penchant for telling dramatic tales. The river curls and twists 287 miles southeast from a point about 15 miles below Cumberland, Maryland, where its two headwaters meet. On its way toward Washington, it crashes through a series of rapids, the largest of which, Great Falls, drops about 35 feet in a single cataract. The Potomac drains the entire area, fed by its tributaries in the north, the Anacostia River and Rock Creek, and by Difficult Run, Pimmit Run, Holmes Run, and Accotink Creek in the south.

The Anacostia River would be a rotund and short Dickensian character, the Potomac's younger brother. Slow and muddy, flat and broad, the Anacostia, known as Eastern Branch until 1927, runs a short, straight, and southwesterly course. It drains the flat Atlantic coastal plain, the low-lying, Eastern-tidewater region, cutting easily through the sand, gravel, and clay that compose its banks. When the rivers join below Washington, they make their way south, joining other rivers to feed the Chesapeake Bay, which eventually drains into the Atlantic Ocean.

In the character of each river lie clues to the distinctive geologic make-up of Washington, a region where two vastly different geologic

Applying the same technique to the Metro's green line in the city's Southeast would have been disastrous. No hard rocks line the banks of the slow-flowing Anacostia River. Instead, bedrock retreats deep beneath the sediment, unconsolidated strata that contain varying amounts of sand, gravel, and clay. Here, engineers used large backhoes to dig the tunnel in the loose material, which over the last 100 million years has been deposited layer

When not enjoying the outdoors, John F. Ross, a native Washingtonian, spends his time writing for print and television on subjects of natural history, science, and history. He lives with his wife and two children in Chevy Chase, Maryland.

after layer—earlier by the rise and fall of ancient seas, and, more recently, by the rise and fall of the Potomac, the Anacostia, and their tributaries during the Ice Ages.

Ingenious as ever, people used deposits from both geologies to build the city. With the hard rocks of the piedmont, they secured the foundations of some of Washington's most prominent buildings: the Capitol, the White House, and the Washington Monument. The Uptown movie theater on the west side of Connecticut Avenue in Northwest Washington hides the remains of an important old quarry for such rock.

The clay found along and near the Anacostia was made into bricks, which helped to build Georgetown. An old brick works still stands on the grounds of the National Arboretum, off New York Avenue, near the banks of the Anacostia. Washington was red brick before it was white marble.

The hard stone of the piedmont meets the soft, often rotten rock of the coastal plain at a junction known as the fall line, which is actually more of a zone, sometimes measuring as much as five miles wide. The rocks of the piedmont do not end abruptly here, but drop quickly—at 125 feet a mile—toward the sea. The coastal-plain sediments lie atop this geologic sliding board.

The fall line itself runs all along the mid-Atlantic seaboard, roughly paralleling the Appalachians, and bisects Washington across a northeast and southwest axis—from Theodore Roosevelt Island to the junction of Florida and Connecticut avenues, then again up 16th Street near Silver Spring, Maryland. The rolling hills of Northwest Washington belong to the piedmont geology, while most of the city, including Capitol Hill and Anacostia, occupies the coastal plain. The hilly, difficult-to-farm topography of the city's Northwest section accounts for its delayed development.

The fall line is not visible except where it crosses a river—the Potomac, in the case of Washington. (The Anacostia never crosses the fall line, remaining entirely in the Atlantic coastal plain.) As a river passes from the hard rock of the piedmont to the soft, more easily eroded rocks of the coastal plain, rapids and waterfalls occur, which is why the fall line was so named.

The Potomac crosses the fall line between Little Falls and Theodore Roosevelt Island. The river narrows and drops, and then widens into the coastal plain, becoming the Potomac familiar to most residents and to tourists, who mostly see it from such sites as the Lincoln Memorial or the Kennedy Center.

It was no accident that Washington was built at the intersection of the Potomac and the fall line, nor that Indians were attracted to this spot long before the coming of the Europeans. Indians as well as Europeans found that the fall line, with its varied geologies, fostered a number of different micro-environments, which in turn supported a wide variety of plants and animals. In fact, most paleo-Indian sites in the East are either on or near a fall line for many of the reasons that were later to interest the Europeans. Fall lines in general afford easy river crossings, good fishing, and a natural setting for commerce.

For later Americans, fall lines became obvious locations for the first north-south post roads, and also served as the farthest inland ports for deep-draft, ocean-going ships. Here, also, abundant power from falling water fostered such useful enterprises as flour milling. Locally, the early

fall-line towns of Alexandria and Georgetown, on the Potomac, and Bladensburg, on the Anacostia, all started off as ports for seagoing vessels under sail. In fact, most major towns from Trenton, New Jersey, south to Macon, Georgia, are located on or near the fall line for precisely these reasons.

None of the built-in advantages of the fall line were apparent to the first known visiting European, Captain John Smith, who used the Potomac as a highway of exploration in 1608. In fact, the fall line on the Potomac probably convinced Smith and his small band of adventurers to turn their boats around at what is today called Little Falls. It was a quest for gold, the vision of an East-Coast Eldorado, that lured Smith and his men away from Jamestown, the early, ill-fated colony in Virginia.

However, in terms of shiny minerals, Smith found only the glitter of worthless mica flakes in the mud along the swampy green banks of the Potomac. But he also found Indians. What a sight this meeting of two worlds must have presented. Even though Smith did not write of his travels until 16 years later, his recollection of the Indians glows with intensity. They were "so strangely painted, grimed, and disguised, shouting, yelling and crying as so many spirits from hell could not have shewed more terrible." He observed that they painted themselves with a black substance that made them look like "Blackmoores dusted over with silver." In the end he reached some kind of conciliation with them, but he harvested no gold.

He could have, had he looked closer. In fact, gold veins rise to the surface near the very spot where Smith and his company landed. Ironically, the remains of a

★ ★ ★ ★ ★

A map from 1792 grossly exaggerates the import of built-up areas, the gridirons of crossed streets. Names like Mount Pleasant, Beall's Levels, and Duddington Pasture impart the proper rural ambiance. The District of Columbia site was virtually in young George Washington's front yard when he was a surveyor, top.

★ ★ ★ ★ ★

Mason's mark, above, appears on a hewn stone from a canal near Great Falls that predates the Chesapeake and Ohio Canal from 1853, right. George Washington imagined that such flatboats would bring wealth to his namesake city, but, instead, roads and undreamed-of rail- and airways emerged to carry the bulk of the capital's cargo.

gold mine are still visible on the road leading into the Maryland side of Great Falls National Park; and flakes of gold can be sifted out of such Maryland suburbs as Potomac, Bethesda, Kensington, and Rockville, the last of which is named for early ore-crushing operations during the region's many mini-gold rushes. Nearby Virginia sports thousands of Colonial-era gold prospects all along the fall line. In fact, from Maine to Alabama, right along the geologically active fall line, prospectors extracted nuggets and dust before the epic California find of 1848.

With regard to Native Americans, far too little is known about the pre-European inhabitants of our would-be Gold Coast. In the District of Columbia today, thousands of buildings and houses and miles of streets and pavement continue to prevent archaeologists from plumbing the earth for clues. Eyewitness accounts and some extant drawings reveal a mélange of Algonquian-speaking tribes who resided here, often banded into loose confederations after several centuries of warfare. To the west of the fall line were Iroquoian and Siouan tribes; to the east, the Conoys, the Patawomeke (after which the Potomac is named), and others. A large confederation of tribes spreading south from the Potomac was banded under the leadership of Powhatan, father of Pocahontas. European imports of guns and whiskey, religion, and concepts of land ownership irrevocably disrupted the Indian cultures.

William Henry Holmes, a prominent Smithsonian anthropologist at the turn of the century, performed the most comprehensive study of Indian life in the area to date. "So numerous indeed are [the remains] in certain localities," he wrote, "that they are brought in with every load of gravel from the creek beds, and the laborer who sits by the wayside breaking bowlders [sic] for our streets each year

passes them by the thousands beneath his hammer; and it is literally true that this city, the capital of a civilized nation, is paved with the art remains of a race who occupied its site in the shadowy past."

One glimpse from the shadows comes from a map—the first one published of the area— that John Smith drew as a result of his travels. It records Indian settlements on both sides of the Potomac, two of which were located within the confines of present-day Washington: an unnamed fishing village below Little Falls and the Necostin village of Nacochtanke on the east bank of the Anacostia. The latter village now is covered for the most part by Bolling Air Force Base and a power plant. Smith calculated that Nacochtanke was inhabited by 300 people, including 80 warriors. Information about the village remains scarce, but, if it was like other woodland villages, the Necostins probably lived in small wooden dwellings scattered near agricultural fields. The chief's house and the village's religious structures may have been protected by wooden palisades.

The name Anacostia comes from a continuing corruption of the Indian word Nacochtanke, first into Latin, then from Latin to Elizabethan English. A general translation seems to be "town of traders." Nacochtanke was probably a major trading center, perhaps in part due to the richness of natural resources. (Smith reports "sporting himselfe" at ebb tide on the Anacostia by spearing fish to the river bottom with his sword.)

Henry Fleet, an intrepid young fur trader who lived among the Indians for five years after an Indian ambush wiped out his expedition, remembered seeing hundreds of Indians gathering in the area to trade animal hides and other wares. Fleet and others joined in a 17th-century rush for beaver pelts, stimulated by a fashion craze for fur-felt hats back in Europe. The trade in skins aggravated an already violent social environment among the tribes.

For what probably was a long time, local Indians mined soapstone from the banks of Rock Creek and carved it into oblong and round vessels, small cups, pipes, and other tools, some of which are on display at the Smithsonian. Old Indian quarry sites are still visible—although the soapstone itself is not—along Soapstone Run, which drains into Rock Creek Park near the University of the District of Columbia. One of the few remaining outcroppings of soapstone is to be found in Fort Bayard Park, at the corner of River Road and Western Avenue.

It's difficult to know what clues to the ancient Indian past are underfoot wherever one stands in Washington. In the dirt excavated in the construction of the White House swimming pool, for instance, archaeologists found stone projectile points, chips, and flakes of Indian manufacture, as well as potsherds.

Of course, one can find clues to an even more ancient and mysterious past beneath Washington's earth. In 1942, while digging the hole for the McMillan Reservoir near the Shrine of the Immaculate Conception, surprised workers pulled out the leg bone of a brachiosaurid, an immense, four-footed, plant-eating dinosaur. Almost 50 years earlier, men digging a sewer on Capitol Hill came upon a large vertebra and bone fragments of a two-legged, meat-eating dinosaur, probably *Dryptosaurus*. Recent finds in adjacent Prince George's County suggest that dinosaurs were active in the D.C. area in the Mesozoic era 250 million to 65 million years ago, though not to the degree found out west. Dinosaurs

roamed about in a steamy, hot climate no doubt similar to August in Washington today.

In 1923, another souvenir from antiquity sparked interest. While digging the basement for the Walker Hotel, which today is the Mayflower Hotel, at Connecticut Avenue and DeSalles Street, workers found fibrous and unpetrified cypress stumps, some of which measured more than eight feet in diameter. The most recent analysis suggests that the cypress swamp in which these trees lived was 100,000 years old, dating back to about the time when modern people began to emerge in the Middle East and Europe. This cypress swamp probably extended as far west as Washington Circle, near George Washington University. And petrified wood from earlier eras has emerged also, with a fossilized palm trunk having come to light on Capitol Hill.

The most likely explanation for the demise of the cedar swamp was a shift in water levels and temperatures during one of the periods of Ice Age glaciation, the same factors that caused the formation of the gravel terraces upon which the District is built today.

Yet perhaps the strangest and even the saddest of all relics lying hidden beneath the surface of this metropolis are the dozens of creeks, streams, and springs that once laced the city. Gone, for example, are Tiber Creek, Slash Run, and St. James Creek, waterways that were relegated to underground sewers once their waters grew polluted or builders coveted the land through which they flowed. Even Presidents once swam in the Tiber, a creek that flowed south to the Capitol and then west along what are today Constitution Avenue and the Mall to

Washington has a well deserved reputation for being fun and free, a town reveling in stylish sport, spirited show-off, and humane conversation at garden get-togethers. At left, Georgetown crews slice Potomac swells at dawn, near Francis Scott Key Bridge. Above, Morgan Dancers, famous in 1923, leap at a downtown sandy beach, now built over.

spill into the Potomac at 17th and Constitution. Other District residents swam there, too, in swimming holes known as "Blue Cork" and "Piggory" that were located between F and H streets. Shad, herring, eels, and catfish were caught as far upstream as the Capitol.

But the refuse of fishmongers and others turned the meandering Tiber into an open sewer, straightjacketed it into a canal, and, finally, buried it. Nothing remains on the surface: the brick sewer runs beneath the Rayburn Office Building on a redirected course to the Anacostia.

So, too, was St. James Creek extinguished, water that once drained the area south of the Capitol into the Anacostia. Today it runs silently beneath Canal Street. Even Rock Creek almost succumbed, so polluted were its banks with ash and refuse. It's easy to forget that during Colonial times Rock Creek was so large that ocean-going ships could travel upstream as far as P Street, and that the point at which Rock Creek met the Potomac served as a busy harbor. There are no obituaries or monuments to these waterways, which nature took hundreds of thousands of years to create but humans obliterated in the course of several generations.

Were we to travel back in time to Colonial days, the number of streams and creeks in this area would astound us. But perhaps more surprising would be the vast expanses of the Potomac and Anacostia, which today are mere shadows of their former selves. Seafaring vessels once headed up the Anacostia one and a half miles to the busy seaport of Bladensburg. Water lapped at what is today 17th and Constitution, and ships sailed up into a large bay where the Tiber spilled into the Potomac.

The clearing of fields for agriculture and settlement, along with run-off from construction projects, speeded the natural sedimentation process along both rivers. Despite repeated dredging, Bladensburg, once a major port, was closed to large ships by the early-19th century. Meanwhile, the building of bridges across the Potomac gradually slowed its waters, permitting sediments to build up quickly.

In 1870, more than 300 acres of tidal flats were situated on the east side of the Potomac. Dubbed the "Potomac Flats," they were exposed during low tide and smelled of Washington sewage. In 1892, Congress voted to reclaim the tidal flats and to rid the city of this potential health hazard by filling wetlands with sediment dredged from the channel. Where once there was water, now there was land. The great saga of the emergence of Washington, D.C., up from the swamps, built high upon broad shoulders of fill dirt, will unfold later in our adventure.

Pierre L'Enfant's thoughts as he first pondered his plans for Washington, D.C., have eluded the historical record. Perhaps he stood on Jenkins Hill, now Capitol Hill, looking west, down where the Mall would be, wondering how a new, sparkling city, a city that was to become the most important in the world, might look. His grand plans could not help but be shaped fundamentally by those two magnificent rivers that have exercised such a profound influence on the region for the past million years. ★

Washington City

Thomas H. Wolf

THE FEDERAL CITY OF WASHINGTON IS UNLIKE ANY OTHER CITY IN THE WORLD. THERE WAS NEITHER A COMMERCIAL NOR A MILITARY REASON FOR ITS CHOICE AS THE CAPITAL OF THE UNITED STATES, AND FOR MANY OF ITS 200 YEARS IT HAS REMAINED MORE AN IDEA THAN A REALITY. IN THE BEGINNING, MOST AMERICANS IMAGINED THAT IT MUST BE LIKE THE GREAT CAPITAL CITIES OF THE LANDS FROM WHICH THEY CAME— LONDON OR PARIS, ROME OR VIENNA.

OH, WASHINGTON WAS FINE IF YOU WERE A SPORTSMAN: YOU COULD SHOOT GAME WITHIN SITE OF THE "CONGRESS HOUSE," AND WHENEVER THE TIDE WAS UP IN THE POTOMAC, YOU COULD CATCH A MESS OF YOUR FAVORITE FISH IN THE SWAMPS RIGHT BEHIND THE "PRESIDENT'S PALACE."

★ ★ ★ ★ ★

From 1832, Thomas Doughty's drawing shows the west front of the U.S. Capitol as seen from City Hall at the base of Jenkins Hill. Above right, cast-aluminum lions guard the front doors of the Justice Department.

21

An early watercolor by the artist William R. Birch depicts the original Senate wing, completed in 1800.

However, for the 32 Senators and 106 members of Congress who arrived in the fall of 1800, along with the approximately 131 federal employees—two of them women—it was no place to live. As Secretary of the Treasury Albert Gallatin would write that winter: "Our local situation is far from being pleasant or even convenient. Around the Capitol are seven or eight boarding houses, one tailor, one shoemaker, one printer, a washing woman, a grocery shop, a pamphlets and stationery shop, a small dry goods shop, and an oyster house. This makes the whole of the federal city connected with the Capitol." No streets were paved, and animals roamed everywhere.

Things were no better a mile and a half away at the President's Palace. "Not one room or chamber is finished of the whole," First Lady Abigail Adams wrote her daughter. "It is habitable by fires in every part, thirteen of which we are obliged to keep daily, or sleep in wet and damp places." And the living conditions did not improve quickly.

It would take almost two centuries and half a dozen wars before Washington would become an important city, would become, in fact, the most important city not just of its nation, but of the entire world. What happened there would affect people in the farthest corners of the Earth. Just how this "wild wilderness" founded on the edge of a marshy hollow became so important is what, in part, this book is all about.

Only after one of the longest and most acrimonious debates of the first session of the First Congress was President George Washington instructed to select a site "on the river Potomac" somewhere between the

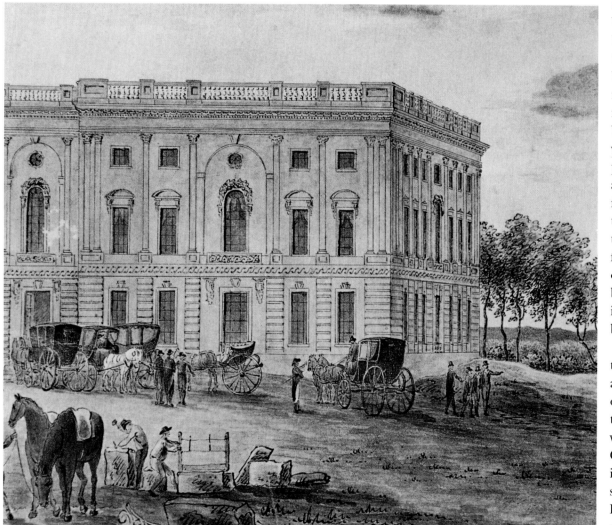

After working for half a century as a print and television journalist in New York, Thomas H. Wolf moved to Washington in 1981. He would never live anywhere else in the world.

Eastern Branch, as the Anacostia River was called, and Conococheague Creek, about 40 miles upstream. Washington had surveyed the country to the west and believed that a canal could be built to join the Monongahela River at Fort Pitt, some 341 miles away, thus enabling a capital on the Potomac to become a great trading center with the vast territories on the other side of the Alleghenies.

It did not take Washington long to choose for the new city the area that encompassed both George Town—as it was then written—and Alexandria, each a thriving port city. By January of 1791 the site of the Territory of Columbia—100 square miles, 69 of them ceded by Maryland and 31 by Virginia—was being staked out by Andrew Ellicott and his assistant, Benjamin Banneker, a free black man. To lay out the capital city the President turned to a gifted French artist-architect whom he called "Langfang" (many announcers on the "Metro," Washington's modern subway, still do). The architect called himself Pierre Charles L'Enfant. At the heart of his plan was the selection of two high spots—Jenkins Hill ("a pedestal waiting for a monument") for the "Congress House" and a second hill a mile and a half away for the "President's Palace"—to be connected in a straight line by a grand avenue 160 feet wide. Pennsylvania Avenue, as this thoroughfare was to be called, would remain a straight line until 1840, when an addition to the Treasury Building extending down 15th Street effectively blocked the avenue.

L'Enfant laid out plans for land stretching only 25 blocks from the Capitol, not the entire District, which at that time embraced five separate jurisdictions: the city and county of Alexandria, Virginia; the city and county of Washington; and the city of George Town, many of whose citizens looked down their noses at Washington. More than five decades later Alexandria, believing that it had gained nothing economically and in fact had lost politically from its association with the nation's capital, would take back its land and leave the District. The governing of the new Territory of Columbia was set out in Article One, Section Eight of the Constitution: "Congress shall have the power. . . to exercise exclusive legislation in all cases whatsoever. . . ." In their wisdom, the framers of the Constitution gave the President the power to appoint the District's chief executive, a mayor. For three-quarters of a century District residents had some electoral power, but to this day they still have never had the right to elect a voting member in the Congress of the nation whose revolution was fought and independence won over the issue of taxation without representation.

In the city's early days the lack of representation may have seemed less burdensome than the lack of amenities, which was partially offset by an

★ ★ ★ ★ ★

The British burn down key sites in the nation's capital. This engraving, published in America by G. Thompson in October 1814, represents scenes from that brief invasion, which culminated on August 24, 1814.

equal lack of formality. First Ladies, for example, called on important newcomers to town. And, according to Christian Hines, an early resident of the District, Presidents were to be seen all over the District, traveling without retinue. President Jefferson, "in particular, was fond of being wherever any improvements were going on," he recalled. Hines also remembered seeing President John Adams passing buckets of water in a fire line. While Congress was in session—six weeks at first, then ten—almost anyone, even visitors, could turn up for food and strong drink in the President's "drawing rooms" every other Wednesday evening.

From the start Washington was a man's town. The first members of Congress did not think the boarding houses suitable abodes for their families. Indeed, a major source of District troubles for years was that so many of its inhabitants considered themselves only temporary residents. As a result, they cared little whether the town prospered or went under. The Wednesday bashes at the President's aside, there was little to do. There were two Christian churches: St. Patrick's had opened it doors in 1792 and Christ Episcopal Church, near the Navy Yard, in 1806. Congress ordered the Marine Band to perform weekly at the Capitol, but the music left much to be desired. (Thomas Jefferson, a violinist, found

★ ★ ★ ★ ★

An armed camp during the Civil War, Washington included such recuperation centers for wounded soldiers as Lincoln Hospital, here depicted in a work by Charles Magnus in 1864.

the brass so jarring that he arranged for 18 musicians to be imported from Italy.) In a man's town, men's preferences prevailed—gambling, drinking, and sports, of which cockfighting and horse racing were the favorites.

One reason that Congress had decided upon the proposed Potomac site was that, being inland, it would be difficult for an enemy to reach should war one day come. When it did, during the War of 1812, Secretary of War John Armstrong proclaimed that with Baltimore within reach the Redcoats would not bother to invade "the sheep walk" on the Potomac. As it

★ ★ ★ ★ ★

Pillars rise at the Capitol in 1857 for the current dome. Soon the Civil War intervened, but construction continued, Lincoln's symbol of an enduring Union. Both inner and outer domes, the ones we see today, were assembled from cast iron, rather than stone.

turned out, of course, the Brits did get to Baltimore—and we got a national anthem—but not before they had sailed up the Potomac, laid waste to Fort Washington (which had been built to make the national capital impregnable from the sea), and burned down much of the young city, including the Capitol and the White House.

War always has played a major role in the history of Washington. The War of 1812 was certainly no exception, although there are two ways of considering the devastation it caused: on the one hand, Benjamin Latrobe, the man most responsible for bringing the classical style to

Washington's buildings, thought that "a great[er] benefit could not have accrued to this city than the destruction of its principal buildings by the British"; on the other, the mess that the British left behind was such that "it was feared that the seat of Government would be removed from Washington." In fact, Congress, many of whose members believed that anywhere else would be a vast improvement, came within a handful of votes of doing just that.

It's difficult today to envision just how primitive life was in the Territory of Columbia for most of its first half-century. Cows and horses were stabled in the domestic-service wing of President James Monroe's White House. James Sterling Young, writing about Washington during the early 1800s, tells of Congressmen getting lost on their way home from a dinner party and spending "until daybreak in their carriage weaving through bogs and gullies in search of Capitol Hill, only a mile away." And, in 1840, the Chevalier de Bacourt wrote that "the nights are so noisy that one can scarcely sleep. There is a continual uproar, the reason for which is that the inhabitants all own cows and pigs, but no stables, and these animals wander about all day and all night. . . . The nocturnal wanderings of these beasts create an infernal racket in which they are joined by dogs and cats."

Spring water was not pumped into the White House until 1833. Hot water and gaslight, which had brightened the streets of Boston and Baltimore as early as 1817, didn't reach Washington until 1848, and there were few hotels in which there was any privacy. Guests sometimes had to double up in bed. While visiting the capital in the 1840s, Charles Dickens described the city's leading features thus: "Spacious avenues that begin in nothing, and lead nowhere; streets, mile-long, that only want houses, roads, and inhabitants; public buildings that need but a public to be complete; and ornaments of great thoroughfares, which only lack great thoroughfares to ornament. . . ." And things did not get better fast. "My God, what

have I done to be condemned to live in such a city?" cried a French diplomat just before the Civil War.

None of this seemed to affect life at the top of the white pyramid in what was then and would remain for more than a century a Southern city—or, more accurately, a Southern town. Margaret Bayard Smith, wife of the editor of the National Intelligencer, remembered the 1850s this way: "Last week I went in to pay some necessary visits and dined at Mrs. Thornton's. After dinner I sent for Brother . . . I took him with me to Mrs. Johnson's. The next evening I was engaged at a large and splendid party at Mr. Wirt's . . . The next evening I went in, Ann with me and Mrs. C. and party waited until near 8 for brother. As he did not come, she told me I had best call for him at the President's where he dined. Mrs. Barbour asked me and all the family, brother included, to spend the next day socially with her and pass the evening. She always receives company on Saturday evening. We agreed. Being engaged early in the evening at Mrs. Rush's, brother left us when we rose from table and we ladies retired to dress for the evening. . . . We passed really a merry hour or two during the unceremonious ceremony of dressing. . . . Thus passed another most agreeable evening. We returned home, all of us in fine spirits. If I could, I would have gone on Wednesday to Mrs. Clay's drawing room, but Mr. Smith had an engagement in the city, and I gave it up."

Perhaps one reason for so much partying was the general unavailability of culture. Stagecoaches moved slowly and people did not want to travel, which made for a provincial city. The Smithsonian Castle aside, there were no museums before the

A big gun at Fort Gaines helps guard Washington, D.C., from Confederate attack. The city's ring of defense during the Civil War included 193 such fortifications.

26

Civil War. Carusi's Assembly Rooms was the city's best known place of entertainment. The Library of Congress was available to all, but Congress did not consider education a function of government. In fact, in 1860, when 78 percent of the children in some Northern cities were enrolled in schools, only 29 percent of Washington's white children of school age were enrolled. African-American children were excluded from public schooling until 1862, when Congress finally voted to require three months a year of formal education for every child. Times would change. After the First World War, Dunbar High School, whose faculty consisted of many superbly qualified blacks who had been unable to get teaching posts at white institutions, offered black youngsters an education equal to that at any white high school. And in 1867 Howard

University, surely the premier educational institution for blacks in America, was founded.

Life in general for African-Americans in pre-Civil-War Washington, however, was not much fun. The demand for slaves skyrocketed toward the end of the 18th century when Eli Whitney perfected his cotton gin, and their value remained high, particularly after Congress banned the importation of slaves in 1808. Sad to say, the District of Columbia became a slave-trading headquarters, of which John Randolph of Roanoke, Virginia, later would observe: "In no part of the earth—not even excepting the rivers of the coast of Africa—was there so great, so infamous a slave market, as in the metropolis, in the seat of government of this nation which prides itself on freedom."

In response, demands for an end to slavery

became increasingly loud. So many petitions for Abolition reached Congress that in 1836 it passed a "gag rule," prohibiting further consideration of such proposals. This did not displease many residents of the District, who worried lest "the Africans" revolt, as a number of incidents suggested they might. After each incident, freedom for blacks became more and more restricted. Nat Turner's rebellion of 1831, for example, led to a "black code" in Georgetown that made it illegal for "a person of color" to possess or circulate Abolitionist literature. In 1835, after the so-called "Snow riot," in which a group of African-American churches, schools, and businesses were destroyed by whites—including a restaurant owned by Beverly Snow, a free black— the right of blacks to own business establishments was terminated. By 1850, with more than three times as many free blacks as slaves in the District, and California petitioning for statehood, Henry Clay worked out his famous Compromise, which allowed slavery to remain in the District. The pressure on Congress from those both for and against Abolition grew to ridiculous proportions. When, for example, a symbolic statue of free-

dom arrived from Italy in 1858 to be placed atop the new Capitol dome, Senator Jefferson Davis of Mississippi noticed that she wore on her head the kind of cap that Roman slaves donned after being freed. He objected, and, as a result, the freedom statue atop the Capitol today sports a helmet adorned with feathers and an eagle's head, and not a cap.

It did not help Washington's situation any that business in the city was far from good. In 1854 work on the Washington Monument was stopped for lack of funds—and because of the hullabaloo that arose when word got out that Pope Pius IX had contributed a block of marble. It disappeared one night, and the consensus of opinion was that the anti-Catholic Know-Nothings had stolen it. The monument was only 150 feet high at the time; it didn't reach its full 555-foot height until 1884, and the color change between the two sections is still clearly visible.

Business, of course, had been a major factor in President Washington's choice for the site of the capital. Georgetown and Alexandria were busy ports, and Rock Creek, the boundary between Washington and Georgetown, was deep enough to accommodate ocean-going vessels. (It would later silt in.) Tobacco, the principal crop at the time, had played a major role in the area from the first: it had rescued the original Jamestown Colony from bankruptcy, and had served as acceptable currency for almost all debts. Some of the District's principal roads— Wisconsin Avenue, for one—were literally pressed into existence by the weight of hogsheads of tobacco being rolled to port.

In the District's early days many people smoked cigars or chewed tobacco—and spat, so often missing the ubiquitous spittoons that Charles Dickens advised strangers "not to look at the floor and if they happen to drop anything, though it be their purse, not to pick it up with an ungloved hand at any account." Tobacco con-

★ ★ ★ ★ ★

Capitol Hill sightseers of the 1890s view Horatio Greenough's toga-clad statue of George Washington. The Romanesque founding father now rests under cover at the Smithsonian's National Museum of American History.

★ ★ ★ ★ ★

Trolley cars and horse-drawn gigs, below right, share Pennsylvania Avenue at the turn of the century. Not quite up to date, except in fashions, the capital's amenities usually lagged behind those of New York and Philadelphia.

tinued to be a major player in the life of the capital right up through the First World War. In 1916 Woodrow Wilson's Vice President, Thomas Marshall, appalled at tobacco prices in the Willard Hotel, achieved immortality with the remark, "What this country needs is a good five-cent cigar." And when the call for scrap metal went out at the start of World War II, public buildings alone donated an incredible 58,000 spittoons.

Tobacco may have been a strong contributor to the local economy, but it wasn't enough. Central to the entire history of the nation's capital has been the fact that its only industry has been the government. Over the years there have been great plans for attracting business. In the early 1800s, when the rotunda between the wings of the Capitol belonged to neither chamber, it was made available to anyone who wanted to display goods for sale. A more ambitious project was the Chesapeake & Ohio Canal, the successor to the canal George Washington had hoped would transform the area into an international trading center. As fate would have it, however, on July 4, 1828, Charles Carroll, of Carrollton, Maryland, the last surviving signer of the Declaration of Independence, was turning over the first shovelful of dirt in Baltimore for the Baltimore & Ohio Railroad on the same day that John Quincy Adams was turning over the first shovelful of dirt for the canal in Washington. The railroad soon would put the canal out of business.

After the Civil War, civic leaders proposed bringing a Centennial Exposition to the capital, but in the end Philadelphia was chosen as the site after Congress said no, influenced in its decision by such comments as that of Senator Stewart of Nevada, who called Washington "the ugliest city in the whole country." At the turn of the century, Congress turned down a Chamber of Commerce proposal to attract industry by creating hydroelectric power at the Great Falls of the Potomac, just west of the city. Congress didn't want the District to become an industrial center. And anyway, a shortage of electricity was not the problem. In 1900, according to Constance McLaughlin Green, all manufacturing concerns in the District combined needed less than 9,600 horsepower—the equivalent of about 70 family cars in 1950. Industry stayed away. By the start of the First World War the capital's biggest business, next to government and real estate, was tourism, in part because of the arrival of the telegraph in 1844 and the District's immediate popularity as a news headquarters. People around the country who read about the "goings-on" in Washington—not about business,

but about politics and society—now wanted to go there and see for themselves. The lack of industry had some advantages. Few immigrants were attracted to the area, and the capital thus avoided many of the labor problems that beset other cities. With little manufacturing in the region, the capital's air remained free of pollutants from smokestack industries. And, best of all, because government—like the play—must go on, federal payrolls sheltered the District from the effects of the worst national depressions, starting with the panic of 1873 and including even the great depression of the 1930s. The down side of this situation, however, is the lack of an industrial tax base, and this has been the key to much of the District's financial woes over the past two centuries: federal buildings and land make up more than 50 percent of the capital, and federal holdings are not taxable.

With no voice in Congress, Washington residents have had to stand by and watch. They had no say in what Congress would do, either with regard to their budget or, going back a ways to some of this country's darkest days, any of the great matters that led to the Civil War—the first of the three wars that would transform Washington irreversibly from a small, sleepy Southern town to an important capital city. In 1861 the enemy was literally at the city's gate: Richmond, the capital of the Confederacy, was a little more than 100 miles from the District, and Alexandria was just a few miles away across the Potomac. As a result, Washington was the headquarters not only for anyone wanting to do war business—as it would be again in later wars—but also for enormous numbers of Union troops, all of whom needed food, shelter, transport, and medical help. At one point, some 50,000 of these troops—more than the entire population of the District just a decade earlier—took up residence in Washington. Louisa May Alcott, serving as a nurse, recalled that "long trains of army wagons

kept up a perpetual rumble from morning until night. Ambulances rattled to and fro with busy surgeons, nurses taking an airing or convalescents going in parties to be fitted for artificial limbs. Strings of sorry looking horses passed. Often a cart came by carrying several rough coffins and no mourners following." At one point as many as 30,000 horses were corralled on the Mall.

The District's population doubled as thousands of war-workers from the North and thousands of blacks from the South poured into the city. The city's sanitary facilities were hopelessly inadequate. President Lincoln's son, Willie, died of typhoid fever and the President himself suffered from a mild case of smallpox. Feeling that on the morrow they might die, Washingtonians partied. For "society" there were parties in the grand old manner; for much of the rest of the community, it was drinking and gambling in the District's estimated 2,000 bars and 100 gambling houses—although public gambling was illegal.

The Civil War would answer once and for all the nation's most divisive question: where would the real power in the United States reside—in Washington or in the capitals of what were then the 34 individual states? The war, of course, also settled the question of slavery. Strangely enough, however, the end of slavery brought to black Washington only a short period of joy. Two events soon turned it to sorrow once again for these Washingtonians, who by then made up more than half the District's population. The problem was that many people were afraid of enfranchising what Senator John Tyler Morgan of Alabama called "this influx of negro population from surrounding States." One of these events was the deal which brought Rutherford B. Hayes to the White House in 1877, and Jim Crow

★ ★ ★ ★ ★
Many a military unit has marched down Pennsylvania Avenue since the Civil War. The Welcome Home Parade for World War I's First Division was photographed from a balloon in 1919.

31

laws to the capital. Full-scale segregation came to the District's schools, hotels, parks, theaters, and other public facilities.

Jim Crow was the second of a one-two punch. The first came in 1871 when the three remaining jurisdictions of the District were combined into a single territory to be ruled by an appointed governor, a bi-cameral legislature (half appointed, half elected), a non-voting delegate to Congress, and two boards appointed by the President. Dominating the more powerful of the two—the Board of Public Works—was Alexander Shepherd, an old friend of President Ulysses S. Grant. Whether "Boss" Shepherd, as he came to be known, was a hero or a crook is still subject to debate, although Congress later would investigate him and not find him guilty of anything illegal. What is not debatable are his accomplish-

Government secretaries illustrate D.C.'s summer heat by attempting to fry an egg on a stone railing near the Capitol, from the 1920s. In 1935, at right, a slum dweller hand-pumps water only a few blocks from the Capitol dome.

ments. He began with the construction of the Washington Canal, a two-mile canal that was built to widen the Tiber River, which connected the Anacostia River with the Potomac just south of the White House. It had opened in 1815, and for a brief period served as a valuable waterway. The Seneca stone for the Smithsonian Castle, for example, was floated up the Mall on it. But the canal soon became an open sewer, receiving much of Washington's effluvia and discharging it into the Potomac. The trouble was that what went into the river on one tide came back again on the next.

Shepherd filled in the canal, covering it with what is now Constitution Avenue and Canal Street, S.W. He ripped up the railroad tracks from the Mall at the foot of the Capitol. He graded more than 150 miles of streets, paving 80 miles of them, including Pennsylvania Avenue. (The last stumps had not been cleared from L'Enfant's streets until the eve of the Civil War). He put down hundreds of miles of sidewalks, planted 50,000 trees, and laid miles of gas, water, and sewer mains.

At the end of three years Washington was a very different city in many ways, one of which, unfortunately, was that the city was $18,000,000 in debt, well over Shepherd's original estimated budget of $6,250,000 for the entire project. That was more than Congress could bear. In 1874 it stripped the District of any remnants of an elected government and instead put in place three commissioners appointed by the President. This form of government became effective with the Organic Act of June 1878, and would remain until 1966, when President Lyndon Johnson selected Walter Washington as the mayor-commissioner. From then on, however, to this day, citizens of a town devoted to politics could not vote for members of Congress. In return, Congress promised to put up half the District's annual budget. The trade-off—no vote but lower taxes—didn't seem like a good deal for long. As Congress increasingly became composed of members from distant states and preoccupied with other problems, the affairs of the small district in which they worked came to concern them less and less. By 1919 the promised contribution of 50 percent of the District's budget had fallen to 40 percent, and was soon to fall below 10 percent.

If, after the Civil War, the District was broke much of the time—and it was—its mentors, the President and Congress, worked to insure that the nation's business tycoons were not. For the last quarter of the 19th century Washington became, in the words of journalist Howard K. Smith, "Wall Street's branch office on the Potomac." Anything the financial powers wanted, they got. District life for those in the chips became one long round of partying, the likes of which had not been seen since the latter days of Rome. It made for great reading in the society pages of newspapers around the country. Once

again, however, it was a war—and not a very big one at that—that brought the center of power back to Washington. The Spanish-American War gave the rough-riding Teddy Roosevelt the national prominence that would put him in the Presidency in 1901. And from that bully pulpit T.R. took on J.P. Morgan and assorted "robber barons" and put an end to Wall Street's reign of unbridled power.

Another event in 1901—far less dramatic than a Presidential assassination (that of William McKinley, in Buffalo, in September of that year)—would have an even greater effect on the future of Washington. Guided by Senator James McMillan of Michigan, Congress appointed a commission of distinguished architects and artists to plan a park system for the nation's capital. A principal member was Daniel H. Burnham, who had been the chief architect of

★ ★ ★ ★ ★

Second Bombardment Group aircraft conduct maneuvers over Capitol Hill on April 23, 1931. The photo, from the Records of the Army Air Corps, demonstrates military preparedness between the world wars.

Chicago's successful World Columbian Exposition in 1893. His motto: "Make no little plans. They have no magic to stir men's blood, and probably themselves will not be realized. Make big plans." And big plans the McMillan commission made, most of them in keeping with the Senate's mandate: "The original plan of the city of Washington, having stood the test of a century, has met universal approval. The departures from that plan are to be regretted and wherever possible remedied." As the commission slowly carried out that mandate over the years,

the city envisioned by Pierre Charles L'Enfant a century earlier took shape. But first there would have to be still another war.

The horrors of World War I captivated the nation, and once again, as Alice Roosevelt Longworth remarked, "Every one looked for an 'excuse' to come to Washington." It was from here that the War Industries Board oversaw the mobilization of the nation's resources and the allocation of food. "Tempos," temporary buildings that in the end stayed around for more than 40 years, were thrown up on the Mall to handle

the thousands of new workers pouring in each month. Many of these new federal employees were women, the Civil Service Commission having discovered toward the end of the previous century that "women can successfully perform the duties of many of the subordinate places under government." As had been the case in the Civil War, the District couldn't handle the crush—and particularly the strains on sanitation. In 1918, more than 35,000 cases of flu were reported in the District—10 percent of them fatal—and no one could guess how many more went unreported.

When the war was over, the Washington that emerged was on the verge of becoming a brand-new city. From the recommendations of the McMillan commission came a remarkable spate of construction: Memorial Bridge, connecting the District with Arlington National Cemetery; the Lincoln Memorial (now that the swamp had been drained); the National Gallery of Art; the Jefferson Memorial; and the great buildings of the Federal Triangle on Pennsylvania Avenue, which symbolized the explosion of the federal bureaucracy in the 1930s. In short, the city took on the appearance of the

nation's capital much as it looks today. In 1926 the National Capital Park and Planning Commission was created to oversee the look of all future building in the District. Height restrictions for fire-fighting purposes had been in effect since the turn of the century, and the height of all national-capital structures remains strictly controlled today.

The 1920s didn't exactly roar in Washington as they did elsewhere, but the city once known as "the city of conversation" was now pictured in the press as the city of leisure—of Easter-egg hunts on the White House lawn, cherry-blossom festivals at the Tidal Basin, and of social climbing at such activities as dances, teas, and dinners. Sports were in: tennis for the active, baseball for the spectators. In 1924 the Washington Senators, behind the stalwart pitching of Walter Johnson, won the World Series. Americans loved their capital.

Well, not quite all Americans, perhaps. Even after the First World War, life in the District of Columbia left much to be desired on the part of African-Americans, despite the fact that it was home to more affluent and intellectual blacks than perhaps any other city in the world. For all of his idealism, President Woodrow Wilson had done little to further the cause of equality. He had refused, for example, to desegregate government lavatories. It is true that in order to grant Mrs. Wilson's dying wish he had pushed through a law forbidding residence in alleys—for decades slum dwellings had choked alleys all over the District, many of them practically in the backyard of the White House—but Wilson's law was an empty gesture and never was enforced.

During the war, many black workers had entered the work force and many others had gone off to fight. Then, with the war's end, their presence at home in Washington was met with resentment on the part of whites. The frustration felt by blacks, combined with a rash of

The National Archives building enshrines documents from the earliest days of the nation. Part of the Federal Triangle complex between the Capitol and the White House, it resides near the National Gallery of Art, top right. Planners for this home of the famed Mellon collection of paintings examine architects' drawings in 1937, right.

strikes and the "Red scare" that immediately followed the war, created a very tense situation that, beginning in 1919, finally erupted into race riots. The ultimate blow to Washington's African-American community would come at the dedication of the memorial to the President who had ended slavery. Black speakers not only were not invited onto the dias but were forced to sit in a segregated section at the foot of the memorial. The icing was put on the segregationist cake in 1925 when people everywhere watched the newsreels and saw the Ku Klux Klan, some 25,000 strong, parade down Pennsylvania Avenue, the famed thoroughfare of L'Enfant's plan. It would take a great depression, a great President, and a second great war to set things right.

From the moment that Franklin D. Roosevelt proclaimed that "the only thing we have to fear is fear itself," Washington—and the nation— would never be the same. But Washington would be even less the same, for among the 30,000 federal employees who came to Washington in the New Deal's first year was a new kind of public servant. He—or she—was young, intense, and dedicated to the tasks at hand. Most of them cared little about Southern society, about cotillions and soirees and socials. And while there would always be moths attracted to the flames of the legendary Pearle Mesta, "the hostess with the mostest," and her latter-day ilk, the character of the area that one day would be called "inside-the-Beltway" Washington changed radically. Not that all was perfect, by any means. Crime had been a problem in the District almost from the beginning. At one time there were areas of the city called Hooker's Division and Murder Bay; by 1941 Newsweek was calling the city the "crime capital of the world."

On December 7, 1941, however, when the 27,000 fans who were packed in Griffith Stadium to cheer their already beloved Redskins heard the loudspeaker ordering senior military officers to report to their commands, the name calling stopped. Once again Washington was at the center of a great war. In a little more than a year the Pentagon, the world's largest office building, would open, with—FDR saw to it—unsegregated lavatories. Thus ended an important rite of passage, for with the completion of this massive, five-sided building the once ridiculed federal city of Washington, born in a wasteland of swamp and forest once called the Territory of Columbia, had become the most important city on Earth. ★

The City of Frederick Douglass

SHARON HARLEY

As the seat of the federal government since 1800, as an administrative city, as a border city, and, eventually, as the municipal center that housed such institutions as Howard University and Freedmen's Hospital, the nation's capital has attracted a large, socially varied black population. Additionally, the post-emancipation public-school system was known nationally  for providing quality education to the city's blacks. Migrants from rural areas in nearby Virginia and Maryland, from urban communities in the North and the South, from hamlets in the Deep South, and from

★ ★ ★ ★ ★

In the early 1800s, the nation's capital was also a well-known slave market. Above right, a "soul-driver" herds a slave coffle past the United States Capitol. At left, Jacob Lawrence's *Frederick Douglass* Series No. 30 panel portrays the famous Abolitionist as the U.S. Marshal of the District of Columbia, an office to which he was appointed in 1877 by President Rutherford B. Hayes.

among Washington's own black population—some with antecedents in the pre-Civil War District of Columbia—merged variously with each other to form one of the largest black communities in the United States. The city of Washington and its large black population was further distinguished when it became home to orator, journalist, and political activist Frederick Douglass and other notable black men and women in the late-19th century.

The Africans, Indians, and Europeans already residing in the Potomac Valley region, which later became the District of Columbia,

early on gave the region an aspect of racial diversity. As a symbol for the principles upon which the country was built, the nation's capital attracted both blacks and whites in search of a greater sense of individual and group freedom, closer proximity to the symbols of power, and, more importantly, better job opportunities.

Initially, many blacks came to Washington as slaves, traveling here with their owners from the neighboring tobacco-raising states of Virginia and Maryland. Often they were hired out to work in the new capital city or sold on the auction block. Disturbing to most free blacks of the

Native Washingtonian Dr. Sharon Harley is Associate Dean of Undergraduate Studies and Associate Professor of Afro-American studies and History at the University of Maryland, College Park. She is the co-editor of *Afro-American Woman: Struggles and Images* and *Women in Africa and the African Diaspora,* and author of many scholarly papers and articles.

time and even to some whites (including foreign observers) was the fact that the cities of Washington, Georgetown, and Alexandria, which formed the unified District of Columbia, were major sites for slave-trading activity. According to the census of 1810 and 1820, enslaved blacks outnumbered free blacks in the nation's capital. By 1830, however, there were slightly more free blacks than slaves—6,152 and 6,119, respectively. On the eve of the Civil War, slavery still existed in the nation's capital, although there were only 3,000 slaves as compared to 11,000 free blacks.

Periods of unemployment coupled with competition from enslaved blacks made the daily lives of free blacks difficult. Not only did they face periods of severe economic distress but they did so in a town that was decidedly Southern in its composition and racial outlook. Consequently, black codes and Southern racial customs restricted the activities of free blacks and denied them certain basic rights. As in the rest of the South, these codes became more severe and tightly enforced following the Nat Turner slave revolt of 1831. After this event, local blacks were banned altogether from pursuing certain occupations and certain types of businesses, and curfews were imposed. The blame for slave revolts was placed erroneously on free blacks, who were thought to inspire an otherwise docile slave population to run away and revolt against their state of perpetual servitude.

Locally and nationally, black and white Abolitionists condemned further encroachments on the already limited rights of free blacks as well as the continued presence of slavery and slave trading, especially in the nation's capital. The glaring contradiction posed by the sight of slave pens in close proximity to federal buildings and monuments was pointed out regularly in the writings and oratory of American Abolitionists and foreign visitors. On a visit to Washington in 1804, Irish poet Thomas Moore composed the following lines:

Even here beside the proud Potomac's streams . . .
The medley mass of pride and misery
Of whips and charters, manacles and rights
Of slaving blacks and democratic whites . . .

Yet, in the midst of slavery and a vibrant slave-trading industry, free blacks managed, with the limited resources available to them, to develop a community life. Benevolent and fraternal societies were formed to assist members during times of illness or the death of a family member. The need for education prompted three free black men, George Bell, Nicholas Franklin, and Moses Liverpool, to establish the first school for black children in 1807. Also, as free black worshipers tired of the discrimination they experienced in white-dominated churches and congre-

gations, they formed their own churches. Blacks at Ebenezer Methodist Church, for example, withdrew in 1820 to form their own congregation. The building of other such institutions that occurred within the ante-bellum free-black population of Washington laid the foundation for post-emancipation life.

Prominent church leaders, successful businessmen and businesswomen, and formally educated African Americans served as leaders in the developing free-black community life. Rarely did they forget their brethren still in chains; they raised their voices in condemnation of slavery and they worked hard and saved to purchase the freedom of kinfolk. Some even expressed their opposition to slavery by participating in the

Underground Railroad, allowing their houses to be used as "stations." Although the numbers of slaves in Washington diminished significantly over time, slavery was not abolished until 1862, one year before the general emancipation. In order to appease some opponents, the District's Emancipation Act offered compensation to slaveholders.

The immediate impact of the Civil War and the Emancipation Act of 1862 was a tremendous rise in the influx of war refugees. According to Elizabeth Keckley, a former slave who purchased her own freedom and that of others, and who became personal seamstress for Mrs. Abraham Lincoln and other well-to-do whites, black war refugees "came to the Capital looking for liberty."

Temporary barracks and tents were erected in order to respond to the increasing demand for low-cost housing. Private relief groups were formed to meet the demand of war refugees and soldiers for food, clothing, and housing. Keckley helped to organize the Contraband Relief Association in 1862 to assist the destitute newly freed blacks.

In 1865, the federal government established the Freedmen's Bureau to provide "relief work, education, regulation of labor, and administration of justice." Educational programs initiated by the bureau ranged from donating land and buildings for schoolhouses to establishing industrial schools and building institutions of higher learning for black Americans. One of the most lasting effects of the Freedmen's Bureau's efforts was the establishment of Howard University and Freedmen's Hospital, which has since been renamed Howard University Hospital.

Chartered in 1867 and named for General Oliver Howard, the head of the Freedmen's Bureau, Howard University initially received $500,000 from the bureau for land purchase and construction of campus buildings. Howard University, considered by many to be "the capstone of Negro education," and the development of an exceptional public-school system for blacks, firmly established Washington as an important center of black intelligentsia.

The government jobs that black people received were usually as messengers and laborers. A few blacks received high-level government appointments, but this was rare. Black Republican loyalists who had held nationally elected positions or were nationally known (and male), were allocated the few political patronage jobs reserved for blacks. For instance, the city of Washington drew Frederick Douglass, and other black men like him, providing them with plum political job opportunities. At various points in time, Douglass held the positions of either Treasurer, Recorder of Deeds, or Marshall of the District of Columbia, as well as Minister to Haiti.

Many of the nation's leading black citizens who made Washington their home during the late-19th century, including Frederick Douglass, Blanche K. Bruce, Reverend Francis J. Grimké, John Mercer Langston, and Mary Church Terrell, were not strangers to the city. Several

★ ★ ★ ★ ★

Denied on the basis of race the right to sing either in the Daughters of the American Revolution's (D.A.R) Constitution Hall or the Central High School Auditorium, contralto Marian Anderson lifts her voice in song at the Lincoln Memorial, above, on April 9, 1939. Right, a group of prominent blacks, known as "Roosevelt's Black Cabinet," who were appointed by President Franklin D. Roosevelt in 1938 to advise federal agencies on problems within the black community.

times before, they had journeyed to Washington to campaign for black civil rights, to participate in national meetings of organizations—the Negro Convention Movement and the American Negro Academy—and to attend social events, including inaugural balls, New Year's Day receptions, and Emancipation Day celebrations.

The social scene and employment outlook for most postwar blacks was not as promising, even for the small percentage who were educated. There were few professional positions, and most of these went to nationally known blacks or to the sons and daughters of Washington's established black middle-class families. The vast majority of Washington blacks were poor, however; thousands were so destitute that the only available housing was in overcrowded alley dwellings that were hidden from the street and often lacked indoor plumbing. By the close of the 19th century, there were more than 300 alleys in which approximately 19,000 people, most of whom were black, lived. The names attached to these neighborhoods— Swampoodle, Bloodfield, and Cowtown—can only begin to suggest the level of depravation that existed.

Earlier, General Oliver Howard of the Freedmen's Bureau had proposed a novel housing program that enabled former slaves to purchase through a payment plan small lots on

which to build housing. This program led to the development of the Barry Farm community (1867-1868) in the Anacostia section of Southeast Washington. Soon Barry Farm residents— primarily blue-collar workers and domestic servants—had their own Baptist church and one-room schoolhouse. Eventually, other schools and some black businesses were established, but, as with most of pre-1954 Washington, blacks and whites lived in separate communities or in separate sections of the same community and were rarely served by the same community organizations.

Local and national figures in the radical wing of the Republican Party made the establishment of racial equality in the nation's capital one of their goals, believing that Washington then could serve as a model for race relations for the rest of the nation. A delegation of blacks, including Frederick Douglass, whom many have called "the father of the Civil Rights Movement," called upon President Andrew Johnson on behalf of the black-suffrage cause. Johnson rejected their petition, expressing the widely

held view among whites, including many local whites, that newly freed blacks were ill-prepared to vote. Despite local and Presidential opposition to local black male suffrage, however, Congress passed a bill in 1866 granting every male District resident over 20 years of age, regardless of color, the right to vote.

A growing black-business spirit in the late-19th century influenced Andrew F. Hilyer, a local inventor and civil-rights advocate, who helped to establish and became the first president of the Union League of the District of Columbia in 1892. The goals of the League were:

To advance the moral, material and financial interests of the colored people; . . . to foster such a spirit of cooperation that mechanical, industrial and professional enterprises may be established and maintained; and to collect and disseminate among the people such data and information as will best tend to promote these ends.

In addition to its business directories, which were published periodically throughout the 1890s, the League published *A Historical,*

Biographical and Statistical Study of Colored Washington in 1901.

Then and throughout most of the early-20th century, the black business and entertainment community that was centered around U Street, in the Shaw neighborhood of Northwest Washington, attracted blacks from all walks of life. In segregated Washington, Shaw was home to the nationally popular Howard Theater and the Lincoln Theater, as well as to the Lincoln Colonnade and the Whitelaw Hotel, which featured their own ballrooms, and Jack's Place and Poodledog Cabaret.

While acceptance into established middle-class social circles did not extend to the masses of unlettered, rural black freedmen and freedwomen, other poor, black migrants, who had preceded the newcomers by varying periods of time, helped them adjust to the ways of the city. Assistance in finding employment, schooling, housing, and a church came from family members and neighbors. With the constant flow of new migrants and the annual homecoming trips that migrants made to the places of their birth,

cultural linkages with rural Southern roots remained strong. White and black middle-class support for the city's poor newcomers came through organized charitable associations, social settlements, and the burgeoning black women's club movement. Often forgotten in the account of the Progressive-era reform is the extent to which, in more loosely defined

Walter E. Washington, the District of Columbia's first elected mayor, is sworn in, above, by Associate Supreme Court Justice Thurgood Marshall on January 2, 1975. Opposite, an aerial view of some of the more than 200,000 people who, on August 28, 1963, participated in the March on Washington, at which the Reverend Martin Luther King, Jr., below, delivered his memorable "I have a dream" speech.

ways, the urban poor cared for their own through the sharing of limited resources—taking in relatives and friends and helping out during times of illness and death.

With education, hard work, and thrift, newcomers and especially their children joined the growing middle class, although most remained part of the working poor. Seasonal unemployment in the construction industry and low wages forced black men and women to join the labor force in order to make ends meet. Children engaged in wage work when the family had no choice, but generally parents and other kinfolk worked in order that the children could attend school.

Recruited to teach in the District's prestigious M Street High School, Oberlin College graduate Mary Church Terrell and other nationally prominent black women and men usually had little difficulty in securing teaching appointments in the colored-school system. The ease with which members of the upper-middle class secured these appointments, especially at the M Street High School and Howard University, caused some tension between the middle-class elite and the sons and daughters of, say, washerwomen. This conflict centered around class as much as skin-color differences, and the issue of favoritism often was played out in the pages of the notable black newspaper, the Washington Bee. From 1882 to 1921, Washington native and vitriolic editor of the Bee William Calvin Chase clearly lived up to the paper's motto: "Stings for Our Enemies—Honey for Our Friends." Alternately a friend and foe of individual members of the black elite, he regularly reported on the use of favoritism that allowed them to maintain a stronghold in the D.C. colored public-school system.

Employment opportunities for the masses of blacks did not open up significantly until World War II. To bring attention to the pervasive racial discrimination in private wartime industries, A. Philip Randolph, labor leader and organizer of the Brotherhood of Sleeping Car Porters, threatened in 1941 to lead a massive march on

★ ★ ★ ★ ★

Appointed to the United States Supreme Court in 1967 by President Lyndon B. Johnson, now retired Associate Justice Thurgood Marshall, left, became the first African-American to serve on the nation's highest court. Above, Sharon Pratt Kelly, who became the District's first female African-American mayor on November 6, 1990. In his *Frederick Douglass* Series No. 32 panel, below right, artist Jacob Lawrence allegorically portrays Douglass's return to Maryland as a free man. "Promise and hope," explained the artist, "are insinuated by the banner, the broad streaming cloud, and the single vigorous flower."

Washington. President Franklin D. Roosevelt's Executive Order 8802, which prohibited racial discrimination in private defense industries that received federal contracts and in the federal government, increased the black presence in Washington and the black clamor for the end of Jim Crow segregation and for local home rule.

Prior to the historic Brown v. Board of Education of Topeka, Kansas, Supreme Court decision of 1954, African Americans locally and elsewhere, along with their white sympathizers, began to work for improved race relations. In December 1945, President Harry S Truman commissioned a President's Committee on Civil Rights and charged it with defining the role of the federal government in improving race relations. Meanwhile, Mary Church Terrell's campaign to end segregation in restaurants and other public facilities in the nation's capital was, according to historian Beverly Washington Jones, "a continuation of [Terrell's] drive to remake the nation's capital into the 'Colored Man's Paradise.'"

As a member of the Coordinating Committee for the Enforcement of the D.C. Anti-Discrimination Laws, formed in the summer of 1949, an elderly Terrell organized the first public demonstration for the enforcement of the 1872 and 1873 "lost" laws that required public eating places to serve "any respectable well-behaved person regardless of color, or face a $100 fine and forfeiture of their license for one year." On June 8, 1953, Chief Justice William O. Douglas spoke on behalf of the court when he declared the acts of 1872 and 1873 enforceable.

This decision, along with Brown v. Board of Education and many others that declared that segregation in public facilities to be unconstitutional, may have brought Washington closer to the 'Colored Man's Paradise' that Terrell and

others in post-emancipation Washington had envisioned.

In the 1960s' activism that followed the Brown decision, a number of local black activists came to the forefront: Walter Fauntroy, of the Southern Christian Leadership Conference (SCLC); the late Julius Hobson, of the Congress of Racial Equality (CORE) and later of the D.C. Statehood Party; and Marion Barry, director of the Washington office of the Student Non-Violent Coordinating Committee (SNCC) and head of Pride, Incorporated. Spurred by the successes of the national civil-rights movements, they soon turned to Washington to wage a full-scale battle for home rule. Yet the city still lacks full home rule, and Washington and its black community continue to reflect upon the sentiment Frederick Douglass so eloquently expressed in the late-19th century:

It [Washington, D.C.] is our national center. It belongs to us, and whether it is mean or majestic, whether arrayed in glory or covered with shame, we cannot but share its character and its destiny. ★

The Rise of Imperial Washington

Adam Platt

IT IS AN IRONIC BUT FAIRLY STEADY RULE THAT NATIONAL CAPITALS PROFIT DURING TIMES OF NATIONAL TRAUMA. WASHINGTONIANS KNOW THIS WELL, BUT RARELY ADMIT IT. "IT IS A DREADFUL THING TO SAY," WROTE THE LATE COLUMNIST JOSEPH W. ALSOP, WHO CAME TO THE CITY IN 1936, "BUT BEFORE NUCLEAR WEAPONS HAD TO BE WORRIED ABOUT, WARS TENDED TO QUICKEN THE PULSE, HEIGHTEN THE INTEREST, AND INTENSIFY THE PLEASURES OF WASHINGTON LIFE." THE CIVIL WAR HAD TRANS-

FORMED WASHINGTON DECISIVELY; THE FIRST WORLD WAR HAD DONE THE SAME. EVEN THE DEPRESSION, WHICH WAS TREATED AS A KIND OF WAR BY FRANKLIN ROOSEVELT'S DYNAMIC YOUNG ADMINISTRATION, INVIGORATED THE CAPITAL. "WE'RE GOING TO TAX, TAX, TAX AND SPEND, SPEND, SPEND" WENT FEDERAL EMERGENCY RELIEF ADMINISTRATION CHIEF HARRY HOPKINS' FAMOUS LINE ABOUT THE NEW DEAL; AND THE FEDERAL GOVERNMENT, AND ITS CITY, HAD FLOURISHED ACCORDINGLY.

BUY WAR BONDS

☆ U. S. GOVERNMENT PRINTING OFFICE : 1942—O—469197   WNS 519-C

But the Second World War was a different circumstance altogether. By the late fall of 1941, monumental Washington was largely complete. The National Gallery of Art, built over an old train depot along Constitution Avenue, had opened in March. The city's first truly national airport, across the Potomac River at Gravelly Point in Virginia, was finished months later, not far from the new building site of a vast, five-sided military complex called the Pentagon. In no way, however, did Washington's pace and manners jibe with these new symbols of national prominence. Pre-war Washington, by the standards of the more northerly East Coast cities, was still a slow, smallish place. It was "a city only a few generations out of the mud," in the words of journalist David Brinkley, "a city that still boasted 15,000 privies."

On December 7, 1941, everything changed. The country went to war, and Washington went with it. The town's frenzy was unique. The attack on Pearl Harbor occurred on a Sunday, and much of official Washington was attending a

Redskins football game at Griffith Stadium. No public announcement was made, for fear of panicking the crowd. But news of the attack spread anyway, as, one after another, journalists, Army personnel, and diplomats were paged over the stadium loudspeakers. The White House appropriated Al Capone's old armored limousine for the President's protection. In time, President Roosevelt was issued a gas mask, which he hung lightly over the back of his wheelchair. All over town, bureaucrats jumped to their work. "Anything beyond right away is too remote to bother with," Life magazine reported; "everyone is up to his ears in the next ten minutes."

Washington had been preparing for war for more than a year, but still the city was overwhelmed. After Pearl Harbor, new federal workers were hired at the rate of as many as 5,000 per month. In 1942, 1,500 building permits were issued each month, and a 6,160-room dormitory was thrown up across the river in Arlington to house the legions of youthful "government girls" drawn to Washington by prospects of secretarial

Adam Platt was born and raised in postwar Washington. He has written for *Esquire*, *Newsweek*, and the American Spectator, and is co-author with Joseph W. Alsop of Alsop's memoirs, *I've Seen the Best of It*.

work, excitement, and fun. Temporary office buildings, called "tempos," sprung up along the Mall. Built with cement and grey plaster board, they made the formerly elegant space resemble "a kitchenette with too many grand pianos in it," in the words of one magazine. Construction of the Pentagon proceeded at a blistering pace; in the end, the building contained 280 restrooms and nearly 18 miles of corridor. Roosevelt thought this vast facility might be used for storage after the war.

Washington was a city of crowds during the war years. Its citizens moved in swarms, elbowing for space aboard trollies, in cafeterias, and in rooming houses. Work schedules for federal employees were staggered to ease traffic congestion. "The Nazis couldn't invade this town," said one cabdriver, "not during rush hour." Lines were the rule—for food, for hotel rooms, for entertainment. Visiting the capital in 1943, writer John Dos Passos couldn't get his laundry done and had trouble finding a place to stay. Rooms renting for $50 per month before the war now went for 10 times that. Appointments with high officials were canceled, half-kept, often forgotten. "But of course it's wonderful and horrible but it's not a city," one man told Dos Passos. "It's more like a vast temporary headquarters during a campaign."

In the press, much was made of the zesty new government recruits and their swinging night life around town. In fact, there was a good deal of disaffection in the ranks, especially among women who came to Washington expecting glamour and intrigue and instead found mind-numbing clerical jobs at $1,440 a year. Helen Tucker, 22, told a Life magazine reporter that she was quitting her job as junior clerk. "She is discouraged by the scarcity of beaux, and afraid the government may freeze her into her job for the duration." At some government agencies, exit-interview stations had to be set up to process all the employees wanting to leave. Longtime residents watched this drama with bemused alarm. "To the cabbies," Life reported, "the name 'bureaucrat' has become an insult."

The bureaucrats, however, were in Washington to stay. After the First World War, the size of the federal payroll had receded. Following Victory-in-Japan, or V-J, Day, September 2, 1945, the numbers of federal workers dropped briefly and then, gradually, began to grow. The war had doubled the city's population, and, inevitably, as the United States took up the burdens of world power, the business of national government spread out into the suburbs. Before the decade was out, several new bridges across the Potomac and Anacostia rivers either were planned or under construction. Following the Pentagon's example, many new federal projects were built outside the old District lines. Ease of access for the now ubiquitous automobile was one reason for this, but with the Cold War looming, Washington also wanted to be able, as one planner put it, "to dodge bombs."

With the end of the Second World War, the capital entered a new era of self-importance. "A growing place" is how Joseph Alsop described the postwar city, "more invigorating than the small southern town of old and more involved with the outside world." Accordingly, the capital took on an earnest, business-like sheen. In 1947, the State Department abandoned its old headquarters at the cranky, ornate State, War, and Navy Building adjacent to the White House for a flat-faced, boxy structure on C Street in a neighborhood called Foggy Bottom. The diplomats needed the space—it would be expanded in 1957—although many, including soon-to-be Secretary of State Dean Acheson, lamented the loss of their personable old home.

Other losses were more ephemeral. The city's ancient social axis was obliterated by the war. The seemly world of diplomats and well-born politicians, dining at the mansion homes of such chosen hostesses as Marie Beale and Mildred Bliss, was replaced by a racier, more pragmatic routine. Business and pleasure mingled in the hazy, new world of the Washington cocktail party. On the more rarified dinner circuit, bloodlines were less important than one's proximity to power. "The guests," wrote Russell Baker, who covered the White House for the New York Times during the 1950s, "will have been carefully selected by the hostess to form a group of men who can be useful to each other." The new order was less mannered than before and more preoccupied with itself; utility, not fun, was the new name of the game.

For a large number of Washington's residents, however, the war changed nothing. The African-American population in the District increased by 41 percent during the '40s, and continued to grow at this rate through the next decade as well. Yet the predominantly black neighborhoods spreading north from the Capitol and east towards the Anacostia River benefited little from the area's wartime boom. The housing to which African-Americans had access was often shabby and overcrowded, and public funding was minimal. Throughout the city, restaurants, schools, and even playgrounds were still segregated. During an early tour of the Pentagon, Roosevelt Administration officials had been shocked to find separate lavatory facilities planned for "white" and "colored." In 1948, actors booked at the whites-only National Theater boycotted their shows, and the management was forced to show movies instead.

Shortly after the war, civil-rights groups led by the National Committee on Segregation in the Nation's Capital began agitating for change. In 1948, in the case of Hurd v. Hodge, the United States Supreme Court ruled that restrictive housing covenants were unconstitutional, over-

55

★ ★ ★ ★ ★

Washington's concentration of government agencies and associated institutions, such as the International Monetary Fund, below, particularly since the New Deal era of the 1930s, attracted ever-growing hordes of lobbyists to the halls of Congress, opposite. Most lobbyists shunned the limelight, although some gained national recognition, such as auto-safety and consumer-rights crusader Ralph Nader, shown above testifying before a Senate subcommittee in 1966.

turning an earlier District Court ruling. Two years later, when 11 black children tried to enroll at the new John Philip Sousa Junior High School in Southeast Washington they were turned away. The resulting legal suit, Bolling v. Sharpe, reached the High Court in 1954, and was ruled on as part of the celebrated Brown v. Board of Education decision that struck down the long-held tenet of "separate but equal." Thereafter, government officials, including President Dwight D. Eisenhower, nervously touted Washington, D.C., as a model for school desegregation throughout the country.

Despite the President's attentions, local government in the District remained, at best, an anomaly. In the 1950s, as before the war, Washington had no elected mayor, and its citizens no national vote. The District's affairs were managed by a three-member commission, two of whom were appointed by the President. Myriad Congressional committees governed city appropriations. The Washington Post rightly called this situation "a poisonous thing." In a 1948 Post poll, 70 percent of the respondents favored home rule. In 1951 the Senate actually passed a home-rule bill, but the measure languished in the House District Committee, which was chaired by a rock-bound Southern Democrat from South Carolina, John McMillan. McMillan's critics said his anti-home-rule stand was racist. McMillan, who did not leave his post until 1972, rarely said much at all.

For much of metropolitan Washington, however, home rule was not a burning issue. With new arrivals flooding into the area at the rate of 50,000 a year, more and more Washingtonians came from someplace else. Beginning in 1951, the city's population actually began to shrink, as

Increasingly frustrated in their attempts to achieve change through the usual political channels, vocal protesters brought—and continue to bring—their grievances to the streets of Washington to try to influence Congress and the President, as well as the press and the public at large.

middle-class families moved out to the bedroom communities mushrooming around towns like Arlington, Virginia, and Bethesda, Maryland. The effective boundaries of metropolitan Washington slowly expanded, enveloping Montgomery and Prince George's counties to the north and east and Fairfax and Arlington counties to the south. With its tax base pinched, the District's "inner city," as it began to be called, suffered, although the Eisenhower Administration kept the streets cleaned and the monuments buffed to military standard.

The outbreak of the Korean War in 1950 solidified the trend toward international government in the nation's capital. The equation was simple: as the modern world shrank, the city's overseas entanglements grew. The World Bank and the International Monetary Fund established their headquarters in Washington in 1945. Massive foreign-aid programs, such as the Marshall Plan and Point Four, soon developed their own bureaucracies. By the 1950s, the city was home to legions of international organizations with such acronyms as IADP (Inter-American Development Bank), ILO (International Labor Organization), and WWF (World Wildlife Fund).

And, in 1955, President Eisenhower authorized $46 million for the building of a new Central Intelligence Agency—or CIA—headquarters in the woods near Langley, Virginia.

For the most part, global events, not rational planning, conspired to make Washington a world capital. "A model for the nation" had always been the cry of politicians preoccupied with the city's public image. But as the region buckled under the postwar population boom, attendant urban problems, such as crime, traffic congestion, and pollution, began to impinge on the city's role as a national showcase. "In the summer," warned Tom Wicker in the New York Times guidebook to Washington, D.C., first published in 1967, "the Potomac is apt to smell." Crime rates in the capital—always a national preoccupation—rose during the '50s and soared thereafter, increasing a staggering 395 percent between 1960 and 1969. Newsweek magazine declared Washington the "murder capital" of the country in 1941, and the cry has been repeated, with varying degrees of accuracy, ever since.

In fact, social conditions in Washington were no worse, and often were much better, than those of cities suffering similar blight. In 1954, the largest urban-renewal project the country had ever seen razed some 450 acres of land near the Potomac River in Southwest Washington. Even more ambitious was a plan for nearly 400 miles of new highway linking the District to the suburbs. Planners envisioned a series of freeways radiating from the city center over three concentric loops, the largest of which would run 100 full miles and circle the entire metropolitan area. Both of these massive projects stirred a good deal of local opposition; in the end, with the freeway plan, only the outer loop of the so-called "Beltway" was built. Even so, between 1940 and 1965 more miles of highway per acre were laid around Washington, D.C., than in any other city in the United States.

Life in the nation's capital was speeding up perceptibly, and nowhere was this trend more apparent than in the federal establishment. President Eisenhower added a chief of staff to the White House and created a new executive office called the National Security Council. Senator Robert LaFollette, Jr.'s Legislative Reform Act of 1946 greatly increased the size of Congressional staffs. In 1934, the House of Representatives employed 992 people; by 1990, that number had

ballooned to 9,683. A second Senate Office Building, later named for Everett Dirksen of Illinois, was completed in 1958. The blocky, drab House Rayburn Building— named for longtime Speaker of the House Sam Rayburn of Texas— opened in 1965, sad evidence, according to then New York Times architectural critic Ada Louise Huxtable, of the capital's new "Penitentiary Style."

Arch comments such as Huxtable's did not prevent successive postwar Presidents from tinkering with Washington's appearance. It was John Kennedy who called Washington, D.C., a place "of Northern charm and Southern efficiency," and yet, perhaps to an even greater degree than his predecessors, Kennedy saw the city as a living symbol of our national culture. The capital, he said, "should embody the finest in its contemporary architectural thought." With dogged support from First Lady Jacqueline Kennedy, he scotched plans to demolish the old federal facades along Lafayette Square across from the White House. He hired architects of international reputation for government projects, and initiated plans for the landmark revitalization of Pennsylvania Avenue, which, like much of the city's center, had fallen into disrepair since the war. "After all," said Kennedy, "this may be the only monument we'll leave."

Lyndon Johnson shared John Kennedy's concern for the capital, although he showed it in less aesthetic ways. In his book *Captive Capital*, Sam Smith points out that historically the city has flourished under such "earthy" Presidents as Andrew Jackson, Ulysses S. Grant, and Johnson. For her part, Lady Bird Johnson assigned a high priority to the beautification of Washington, and carpeted dog-eared corners of federal land with daffodils, tulips, and flowering bushes and trees. Funds for the Washington area's first subway system, or Metrorail, were approved in 1965. In 1967 (Washingtonians had received the right to vote in Presidential elections in 1961), Johnson revamped local government, replacing the old commissioner system with a nine-member city council that was overseen by a single commissioner. To this post the President appointed a

★ ★ ★ ★ ★

The capital of a cold-war superpower and secure in its monopoly on national political power, imperial Washington attracted money and influence for the arts. Splendid new museums of art, science, and history joined those already in existence on the Mall and elsewhere in the city. In 1971, the John F. Kennedy Center for the Performing Arts, right, opened on the shores of the Potomac as one of the nation's premier cultural centers.

stolid, if somewhat benign bureaucrat named Walter Washington, who, four years later, would become the city's first mayor.

On a broader level, the Johnson Administration's "Great Society" programs brought to the city a sense of national activism not seen since the New Deal. During the mid-'60s, industry lobbyists, backroom lawyers, and public-interest mavens, such as the intense, angular, former journalist Ralph Nader, all flocked to the capital. This quasi-official world of advocates and influence peddlers began to grow up around the old federal core and, with time, became part of it. As such issues as civil rights and Vietnam buffeted the country, the number of journalists in town increased exponentially, as did the number of

lawyers. In 1969 there were 15 public-interest litigation groups registered in Washington; by 1980, according to *Washingtonian* magazine, there would be 112 such groups, spending a total of $50 million annually.

No cause had deeper resonance in Washington during the 1960s than the struggle for civil rights. The District had always been a segregated city. With the influx of middle- and upper-income professionals during and shortly after the Second World War, large numbers of low-income families, many of them African-American, were priced out of old neighborhoods like Georgetown and Foggy Bottom. The desegregation of the schools in 1954 had accelerated "white flight" to the suburbs. The city, mean-

while, remained the gateway to the North for large numbers of African-Americans moving up from the South in search of economic opportunity. By the summer of 1962, when Martin Luther King Jr. led his celebrated march on Washington, African-Americans composed nearly 60 percent of the city's population; by 1970, the figure was 71 percent.

By contrast, Alexandria, Virginia, did not hire its first black policemen until 1965. Fearing violence during King's march on the capital, the Washington Senators baseball team canceled two successive home games. "Lord help us if [they] ever get home rule," one suburbanite told the Washington Post. This ill will was reciprocated in neighborhoods like Shaw, east of 15th Street, and in the decrepit alleys along the Anacostia River in Southeast Washington. By 1968, roughly 40 percent of the city's African-American families earned less than $8,000, and unemployment among black men under 21 was as high as 17 percent. "It's not so much hate exactly," Rufus Mayfield, former head of Pride, Inc., a local youth organization, told Newsweek magazine in 1968, "but a black man has a deprived feeling when he looks at a white man, a depression, an agony, a pain."

This pain surfaced violently after the assassination of Martin Luther King Jr. on April 4, 1968. The riots began on 14th Street and lasted three days, devastating 57 blocks in the city's center. There were nine deaths, as well as considerable arson and random violence; but mostly there was looting. D.C. resident Sam Smith

observed "a slow stream of people walking down the street with liberated objects: hangers full of clothes, a naugahyde hassock, a television set." Twelve thousand troops, including U.S. Marines and paratroopers, were needed to restore order. The eventual calm was fitful, but in its wake came political reform. In 1970 the District won a non-voting seat in the House of Representatives, and in 1973 Congress passed a home-rule bill allowing citizens of Washington, D.C., to elect their own mayor and city council for the first time.

Metropolitan Washington continued to boom throughout the 1970s and '80s. During this period, Fairfax County, in northern Virginia, surpassed the District of Columbia in total population. The federal government, which had always provided regional economic stability, also continued to grow, but the area's new service and retail economies grew faster. Between 1970 and 1980, demand for office space in the D.C. area increased an astounding two million square feet per year. Many of the region's new arrivals, including some 800,000 people between 1975 and 1985, were young, and many were monied. Seeking to tap this new market, Bloomingdale's opened its first department store outside New York at a bustling Beltway intersection in northern Virginia called Tyson's Corner. Other giant retailers followed, along with such Fortune-500 corporations as Mobil Oil, which moved its entire headquarters to the area's suburbs in 1980.

As the region entered the economic mainstream, Washington began to be touted, for the first time, as a cultural capital. In 1971, the John F. Kennedy Center for the Performing Arts opened its doors on the banks of the Potomac, offering the community an opera house, a theater, and a concert hall in one impressive, if mildly unsightly package. The National Gallery of Art's East Building, a medley of shining glass

★ ★ ★ ★ ★

Old enmities almost buried, Soviet Prime Minister Mikhail Gorbachev joined President George Bush to review the White House Honor Guard on May 31, 1990, below. Soviet and American flags draped official buildings in honor of the visit, opposite. Within a short time, the Soviet Union fractured into ethnic pieces, and Gorbachev was a prime minister without a state. Almost exactly 50 years after the beginning of World War II, the war that had propelled Washington into world pre-eminence, the once sleepy city on the Potomac was the capital of the sole surviving superpower.

and scissoring granite designed by architect I.M. Pei, opened in 1978. Under the rigorous stewardship of J. Carter Brown, the National Gallery staged ambitious international exhibitions, often persuading foreign museums to forgo New York for Washington in return for federal favors. Manhattan's cultural czars complained bitterly, but in increasing numbers New Yorkers traveled south for the capital's music, shows, and even movie premiers.

Through all the cultural and commercial hubbub, the business of Washington remained national government. Ronald Reagan arrived in 1980 with a promise to "privatize" vast sections of the federal bureaucracy. Inevitably, many government contracts landed in the hands of local "Beltway bandits," adding to the region's economic largesse. Real-estate prices soared. Inside the Beltway, the extra-governmental groups mutated and spawned. Between 1973 and 1981, the number of lawyers in town tripled. So did the number of psychiatrists. Seemingly identical in their grey suits and red ties, politicians, consultants, and even journalists vied for "sound bites" in the electronic press. The sparkling new Metrorail system, 110 miles in all, whisked citizens from city to suburb. In 1989, a local publication proclaimed the capital "Fat City," while another magazine came up with the label "power town".

Not all residents were pleased with Washington's new facade. "It was a gentle city when I came," writer Scott Hart told the New York Times in 1972. "Now there's a core of savage competition here." Growing old in the nation's capital, veteran columnist Joseph Alsop cast his sour eye over "the avenues of storage warehouses for government clerks, so prominent today." North-west Washington was still an exceedingly pleasant place to live for those who could afford it. For those who could not, muggings, drug use, and random gun play were increasingly common hazards. Despite the largest per-capita police force in the nation, 472 murders were committed in the District in 1990, the same year the city's mayor, Marion Barry, was convicted of cocaine possession. The modern capital was a rougher, more harried place, but then the entire country was more harried, too.

"Look at the United States," says Frank Waldrop, former managing editor of the old Washington Times Herald, "tell me what it's made of: that's Washington." Approaching the year 2000, then, the capital remains what it has always been: a reflection of the state of the nation. Following the Second World War, the town became a city; the nation, a world power. By 1990, Washington was the wealthiest of the 10 largest metropolitan areas in the country, the United States the wealthiest country on Earth. Washingtonians were no more rooted than they ever had been, but modern Americans were less rooted, too. As monuments collected around the Mall, ego and confidence, compassion and conflict emanated from country and capital alike. The United States had grown up since the Second World War, and its national capital had grown up, too. ★

A Capital City

A Man with a Map

Marjorie Ashworth

A NEWCOMER TO WASHINGTON SOON FINDS THAT THE CITY HAS DIMENSIONS FAR BEYOND THOSE OF JUST ANOTHER AMERICAN TOWN WITH FEDERAL BUILDINGS AND MUSEUMS SUPERIMPOSED ON IT. WASHINGTON CAN LOSE THE VISITOR ON RIGHT-ANGLE STREETS SUDDENLY CUT BY SLANTING AVENUES, CONFUSE WITH TRIANGULAR PARKLETS, BEDEVIL AROUND CIRCLES AND SQUARES, EXHAUST AND DELIGHT WITH ITS LONG MALL AND BROAD AVENUES.

★ ★ ★ ★ ★

The City of Washington lithograph, left, printed by Charles R. Parsons in 1880, depicts the burgeoning federal city designed by French architect Pierre Charles L'Enfant in 1791. Bryan Leister's oil portrait of L'Enfant, above, is based on a silhouette of the Frenchman and a painting of his father, Pierre L'Enfant.

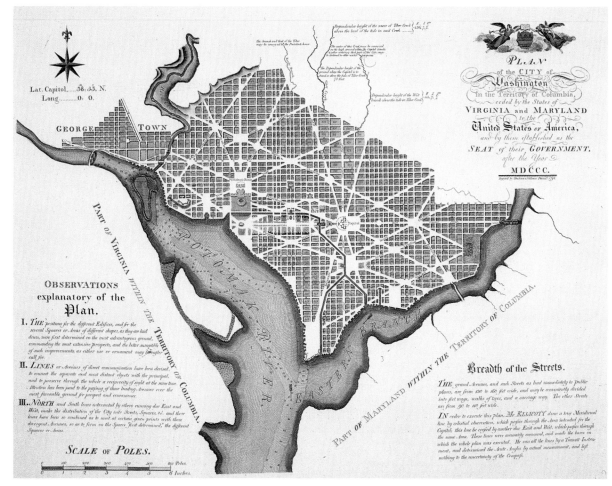

The city of Washington has such unique characteristics because a gifted man stamped his personality on it some 200 years ago. He was, of course, Pierre Charles L'Enfant: Frenchman; American Revolutionary War hero; intimate of the likes of Washington and Hamilton; and surely one of the most tactless, obstinate, arrogant, and tunnel-visioned people around in an era filled with strong personalities. Had he tried deliberately to provoke those most crucial to his success, he could not have done a better job. He was also uncommonly willing to take on any project asked of him, from designing a medal to planning a gala for several thousand guests. However, cost, time, compromise had no meaning for him.

It is remarkable that America's capital was designed with such a sense of grandeur and sureness when one thinks of how it was back in 1791: the country's towering debts, a government barely born, strong separatist feelings in many states, and lingering loyalties to England. It was L'Enfant's personality and the heritage he brought from his homeland that made the city's lofty character possible.

Born in 1754, Pierre Charles L'Enfant grew up surrounded by gems of architectural and landscape planning from an earlier era. Rulers of those days liked to enhance their prestige by adorning their cities with beauty. Public gardens, fountains, and buildings were created in the "grand manner" with space to pause and contemplate the order in fine design. Commissioned by European leaders, landscape architect André Le Nôtre left his imprint on many cities as he emphasized the adaptation of a plan to the natural contour of the land. The landscapes of L'Enfant's youth included Versailles, the

Tuileries, the Palais Royal, and the Luxembourg gardens.

Details of his early life are sketchy, but his father's influence also helped chart his way. His painter-father worked for Louis XVI in the manufacture of Gobelin tapestries that depicted French fortifications and battlegrounds. Under the elder L'Enfant's tutelage, he learned the rudiments of architecture and engineering, even studying under him at the Royal Academy of Painting and Sculpture.

L'Enfant was in his early 20s when France was quarreling with England and the people were stirring with ideas of freedom. France had lost Canada to England just a few years earlier, and had been humiliated on the sea by the English navy. America's Declaration of Independence gave young Frenchmen a chance to fight for freedom and, at the same time, to even the score with their old enemy. Besides, there was no higher adventure in those days than to set off for the "New World," about which they had heard so much.

L'Enfant was among the first Frenchmen to decide to take his chances in America, and arrived on her shores with Major General Tronson du Coudray and some 30 or 40 companions in spring 1777. After a short time helping to defend the lower Delaware River area, du Coudray drowned in a freak accident as he and his men were going to join General George Washington that September at the Battle of Brandywine. This must have left L'Enfant a somewhat bewildered young man, torn between returning home or trying to attach himself to another part of the fragmented Continental Army.

The next few years of his life were a wild mix of drawing, fighting, and suffering severe hardships. He joined Prussian General Frederick von Steuben's staff, and eventually moved with this group to a farmhouse near General Washington's headquarters at Valley Forge, Pennsylvania. While von Steuben began the task of turning raw Colonial recruits into soldiers, L'Enfant spent the long winter doing pencil portraits of American officers. At Lafayette's request, he also painted a portrait of General Washington.

After von Steuben was appointed inspector general of the troops, he insisted on a standard book of Army regulations and set about preparing it with his aides. L'Enfant meticulously drew the illustrations for what was published as Regulations, Order and Discipline for the Army of the United States, but came to be known as the Continental Army's famous "blue book."

L'Enfant then moved to the Savannah-Charleston region with the American and French forces under the Polish patriot Casimir Pulaski. Both he and Pulaski were wounded during the battle for Savannah on October 9, 1779. L'Enfant managed to escape to Charleston, but two days later, Pulaski died. "My weak state of health did not permit me to work at the fortifications of Charlestown," L'Enfant later wrote to General Washington. But in 1780, with the aid of a crutch, he fought in the battle for Charleston, which the American forces also lost. L'Enfant was captured by the British, but was freed

★ ★ ★ ★ ★

This view of Versailles, painted by Pierre Patel in 1668, resembles the western vista from the U.S. Capitol, looking towards the Washington Monument. Pierre L'Enfant was influenced early on by the famous landscape architect André Le Nôtre and his design of Versailles.

through a prisoner exchange in January 1782. By the next year, Congress had recognized L'Enfant's gallant service and commissioned him Major in the Army Corps of Engineers.

Things finally began to change for the young Frenchman. When there was to be an important public event or celebration, L'Enfant was asked to plan it. When Revolutionary War heroes formed the prestigious Society of the Cincinnati, they turned to L'Enfant to design a distinctive medal and certificate of membership.

New doors continued to open. In July 1788, L'Enfant designed a banquet hall and pavilion to accommodate the more than 6,000 people who would be gathering in celebration of New York's ratification of the U.S. Constitution. He worked closely with famous cabinetmaker Duncan Phyfe and hobnobbed with such notables as John Jacob Astor, Alexander Hamilton, and George Washington himself. When New York's City Hall was designated the temporary headquarters for the new federal government, L'Enfant was commissioned to redesign it, and it was here, on April 30, 1789, that George Washington took the oath of office as the first President of the United States. It was here, too, that the first Congress

under the U.S. Constitution convened. For compensation, L'Enfant was offered 10 acres of land in the heart of Manhattan—a plot east of what is now Central Park near 68th Street which even in the 18th century would have been valuable. Curiously, he refused it, presumably because he did not consider it adequate payment.

L'Enfant was at the top of his prestige at this time. Consequently, when an agreement was reached for the capital of the country to be located on the banks of the Potomac River, he was determined to be the person who would design it. As he wrote to President Washington, "no nation, perhaps, had ever before the opportunity offered them of deliberately deciding on the spot where their Capital should be fixed. . . . The plan should be drawn on such a scale as to leave room for that aggrandizement & embellishment which the increase of the wealth of the Nation will permit it to pursue at any period however remote. . . ."

Impressed with L'Enfant's talents over the years as well as with his view of the future of the nation, Washington gave approval in 1791 to L'Enfant's proposal to survey and draw up a plan for the new capital. The President was preoccupied with affairs of state, however, and neither he nor his aides had a firm agreement with L'Enfant that spelled out terms of payment or enumerated exactly what his duties were and to whom he would be responsible.

"Wednesday [March 9] evening arrived in this town Major Longfont, a French gentleman employed by the President of the United States to survey the lands contiguous to Georgetown, where the Federal City is to be put," announced the Maryland Journal & Baltimore Advertiser. Andrew Ellicott, a well-known Philadelphia surveyor, already had been named to begin setting the boundary for the District. He would be working with his assistant, the free black man Benjamin Banneker, a talented, self-taught mathematician and astronomer. Ellicott did not think much of the semi-wilderness selected for the capital's site. "This country intended for the Permanent Residence of the Congress, bears no

★ ★ ★ ★ ★

Anticipating the appearance of the completed capital city, Baltimore artist Edward Sachse depicted the U.S. Capitol in 1852 with both the Senate and House wings completed but not its new iron dome. The Washington Monument, seen at upper left, was not completed until 1885. It rises here from Robert Mills's original temple-base design.

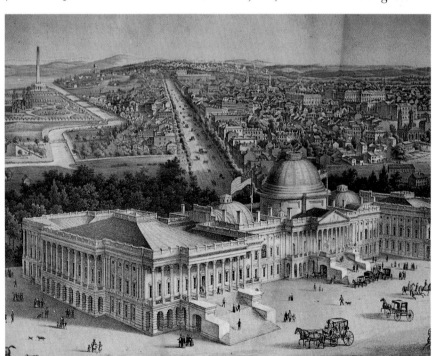

70

In his 1931 painting *The Planning of Washington,* artist Garnet W. Jex assembled some of the major characters who contributed to the creation of the capital city. From left to right: District commissioners Thomas Johnson (with cane) and Daniel Carroll; Dr. William Thornton; Pierre Charles L'Enfant, holding his map; President Washington (mounted); surveyor Andrew Ellicott (kneeling); and black astronomer and mathematician Benjamin Banneker.

more proportion to the country about Philadelphia and German-Town, for either wealth or fertility, than a crane does to a stall-fed Ox!" he wrote to his wife.

L'Enfant, however, was able to look beyond the swampland, scrubby elder bushes, and scanty farms that made up the scene and to visualize the great capital of a vast nation. So clear was his vision of what he wanted to do that he moved ahead with single-minded effort, drawing on such youthful memories as the spacious vistas of Versailles. Jenkins Hill, a wooded rise that was to be the site of the U.S. Capitol, particularly attracted him. It "stands as a pedestal waiting for a monument," he wrote. He wanted a triangle at the heart of the city: the Capitol at one point, the President's House—as the White House was then called—at another, and a proposed statue to George Washington at the third. The city design as a whole was to be a right-angle grid system of streets combined with broad avenues. Circles, parks, and squares added even more variety.

Matching his plans to the contour of the land, he placed the President's House on high ground to the northwest of Jenkins Hill, the two "connected with the public walk and avenue, grand as it will be agreeable and convenient to

the whole city . . . and all along side of which may be placed play houses, rooms of assembly, academies and all such sort of places as may be attractive to the learned and afford diversion to the idle." This thoroughfare was to become Pennsylvania Avenue, the ceremonial way for hundreds of parades, military marches, celebrations, and demonstrations.

Down below Jenkins Hill flowed Tiber Creek, a stream that meandered westward to the Potomac and overflowed with heavy rains and changes in Potomac tides. L'Enfant envisioned a canal that ran from the Eastern Branch, or Anacostia River, to the Tiber, turning the whole into a commercial, scenic waterway. Produce would be brought in from distant farms, the swampland would be brought under control, and the banks of a beautiful waterway would give residents a place to stroll. It could be that L'Enfant was remembering the banks of the Seine in Paris. Indeed, in 1801, the "Centre Market" opened for business on Pennsylvania Avenue between 7th and 9th streets, and farmers and watermen brought in their produce by boat on the canal. L'Enfant's city design also included some 15 squares, a national church, colleges and academies, an arcade of shops, and a splendid vista—the Mall—that stretched down from the Capitol towards General Washington's statue.

While L'Enfant dreamed and planned, there was an urgent need to make haste. Other cities had not given up on their bid to become the capital. Philadelphia, long the center of national activity, was pressing to have the national government there. As reports came from the untamed land to the south that had been chosen, it seemed more and more likely that it would be impossible for the government to move to the Potomac by the target date of 1800.

Letters were dispatched back and forth between the visionary planner and the more practical government. L'Enfant described his great design for the future; Washington and Jefferson urged that there be basic requirements such as streets, buildings, and drinking water for the residents. To get things moving, money was needed to build structures, hack through undergrowth, pay workers, and buy construction equipment. L'Enfant favored floating a loan, but Jefferson and Washington knew the condition of the national budget and wanted to pay expenses by selling land. Local landowners had been persuaded by Washington to give up some of their property to the federal city, and from the sale of these lots the government hoped to finance the building of the Capitol and the President's House. Fearing it might interfere with his city plans, L'Enfant was unhappy with the scheme, but the landowners hoped to make a killing by selling the remainder of the land that they owned.

Other problems arose when L'Enfant refused to report to the three city commissioners—Thomas Johnson and Daniel Carroll of Maryland and David Stuart of Virginia—appointed by Congress in January 1791. All three were influential, proud gentlemen, patriots and friends of Washington. L'Enfant, who also considered himself a friend of the President, began bypassing the commissioners regularly and sending his designs, new ideas, and problems directly to Washington.

The auctioning of lots turned out to be a disaster. When the day of the sale arrived, copies of the map illustrating the preliminary layout of the city were not available, and prospective buyers had no idea where streets and avenues or future government buildings were to be located. Everyone blamed everyone else, and to many L'Enfant looked like the culprit. It was well known that he had opposed the land sale all along and had kept his own copy of the map to himself. It seemed strange that he would have encountered so much difficulty getting the maps printed in Philadelphia in time for the auction.

A second disaster involving L'Enfant directly involved the already exasperated city commissioners. Daniel Carroll of Duddington, nephew of commissioner Carroll, had begun building a home near the future site of the Capitol, and part of it extended onto L'Enfant's proposed New Jersey Avenue. According to L'Enfant's plan, New Jersey and Pennsylvania avenues were key thoroughfares radiating out from the Capitol. L'Enfant notified Carroll that the house had to be removed. Commissioner Carroll appealed to Washington, who had to turn from affairs of state to settle the squabble. The President courteously told Carroll that he had two choices: either have the building pulled down and rebuilt in line with the street without expense to him, or build the house and live in it for six years and then have it removed. Washington sent a copy of his letter to L'Enfant, but the Frenchman already had taken the matter in his own hands and had begun to have the building torn down, informing the city commissioners only after the work was underway. Commissioner Carroll furiously ordered the workmen away; L'Enfant hired more workmen and the building was completely torn down. Washington soothed the Carrolls with payment for loss of property, but L'Enfant's effectiveness was over. The relationship between him and the commissioners continued to worsen, and L'Enfant finally was relieved of his job in March 1792, one year after he had arrived. Andrew

Ellicott and Benjamin Banneker took up his work, making few changes in the original city plan. It is doubtful that L'Enfant ever really understood why his dream assignment had been cut short so miserably.

After the Washington debacle, a number of highly placed friends reached out to help L'Enfant. They knew of his bravery in the Revolutionary War and of his eagerness to take on almost any kind of project asked of him. Perhaps they also understood his inability to compromise and his imperious ways, which went against the grain in America. Alexander Hamilton was the first to offer help, arranging for him to plan the city of Paterson, New Jersey, a pilot model city devoted to manufacturing. Once again L'Enfant threw himself into the project, but his design for Paterson was too grandiose for the backers, money ran out, and a year after he began he was relieved of his job.

After a series of failures, Secretary of State James Monroe urged him to accept a position as a professor of engineering at the U.S. Military Academy at West Point. L'Enfant's reply was that he had neither "the rigidity of manner—the tongue—nor the patience, nor indeed any of the inclinations peculiar to instructors."

Others recognized the country's debt to L'Enfant, but the pride and prickly disposition of this lonely eccentric made it very hard to help him. Trying to get paid for his work in designing the capital city became an obsession with him in his later years. He had refused an earlier offer of money and a "lot on a good part of the city" near the President's House or the Capitol. Now, without funds, he made repeated appeals to Congress for amounts its members would never

honor. In 1810, when he finally was awarded a small sum, the money immediately went to his creditors.

L'Enfant's final project was the reconstruction of the fort at Warburton, now known as Fort Washington, on the Potomac below the capital. For 12 months, L'Enfant designed and superintended the building of the fortification, but, true to his usual pattern, the project became ever more extravagant and he was replaced.

In February 1824, elderly and eccentric, he was invited to take up residence with William Dudley Digges, at Green Hill, in Maryland. Ironically, William Dudley Digges was married to Eleanor Carroll, daughter of Daniel Carroll, the very man whose house L'Enfant had ordered torn down. By now, L'Enfant was an impoverished solitary who still clung to his pride. He died on June 24, 1825, at 71 years of age. At his death, his property—watches, a compass, surveyor's instruments and books, and maps—was valued at about $45.

Some have written critically of L'Enfant's design for the nation's capital as too complicated, even too wasteful of space. The Frenchman's difficult personality did little to invite objectivity, which undoubtedly remains one of the reasons for the long-standing debate over the durability of his ideas. There are few today, however, who would disagree with writer Howard Means, who pointed out that L'Enfant "gave the city something unique and imposed a logic that carried beyond the space he planned and the time he lived in. Washington is not Philadelphia or New York or any other place on the face of the nation. It is Washington, absolutely." ★

★ ★ ★ ★ ★

The most celebrated change to L'Enfant's plan for the capital came with the expansion of the Treasury Department building. Begun in 1836 along 15th Street and across Pennsylvania Avenue, the extension interrupted the direct line from the White House to the U.S. Capitol. Freedom Plaza intersects the famous avenue at 13th Street Northwest.

The Capitol

C. M. HARRIS

THE UNITED STATES CAPITOL IS A UNIQUE BUILDING, OR, MORE ACCURATELY, GROUP OF BUILDINGS—A GREAT SYMBOL OF AN EVER-CHANGING NATION THAT GREW FROM 13 SMALL COLONIES TO FORM THE MOST POWERFUL AND INFLUENTIAL COUNTRY IN THE WORLD. SINCE 1800, WHEN THE CITY OF WASHINGTON BECAME THE PERMANENT SEAT OF GOVERNMENT, CAPITOL SQUARE HAS FORMED THE SYMBOLIC CENTER OF THE UNITED STATES. THE SITE ON JENKINS HILL WAS FIXED ALMOST 10 YEARS EARLIER BY PRESIDENT GEORGE WASHINGTON AND HIS ENGINEER AND CITY PLANNER, PIERRE L'ENFANT, WHO ENTHUSIASTICALLY PRONOUNCED IT "A PEDESTAL WAITING FOR A MONUMENT." L'ENFANT WAS DISMISSED BEFORE HE COULD PRODUCE AN ACCEPTABLE DESIGN FOR THE BUILDING, BUT HE MADE THE SITE THE FOCAL POINT OF HIS PLAN FOR THE NEW CAPITAL CITY, AND IT REMAINS TODAY THE CENTER THAT DIVIDES THE FOUR QUADRANTS, OR SECTORS, OF THE DISTRICT OF COLUMBIA AND ORGANIZES THE NUMBERING OF ITS STREETS.

★ ★ ★ ★ ★

Pediment over the east-front portico of the Senate wing, left, depicts Thomas Crawford's design for "the Progress of Civilization." Modeled in Rome, the figures were carved between 1855 and 1859, and erected in 1863. At right, a bicycle enthusiast tests his skill down the front steps of the House wing. Both Senate and House wings were added to the Capitol in the 1850s and 1860s.

From the day in 1792 when the first competition for a suitable design was announced, architects and artists have aspired to leave their stamp on the United States Capitol, and their skills and tastes—as well as their egos—are well exhibited in its many parts. Much to their dismay, however, but not inappropriately, politicians have shaped the nation's principal public building more than have artists. Political figures conceived it, named it, and have prevailed in most of the design decisions. But the Capitol has never yielded to the individual ideas of politician or artist, and it remains, in fitting fashion for a democracy, a

ancient Roman Republic, which, through literature and art, had inspired the Enlightenment ideal of a modern commonwealth. While serving as U.S. minister to France, Jefferson had gone to great lengths to identify and copy an appropriate Roman model (the Maison Carrée, in Nîmes) for the design of the new Virginia state capitol in Richmond. This interest expressed more than his love of architecture and the antique: Jefferson's larger purpose was political—to adapt from history a useful form and process that would help to secure republican government in America.

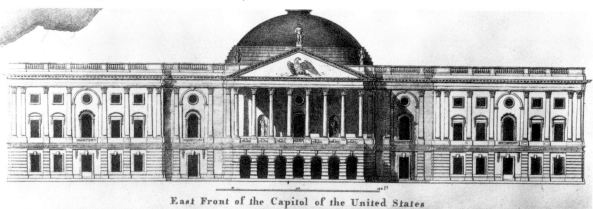

East Front of the Capitol of the United States
as originally designed by William Thornton—and adopted by General Washington, President of the United States.

composite structure as well as a unifying emblem of self-government.

The decision to build a "federal Capitol" was made by President Washington at the urging of his Secretary of State, Thomas Jefferson. The first home of the Federal Congress, in New York City, had been known simply as Federal Hall, and in his preliminary plans for the new capital, Pierre L'Enfant had envisioned a large, imposing, and not too accessible "Congress Hall." Jefferson and Washington were familiar with the term "Capitol," having served in the House of Burgesses that sat in the Virginia Capitol in Williamsburg. But the precedent they had in mind in choosing it was not that of Colonial Virginia. The United States Capitol was conceived as a national temple, a living link with the

The term Capitol was derived from Rome's great national temple to their principal god, Jupiter Optimus Maximus (Jupiter Greatest and Best), which stood on the highest of Rome's seven hills, the Capitoline, and came to be known as the Capitolium. The Jupiter temple had been inaugurated in 509 B.C., the year in which the Romans expelled their Etruscan kings and established a republic. At this temple the Roman people and Senate gathered to deliberate on important political occasions, to commemorate their gods, and to celebrate state festivals and military triumphs. It was precisely this

role of national temple and center of public life that Jefferson had in mind and convinced Washington to implement. The United States Capitol, however, would not contain images of pagan gods; it would house the national legislature, thereby enshrining the law-making process upon which the success of the republic would depend. It was to be, as Jefferson put it, "the first temple dedicated to the sovereignty of the people."

The design that struck Jefferson and Washington as the best and most appropriate for "a Capitol" came from a cultivated physician, Dr. William Thornton, of Tortola, in the British West Indies. Thornton was a naturalist and philosopher, and, less regularly, a practicing physician who had studied the modern sciences at the University of Edinburgh. Of the several entries in the design competition, his gave the clearest expression to the political ideas that lay behind the concept of the national temple. His design was in the neo-Roman architectural style. In the center of the building was a "grand vestibule" surmounted by a low, saucer-like dome—modeled after that of the Roman temple best known to the 18th century, the Pantheon. Historical references and purpose were reinforced by architectural details and by the inscription Thornton planned for the pediment of the

east front of the Capitol—"Justitiae Fidei Sacrum," which he translated: "[this temple] sacred to justice and faith (national)."

The first cornerstone ceremony was held on September 18, 1793, and presided over by George Washington, acting as President and as past Most Worshipful Master of the Alexandria Lodge of Freemasons. A silver plate placed under the cornerstone was inscribed with the year of Masonry 5793. The Capitol, following the masonic tradition of Solomon's Temple, faced the rising sun, but its orientation to the east also signified to the monarchs and people of Europe the dawning of a "new order of the ages."

Early construction of the Capitol proceeded haltingly amid continuous controversy and precarious finances, eroding the high purpose imparted to the building by Washington, Jefferson, and Thornton. Interested parties in Philadelphia, the temporary capital until 1800, worked throughout the decade to prevent the government's removal to the Potomac; and superintending architects tried to substitute their own plans for the Capitol for the modified version of Thornton's that had been approved. Congress, suspicious of the monumental scale of the architecture, provided funds grudgingly. Labor and materials were expensive and often difficult to obtain. By the end of 1795, only the foundations of the building and one story of the north wing had been raised. As 1800 approached, "true republican" opponents of Federalist Presidents Washington and John Adams called for more practical use of the federal buildings, some demanding that the nearly completed President's House be given over to Congress and that the Capitol be used for the offices of the executive departments.

The Republican coalition gained political ascendancy in 1800 with the election of Thomas Jefferson to the Presidency. Their influence behind the scenes accounts for Congress's fail-

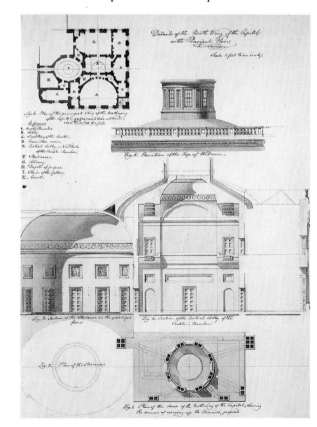

★ ★ ★ ★ ★

A 19th-century pen-and-ink sketch by Benjamin Latrobe includes details of the floor plan for the Capitol's north wing and Senate chamber. Appointed by President Thomas Jefferson in 1803, Latrobe was the first professional architect to work in the United States.

ure to carry through with one of the key elements in Thornton's temple design—the entombment of George Washington in the crypt on the ground level at the center of the building. Although Martha Washington reluctantly had assented to Congress's formal request to do this after the General's unexpected death in December 1799, the newly ascendant Jeffersonian Republicans had no intention of making the Capitol into a shrine for the popular Federalist President.

Jefferson kept the members of his party from going further, however, and the necessary funding was voted to continue construction of the principal public buildings. The new President also secured the services of Benjamin Henry Latrobe, the foremost architect and engineer then practicing in America. As Surveyor of the Public Buildings he introduced a new level of competence in construction. Latrobe also wanted to introduce significant changes to the Capitol design after his own neo-Greek taste, but Jefferson insisted that the neo-Roman Thornton design—as modified to his taste—not be altered. With much grumbling, Latrobe completed the south wing and rebuilt much of the north wing (first put together with wood and plaster) by 1810. When the chambers and functional rooms were largely finished, Congress showed its appre-

ciation by denying an appropriation for the "middle building" of the Capitol and referring to Latrobe as "the late Surveyor of the Public Buildings." The embittered architect set out for Pittsburgh in 1813, hoping to make money building steamboats on the Ohio River for Robert Fulton. Capitol construction all but stopped. The two wings remained connected by nothing more than a crude passageway of brick and pitch-pine boards.

Three years later, as the newspapers proclaimed it, calamity descended. The British determined to exact revenge for the American burning of the provincial Canadian capital of York (today's Toronto) in the War of 1812 and targeted the Federal City for destruction. In 1814 they made their way up the Chesapeake Bay and deployed a detachment of troops in southern Maryland, meeting only feeble resistance. Having entered Washington, they methodically set about the business of burning the public buildings. The republic's humiliation was complete. After rockets were shot through its roof and fires set in each of its rooms, the Capitol—"the harbor of Yankee democracy," as the British commander called it—went up in flames. Such was the intensity of the heat in the House chamber that Latrobe, on visiting the site a year later, found lumps of glass formed by the melting skylights that weighed more than a pound. He reported the scene to Jefferson, in retirement at Monticello, taking care to add that his brick dome over the Senate chamber was still standing, forming "a most magnificent ruin."

After a brief period of hesitation, Congress determined to reconstruct the United States Capitol. The work became a patriotic cause, a defiant expression of national will. Britain would not have its way. The building now took on a new identity, becoming a powerful symbol of the nation's hard-won independence and enduring commitment to republican government. Latrobe was reappointed architect, and, during his second "campaign" at the site, exerted much more influence on the design. The east portico was completed and extended across the entire facade of the central section of the building. Thornton's elliptical House chamber was redesigned in the form of a semicircular amphitheater.

Work on the north and south wings was completed by Charles Bulfinch, of Boston, who replaced Latrobe in 1818. An unusually agreeable and accommodative architect, he showed greater sensitivity to the ideas of his predecessors. The modified central block of the building was completed at last in 1827 with a bell-shaped wooden dome covered with copper.

The first Capitol had taken 34 years to complete, at a cost of $2,433,000. It had stretched more than 351 feet, and covered about one and a half acres, but it was outmoded within two decades. Some modernizing was done: running water was brought in from neighborhood springs in 1832; candles and astral oil lamps were replaced by piped gas lighting during the 1840s. But the design that appeared imposing, even intimidating, to the first Federal Congresses soon was perceived as quaint and confining. And seemingly little could be done to rectify the long-standing problems of bad acoustics, poor ventilation, and inadequate heating.

By 1850, when a second design competition was legislated, the United States had grown from 13 to 31 states, spanned the North American continent, and fronted on the two great oceans, the Atlantic and the Pacific. The sizable increase in Congressional membership mandated larger chambers for the Senate and the House and additional space for Congressional committees and offices. Visitors flooded the Capitol in numbers inconceivable to the previous generation.

But something more than additional space was required. The elected representatives had begun to expound and reflect upon what appeared to be a limitless future for the American people. By mid-century, through their writers, orators, and poets, Americans had begun to think in expansive, continental terms, and to express ideas of Manifest Destiny. The American sense of space and scale had been altered forever. Monumental architecture no longer was viewed suspiciously, nor, with the great increase in national wealth, perceived as extravagant expenditure.

In early 1850, Robert Mills, then Architect of Public Buildings, prepared a scheme for the enlargement of the Capitol that projected new Senate and House wings to the north and south of the original building, and a tall, colonnaded central dome—elements that eventually were adopted. The visual impact of such a change, however, proved difficult to digest. In the fall of the same year, the Senate Committee on Public

★ ★ ★ ★ ★

A painting of the old House chamber depicts a night session in 1822. Artist Samuel F.B. Morse captured many details—including individual members—and went on to invent the telegraph.

★ ★ ★ ★ ★

Italian artist Constantino
Brumidi painted "the
Apotheosis of Washington"
allegory on the inside of
the Capitol dome.

Buildings invited plans and estimates for extension of the Capitol either by additional wings or a totally separate building to the east, within the Capitol grounds. None of the entries was accepted, for no one idea struck the right chord, as Dr. Thornton's had in 1793. Some entries proposed to expand the old building to the east and west, but Congress hesitated to build over the structure of the old Capitol. Mills was instructed to combine the elements of the four designs judged best by the committee.

The need for space was so acute, however, that a Democratic Congress went ahead, and, on September 30, 1850, appropriated $100,000 to get work on the Capitol enlargement started, even authorizing the Whig President to appoint the architect. Millard Fillmore chose Thomas Ustick Walter, a prominent Philadelphia architect who had submitted a design in the 1850 competition. The extension that was approved by the President more than doubled the area of the Capitol without altering the old building and its copper-clad dome. It placed two large rectilinear wings (oriented on east-west axes) on the north and south ends, connecting them to the old building by corridors. These provided grand new House and Senate chambers and much needed office space. But the overall visual effect was to create a bulky, horizontal grouping of classical buildings. The combined fronts of the new Capitol complex were to extend 746 feet, more than twice the span of the old building. The scale first envisioned by L'Enfant when he laid out his immense Capitol Square thus was realized, but not without a loss of symbolic clarity. The temple design of the original building was now obscured.

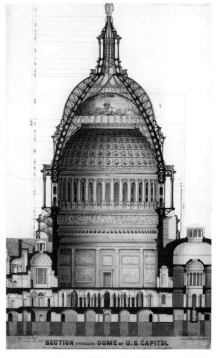

★ ★ ★ ★ ★
Architect Thomas U. Walter's 1859 section drawing, right, details the current 4,500-ton, cast-iron dome, which, beginning during the Civil War, was crafted to replace Charles Bulfinch's original. Brumidi's painting appears at the top of Walter's unique double dome.

★ ★ ★ ★ ★
Constantino Brumidi, left, spent 20 years of his life painting his Capitol masterpiece. At right, a 19-foot statue of Freedom caps the dome.

President Millard Fillmore laid the cornerstone of the extension on July 4, 1851, assisted by the Grand Master of the District of Columbia Grand Lodge, who was dressed in the same Masonic regalia George Washington had worn in 1793. There was suitable oratory from Senator Daniel Webster, who prayed that "the walls and arches and domes and towers, the columns and entablatures, now to be erected . . . endure forever."

Construction at first progressed rapidly despite the fact that Walter was not permitted to award a general contract, and many large portions were done day by day. Stone supply, however, was a constant source of trouble. The larger exterior marble blocks from quarries in Berkshire County, Massachusetts, cost the United States $1.98 per cubic foot (a price that a House investigation judged to be unnecessarily high). Controversies over charges of employment fraud, the method of awarding con-

A bill rests on a table in the Senate Appropriations Committee Room, on the first floor of the Capitol's north wing. Mythological marine figures on the walls and ceiling hint at the room's former use by the Senate Committee on Naval Affairs.

sessed considerable talents, but, much to his regret, was unable to avoid the inevitable political pressures of a huge government undertaking. The political affiliation of workmen once again became significant. Despite strict official hiring policies, Meigs was plagued by requests from Congressmen to give employment to their constituents. He turned over the matter of hiring to his foremen. In June 1853 Secretary Davis wrote to Meigs, "unofficially and without intent to interfere . . . that complaints are frequently made that your subordinates decide against employing workmen because they are Democrats."

Meigs concentrated on what he saw as the deficiencies of the Walter scheme. The changes he made to the plan for the Capitol extension, while frequently challenged in Congress, were consistently and ably defended by Davis, who in fact originated many of them. The most significant alteration to the adopted scheme involved relocating the new legislative chambers to the centers of the new wings, rather than to their western extremities, as Walter had intended. Meigs also substituted brilliantly colored English Minton encaustic tile for Walter's proposed brick floors; monolithic rather than sectional columns for the porticoes; and iron, rather than wooden, roofs and ceilings, window and door casings. He improved the design of the acoustics and that of the heating and ventilating systems, also supervising a myriad of other engineering improvements—all at little increased cost. The best modern style of the mid-19th century was introduced into the interiors of the Capitol. Italian marble was used throughout, its cost no longer considered prohibitive.

As work on the wings for the new legislative chambers progressed, however, the Bulfinch dome seemed more awkward and ill-propor-

tracts, and quality of materials and workmanship—in no small way colored by politics—led the newly elected President, Franklin Pierce, a Democrat, to remove responsibility for the Capitol extension from the Secretary of the Interior and to place the entire business of completing the Capitol in the hands of his Secretary of War, Jefferson Davis. Soon after March 1853, architect Walter, who had been appointed by a Whig President, was subordinated to the chief military engineer, Captain Montgomery C. Meigs.

Trained as an engineer at West Point, and a descendant of Benjamin Franklin, Meigs pos-

tioned. The horizontality of the extended Capitol was overwhelming. Consensus grew for a new dome, and in March 1855 Walter gained approval for his design for the great cast-iron dome that since has become a worldwide symbol of both Washington, D.C., and the United States. The new House chamber opened in December 1857, the Senate chamber in 1859. The dome was still under construction when the Civil War commenced, but President Lincoln insisted that the work continue, aware that the structure formed a strong visual symbol of the Union. With the placement of Thomas Crawford's statue of Freedom at the pinnacle of the dome in December 1863, the United States Capitol attained the form and appearance it would have for almost another century.

After the Civil War there was a pause in major construction at the Capitol. The redesigning of the grounds and construction of the monumental terrace and staircases on the west side of the Capitol were the major undertakings of the last quarter of the 19th century. Building activity within the Capitol walls picked up after 1900 when the rooms vacated by the Library of Congress, finally established in its own building, were converted into 28 committee rooms. Space used by the Supreme Court and Law Library was available upon the completion of the Supreme Court Building across Capitol Square in 1935. Extensions of the Capitol have occurred infrequently, but efforts to improve the internal systems of the building have been constant. It was not until the Great Depression that air conditioning of the Capitol was feasible, and in 1936, at a cost of more than $2.5 million, the first system was installed.

Long debated plans for further enlargement of the Capitol finally moved forward in the Eisenhower era with the extension of the east

walls and portico of the old Bulfinch structure. The case for enlarging the central block focused on the Walter dome. Although this dome was undertaken because the Bulfinch dome had become disproportionately small for the extended Capitol, it was soon perceived to visually overwhelm the building, especially the east front. Many agreed with the flamboyant Senator Roscoe Conkling of New York, who more than once remarked that the Capitol was "a dome with a building under it, rather than a building with a dome upon it."

Several proposals to gain additional bulk and space by extending the west front have been made since the mid-19th century. Thomas Walter and many subsequent architects have envisioned a pedimented portico under the dome on the west side of the central block to give the enlarged Capitol more harmony and monumentality. In recent years plans to extend the west front rested on the argument that the west wall was about to fall down, which proved to be exaggerated. Congress's determination in 1983 to restore the remaining original features of the Thornton-Latrobe-Bulfinch structure seems to have ended the debate, at least in this century. Restoration work was completed in 1987. ★

★ ★ ★ The West Front and Terraces ★ ★ ★

THE WEST FRONT of the Capitol has had a curious evolution. William Thornton, whose design for the Capitol had won the approval of both Washington and Jefferson, originally had planned a second large circular space behind the Rotunda, the Grand Conference Room, a magnificent chamber intended for joint sessions of Congress. This space would have projected partially from the west front, and been open through windows to the distant western horizon. Like President Washington, and, later, Jefferson, Thornton had little difficulty foreseeing the country's westward destiny, and responded in this design, not unintentionally, to the westward pull of the interior of the continent.

Very little work had been done on the center of the building when the death of George Washington in December 1799 led Thornton to rethink the design of the west front and consider a temple-like monument to the first President. The abandonment of plans for the conference room, as well as those for the entombment of Washington, left the space in the center of the

west front available for other purposes. Under Charles Bulfinch, and with Congressional mandate, that space was finished off with a rather modest colonnade, behind which, on the principal floor, were the quarters of the Library of Congress. Visitors soon discovered, much to the dismay of serious readers, that the library reading room, considered the most beautiful in Washington, offered the best scenic view in the city.

The foundations of the Capitol were laid too close to the brow of Jenkins Hill, which falls off sharply in the direction of the Mall and the Potomac River. This made the appearance of the exposed basement wall of the west front a problem from the outset. Bulfinch effectively diminished the defects in siting the Capitol by creating a grassy, earthen embankment that helped to give visual support to the structure. Below the central section of the building, he interrupted the earthen berm with a simple terrace and staircases that created for the first time a direct

approach to the Capitol from the Mall and the center of the city.

For many decades the grounds of the Capitol and the Mall formed an ill-kept, if vaguely pastoral landscape at the heart of the Federal City. The Capitol grounds had been enclosed and encircled by a road in the very early 19th century. By 1820 Bulfinch's elegant sandstone piers, gatehouses, and iron railing had been set around "Capitol Square." Only a few years later, however, the Commissioner of Public Buildings, when asked about progress of plans for improving the Square, reported to Congress that the Capitol grounds were so cluttered with shops and materials that it was impossible to estimate the cost of improvements, and therefore no plan existed. Several years later, during Andrew Jackson's Presidency, seven acres were added to the grounds on the west. James Maher, the Irish gardener in charge, planted many fast growing trees that, in the wet, warm Washington climate, soon gave the grounds the appearance of a small forest.

The extension of the Capitol in the 1850s required a complete rethinking of the surrounding landscape. Senator Justin Morrill of Vermont, Chairman of the Senate Committee on Public Grounds, called landscape architect Frederick Law Olmsted to Washington. In March 1874, Congress appropriated $200,000 for grounds improvements and put Olmsted, best known for his design of New York's Central Park, in charge. At this time the view from the west front took in railroad tracks that crossed the Mall as well as the abandoned

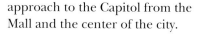

★ ★ ★ ★ ★
Another William Thornton drawing, this one of the west front of the Capitol, depicts an alternate dome and, behind the Rotunda, the circular hall designed for joint sessions of Congress.

★ ★ ★ ★ ★

Originally planned to house the Library of Congress, Bulfinch's west-front Capitol colonnade, along with Frederick Law Olmsted's terraces, provides a sweeping view of the nation's capital.

waterways of the Washington City Canal, which had become a fetid open sewer.

Despite the recent Capitol extension, Congress was already demanding additional storage space when Olmsted's design work began. That need helped to shape Olmsted's inspired solution: Bulfinch's earthen berm was replaced by a huge, architectural, marble terrace, beneath which a vast new storage area was created. Grand staircases descended the western slope of Capitol Hill, connecting with broad walkways that picked up the axes of Maryland and Pennsylvania avenues. Refuge from Washington heat was provided by shading the 46 carriage ways and footpaths with dense, low-growing trees. These plantings insured that the views of the building afforded by Olmsted's broad new lawns would not be interrupted.

Although the aged Thomas Walter declared that Olmsted's terrace "would be the making of the building," it took Congress 10 years to approve the terrace design. Some members feared that it would overwhelm the Capitol. Funds to start the terrace and stairways finally were voted in 1884, and then Olmsted had to fight—and was only partly successful in his efforts—to keep the terrace from becoming pierced with openings to accommodate offices rather than storage in the space below. In his opinion, such an alteration diminished the role of the terrace as a base for the building. "I would much rather the work be arrested for years than have it go on with that condition," he told Architect of the Capitol Edward Clark. Although he had numerous great city parks to his credit, Olmsted considered the Capitol improvement his most important work.

With the completion of the Olmsted terrace in 1892, the west front of the Capitol assumed its present appearance. As early as the mid-19th century, ominous bulges were noticed in portions of the west-front foundation and basement, portending problems that construction of the terrace had not solved. The original Aquia Creek, Virginia, sandstone of the exterior walls was painted almost every four years, as it had been since 1819, but beneath the clean white surface the structure continued to deteriorate well into the 20th century.

Much controversy had been provoked by the east-front extension of 1958-1962, but arguments for and against preservation of the crumbling original west front were even more intense and heated two decades later. By that time, the west portico had been reinforced for some time by an ugly grid of highly visible timbers. The collapse of a portion of the sandstone veneer in April 1983 strengthened the hand of the pro-extension forces, but preservationists ultimately triumphed in this battle. The process of restoration showed that the west front was not quite as weak as had been supposed, although almost 40 percent of the original Aquia sandstone had to be replaced with more durable Indiana limestone. ★

Capitol Gallery

Michael Richman

As the legislative home of the American people, the United States Capitol daily celebrates the achievements and shortcomings, successes and failures of our democracy. For the first-time visitor as well as the dedicated Beltway-insider, the Capitol is a building that both creates and recreates history. This magnificent edifice also deserves recognition as a museum of American art and history, with an impressive collection of nearly 700 paintings and sculptures.

There is an adventure awaiting those with the time to explore the bronze and marble effigies in Statuary Hall. Much can be learned here about the reputations and contributions of the 89 men and 6 women from 50 states (Colorado, Nevada, New Mexico, North Dakota, and Wyoming have contributed only one statue) whose statues stand in the halls and corridors of Congress. These statues of distinguished Americans, many of them veterans of service in the House and Senate, are an unexpected treasury of America's past.

★ ★ ★ ★ ★

A special realm within the National Capitol Building, Statuary Hall holds works that transcend artistry—they are truly icons of our nationhood. Detail of hand at right is part of a standing figure of Lewis Cass, a Michigan legislator.

In the 1864 Congressional debate that established Statuary Hall, Justin S. Morrill, Senator from Vermont and principal sponsor, proclaimed: "pilgrims from all parts of the Union, as well as from foreign lands, may come and behold a gallery filled with such American manhood [and womanhood] as succeeding generations will delight to honor, and see also the actual forms and mold of those who have 'inerasably' fixed their names on the pages of history."

Passed on July 2, 1864, the law directed President Lincoln "to invite each and all the States to provide and furnish statues, in marble or bronze, not exceeding two in number from each State, of deceased persons who have been citizens thereof, and illustrious of their historic renown or for distinguished civic or military services, such as each State may deem to be worthy of this national commemoration."

In spite of these lofty pronouncements, the down-to-earth reality was that since the House of Representatives had moved to its new location seven years earlier, "the old Hall, empty and deserted, remains an unappropriated waste, draped in cobwebs and carpeted with dust, tobacco and apple pomace—a conspicuous nuisance."

It may well be that, just as Lincoln had urged the continuation of construction of the Capitol

during the Civil War, Congress enacted legislation creating an American pantheon during the last days of the 38th Congress as a harbinger of Union victory, even though the military outcome was still uncertain. Nowhere in the debate were the 11 Confederate states mentioned; they were missing.

In exercising its new role as art patron, Congress assumed that the states would determine who their two submissions should be, and would select the appropriate artists. Quality would be assured by competition, producing "worthy monuments to the genius of artists who will vie with each other for distinction in the execution of the various works that will be required."

Although the Secretary of State mailed invitations to the governors of 25 states in early January 1865, it would be five years before Rhode Island became the first state to respond. Its impressive submissions included statues of Revolutionary War hero Nathanael Greene, and of Roger Williams, the Puritan minister who founded the state in 1636. Greene's statue, by Henry Kirke Brown, was the first to be placed, on January 2, 1870. Remarking on the effort, Edward Clark, having recently replaced Thomas U. Walter as Architect of the Capitol, wrote: "Your 'Greene' is admired by everyone

whom I have heard speak of it, by some enthusiastically. It is in my judgment, an honor to the Nation, and the State that presented it, to say nothing of the genius who formed it."

Although Rhode Island's second entry bears inscribed markings to the effect that it was carved in Rome in 1870, Franklin Simmons's statue of Williams was not unveiled in Statuary Hall until January 9, 1872. Although no likeness of Williams survived, Simmons gathered information about the minister's personality and beliefs and carefully read accounts of Puritan lifestyle and apparel before making his imagined effigy.

For Daniel Chester French, the commission from the State of Michigan to make the Lewis Cass statue helped this Massachusetts-born sculptor build a national following. Of the statue, the 19th to be added to the Statuary Hall collection, historian Lorado Taft wrote: "Mr. French had a sturdy subject to deal with and selected the position best suited to reveal the character of the man. With all its solidity, the artist has so well treated the surface and made the flesh so mellow and the drapery so crisp and full of color that the figure easily takes its place among the best portrait statues of the country. Among its hard, conventional companions in that extraordinary collection of the Capitol, it stands almost alone."

French was able to model his portly subject faithfully and inspirationally by planting the feet apart in order to understate the figure's ponderous bulk, and by subtly draping the ubiquitous cloak off the column-like lectern and onto the floor as a tangible compositional balance to Cass's ample belly. The successful portrait sculptor must focus on details that enhance rather than dominate. There are too many hands frozen in awkward gesture that leave a great many statues lifeless and uninteresting.

No finer example of this detailing skill exists in the Statuary Hall collection than French's lifelike precision in modeling the right index finger and thumb of Lewis Cass as they press firmly into the rumpled pages of a lawbook. That hand is alive, and it imbues the figure with an expanding energy and down-to-earth believability. French has given Cass an unmistakable legislative rebirth, as though the Senator were still on the floor of the Senate, pausing during a debate.

Of the 58 sculptors represented in Statuary Hall, 11 are women, reflecting the fact that, well into this century, women were more widely represented in the profession of sculpture than in those of painting and architecture combined. One of the more competent of these female artists was Elisabet Ney, whose marble statue of Samuel Houston was presented in 1904.

Although Houston served as Representative and Governor of Tennessee and Senator and Governor of Texas, he is portrayed with a deer-skin jacket and a marvelously etched blanket that represents the four years he lived on an Indian reservation in the Oklahoma Territory. Only the sword and the haughty stance suggest Houston's exploits in securing Texas independence.

In 1905, Frances Emma Willard, of Illinois, became the first woman to be honored with a portrait statue in the Capitol, a slightly larger

than life-size marble by Helen Farnsworth Mears. Modeled in New York City, this statue may be one of the first marbles in Statuary Hall executed by the popular Italian carvers, the Piccirilli Brothers. The marble portrays the renowned educator, orator, and reformer in a reflective pose, gently leaning on a podium during one of the many lectures that earned her the title "best known and most universally loved woman in the United States."

The dignified calm of Miss Willard presents a dramatic contrast to the sprightly bounce of Henry Clay, of Kentucky. The most impressive of Charles Henry Niehaus's eight contributions to Statuary Hall, this willowy thin figure strode into a room, hat in one hand, with cane, overcoat, and a single glove clutched in the other, eagerly ready to get down to business.

At the time of the Clay unveiling in 1929, Statuary Hall was filled to overflowing. A bill introduced that year proposed a National Hall of Fame. Apparently this legislation never left the House Committee on Public Buildings and Grounds, but, by 1933, the Architect of the Capitol had been authorized to relocate some of the statues to other areas of the Capitol.

Around this time, Georgia and Mississippi contributed statues of Alexander Stephens and Jefferson Davis, respectively. Although both men had served in Congress, they are perhaps better known as the President and Vice President of the Confederacy. Jefferson Davis, who before the Civil War had served as U.S. Secretary of War (with oversight responsibility for the construction of the U.S. Capitol extension), and as Senator from Mississippi, is remembered with a bronze statue by Augustus Lukeman.

While there was no protest over the placement of the Davis statue, the Alexander Stephens monument drew a rebuke from the District of Columbia chapter of the National Association for the Advancement of Colored

Vinnie Ream sculpted her evocative statue of Lincoln in the late 1860s, opposite. Above and right, Hawaii's Father Damien, by Marisol Escobar; today it stands in Statuary Hall after its 1969 dedication in the Rotunda, at right. The priest served at a leprosy colony on the island of Molokai.

People, which claimed that "when he and others had been forgiven of their treason, the ungrateful South sent him to Congress again, where he obstructed every wise measure of Reconstruction statesmanship."

Careful examination of the marble Stephens statue, sensitively carved and one of only five seated sculptures in the collection, reveals Gutzon Borglum's modeling talents. The sculptor has captured faithfully the frail and wiry demeanor of the Georgia legislator, whose bony fingers are locked to the arms of the chair as he stares at the world, his cocked head intractably defiant.

Another member of Congress who also holds a special place in American history is Hannibal Hamlin, the Democratic Senator from Maine, who served as Lincoln's first Vice President. Portrayed by sculptor Charles E. Tefft, Hamlin here is an ageless, gentle old man, his wonderfully accentuated fingers gingerly gripping his cane. Little is known about Tefft, the Maine-born, New York City-trained sculptor, but the statue he produced is full of spirit and charm. It ranks right up there with the irreverently informal, hands-in-his-pockets, twinkle-in-his-eye statue of Will Rogers by the noted portraitist Jo Davidson. These works, placed in 1934 and 1938, respectively, offer adequate proof that the talents of American portrait sculptors await discovery in this collection.

Certainly the most refreshing and triumphal portrait in Statuary Hall is the blocky bronze of Father Damien, of Hawaii, by the internationally renowned American sculptor Marisol Escobar, born of Venezuelan parents in Paris. Nearly all of her life-size sculptures have been carved in wood, and, characteristically, her figures are stylized, bulky forms on slender legs, with tantalizing facial imagery and pervasive witty fantasy. What is remarkable in this portrait of Joseph de Veuster, the Catholic priest who spent 16 years

on the island of Molokai attending to a leprosy colony before contracting the disease himself, is the degree to which Marisol captures the likeness and character of this man, especially in the pock-marked face, the straggly beard, and the leprosy-twisted right hand.

Of the statues that were ordered directly by Congress, one of the first and perhaps historically the most important was the marble of Abraham Lincoln. That young Vinnie Ream was able to secure a $10,000 commission from Congress in July 1866 was in large measure possi-

ble because she had modeled a bust of Lincoln in March and April 1865. By June 1868, the perplexed young sculptor wrote to John Quincy Adams Ward: "as an eminent and experienced artist [to learn] your opinion as to the probability of moving with perfect safety a life-size clay model of Mr. Lincoln. . . . Clark Mills and a Mr. Flannery assured the House that my model can be moved out of the capitol, without the least probability of injuring it. They desire to delay me in my work, and offer to move the statue, and I believe they would rejoice at an opportunity to destroy it."

Writing in 1903, sculptor Lorado Taft offered this assessment of Ream's first monumental effort: "The 'Lincoln' is an extraordinary work for a child, and really is a far more dignified portrait than many of its neighbors in the National Hall of Statuary. It is neither grotesque in expression nor absurd in gesture. Closer examination reveals an absence of body within the garments. One feels that the girl sculptor approached her subject with reverence and, although her work is quite devoid of strength, it has its own melancholy expressiveness."

It is fitting that Ream's Lincoln joins Charles Tefft's Hannibal Hamlin, Augustus Lukeman's Jefferson Davis, and Gutzon Borglum's Alexander Stephens in forming a unique, four-way, sculptural tribute to the leaders of America during the Civil War.

A second Lincoln monument resides in the crypt of the Capitol. The three-times life-size beardless head was Gutzon Borglum's first sculpted portrait of the martyred President, and a precursor of his gigantic Presidential group at

Mt. Rushmore, South Dakota. The head, emerging unexpectedly out of a block of rough-hewn marble, was apparently purchased by Wall Street business tycoon Eugene Meyer, Jr., and presented to Congress to celebrate the 100th anniversary of Lincoln's birth. About the bust, Robert Todd Lincoln remarked, "I think it is the most extraordinarily good portrait of my father I have ever seen, and it impresses me deeply."

Congress's "official" art patronage may well have begun in 1832. Marking the 100th anniversary of the birth of George Washington, it commissioned the well-respected, Harvard-educated sculptor Horatio Greenough to make a monumental marble for the Rotunda. Displeased with Greenough's toga-clad, sandal-shod rendering of the father of his country, Congress banished Greenough's statue to the grounds within three years, and in 1908 transferred it to the Smithsonian Institution for safer keeping. It can be seen today in the National Museum of American History.

The other two painted images of Washington were more grandly received. John Vanderlyn produced a full-length portrait of Washington based directly on the famous Lansdowne portrait by Gilbert Stuart, which the young artist had seen in Stuart's Philadelphia studio. In 1834, a grateful Congress supplemented Vanderlyn's $1,000 fee with a $1,500 bonus "as evidence of the faithfulness of the copy." Today the painting is located on the south wall of the House Chamber, where it was installed in 1859.

Perhaps the most compelling of this early patronage was the purchase of Rembrandt Peale's Pater Patriae, known affectionately as the "Porthole" Washington, in 1832, for $2,000. For many years it hung "out-of-view" in the Vice President's office, and only recently was it installed in the exquisitely restored Old Senate Chamber. Like his father and brothers, Peale was the consummate promoter: in 1823, he claimed

Rembrandt Peale's portrait of George Washington, opposite, was purchased for the Capitol in 1832 and today hangs in the old Senate Chamber. Below, a masterful statue of Henry Clay, the "Great Compromiser" from Kentucky, the work of Henry Niehaus, had its unveiling in 1929.

that after 16 failures he had made the "last life portrait" of George Washington, even though the sitting took place in 1795. It is obvious that Congress felt more comfortable with Peale's mythologizing image than with Greenough's attempt to transform Washington into the Olympian Zeus.

While most of the portrait paintings of leaders of the House and Senate rank below their sculptural counterparts in artistic merit, a notable exception is the oil painting of Thomas Brackett Reed, of Maine, by John Singer

Sargent, commissioned by 21 fellow members of the 51st Congress. Sargent ignored Reed's 300-pound body, creating a closely cropped, half-length composition that captures the Congressman's brilliant intellect and razor-sharp wit, as evidenced in a memorably pithy evaluation of two colleagues: "They never open their mouths without subtracting from the sum of human knowledge." Cramped unceremoniously among larger and lesser canvases in the Speaker's Lobby, the Reed portrait remains a Capitol masterpiece. ★

The White House

William Seale

Seeing the White House for the first time, two things come to mind: first, it appears smaller than you thought; second, aside from that, it brings no surprise; it looks just like it does on postcards. It is arguably the most familiar house in the world, the very symbol of the Presidency it houses. What is life in the White House like for a President? Here, in the mansion's columned center section, he eats, sleeps, and ties his tie. In a wing to the west is the office in which he works, meets his cabinet, endures his trials, and perhaps pauses to enjoy the idea of who he has become. History's prospects puzzle him at these rare moments, but for now in a distant way.

★ ★ ★ ★ ★
Sunset falls on the north facade of the White House, in this recent photo taken in Lafayette Square, foreground. An equestrian statue of General Andrew Jackson salutes the city's current residents. Above, the Presidential seal, first used officially in 1877.

For the most part, however, Presidents save self-reflection for that time, at some predictable junction, when they retire and build their own splendid, monumental libraries. With some variations, the stories of Presidents and their personal response to holding the Presidency are all somewhat the same. Similarly, their assigned house also has remained the same, so much so that past Presidents, except perhaps for George Washington, would recognize the White House's postcard image today if they were to come back and see it.

The building of the White House was stipulated in the Residence Act of 1790, which created the new national capital. Congress specified nothing in this act other than that there be one house in the capital for itself and one for the President. The White House we know so well today developed out of President George Washington's desire to produce the appropriate imagery for the new American Presidency. He was the one who was most concerned about this subject, as well as the one who would make the ultimate decision. Secretary of State Thomas Jefferson attempted to advise him on the design but got nowhere. Instead, the President turned to a peculiar, tall, lanky Frenchman named Pierre Charles L'Enfant, whom he had known during the War of Independence. L'Enfant claimed to be an engineer, but he was also an artist.

L'Enfant stayed on after the Revolutionary War and became something of an artist-in-residence to the founding fathers, designing parades and testimonial dinners through the late 1780s to promote the new Constitution.

L'Enfant wanted very much to design a capital for the United States of America, and in 1791 Washington put him to work doing just that. The house L'Enfant planned for the President remains somewhat shrouded in mystery. Washington and L'Enfant established the site a little south of where L'Enfant had wanted it, but on a spot where Washington believed it should be.

The White House is only about a quarter of the size Washington and L'Enfant originally had in mind. Imagine a building about the scale of the National Gallery of Art, approached by two grand avenues—Pennsylvania and New York—that would have crossed had this edifice not intervened. That was the "palace." L'Enfant claimed he sketched it and Washington approved the idea.

L'Enfant refused to work with bureaucrats and committees, and so was short-lived on this job. Following his dismissal, Thomas Jefferson persuaded the President to hold a public competition, from which the winning White House design would be selected. Advertisements were distributed, but the homely entries only served to confirm Washington's belief that no one had a worthwhile plan except him. Fortunately, he recalled meeting a young, Irish-born architect and builder by the name of James Hoban on his trip through the South in 1791, and prudently contacted him. Hoban was from County Kilkenny, of peasant stock. He had been a pupil of the well-known Irish architect Thomas Ivory, and was full of ambition. He met with the President, and they reviewed the problem. At the judging of the competition Hoban won, hands down. He took for his prize a medal, which over time has found its way through the generations of his family to the White House, where it hangs today.

The house Washington finally agreed to have built in 1793 was a revised version of the palace of the Duke of Leinster near Dublin. Hoban

BUILDING THE FIRST WHITE HOUSE

WASHINGTON D.C. 1798

knew the original well, but Washington had his way with the design in most respects. He demanded and got a house of stone, even though the commissioners feared no quarry would be adequate to supply so ambitious a building, and Jefferson thought it pretentious. The pale, somewhat porous and grainy Aquia Creek sandstone, which also was used a little later for the Capitol, was quarried below Mount Vernon—hence the legend that Washington sold stone from his lands to the government. In fact, he was not opposed to this possibility, but no good stone turned up at Mount Vernon.

A dearth of specialized labor sent the building commissioners to Britain and Europe to inquire about tradesmen. At last, in 1794, qualified stonemasons were secured in Scotland. They came and built the stone walls of the house at a constant pace and with distinctive execution. The lovely, rich carving on the outside was Washington's wish, and it culminates in the sumptuous swag that crowns the front door. Restoration architect Charles E. Peterson notes the similarity between the style of this work and the carving on medieval cathedrals in Scotland. Cleaned in recent years of its many layers of paint, the carving stands out as the finest example of its time in this country. From the beginning the walls of the First Residence were protected with the Scotsmen's own mix of whitewash. Conservators in 1988 found this the toughest coat to remove. As early as 1802, when it was fresh, the whitewash gave rise to the nickname the "White House." It must have seemed very white indeed against the new capital's vast, empty landscape of earth, greenery, and sky.

It is tempting to think that, in retirement, George Washington returned to see the house in some semblance of completion. If so, the event was not recorded. His last known visit was in March 1797, while on his way home to Mount Vernon after his retirement from the Presidency. For accepting the end of his Presidency, he was idolized all over the world as the hero who declined to found a dynasty. He paused before the house as he passed toward the Potomac, and the workmen waiting there saluted him generously from the unfinished walls with huzzas and cannon blasts. This was the first ceremony at the White House.

John Adams, the first President to occupy the White House, was defeated for re-election in December 1800—just one month after he arrived. His wife, Abigail, had complained of most everything about her station, including the difficulties of following a rich man like George Washington into office. She had her wash hung out to dry in the unplastered East Room, probably to keep the Presidential laundry out of view.

Jefferson, whose election marked a change from Federalist to Republican government, thought that the house was too pompous and too large. Had Washington been any less associated with it, Jefferson might have moved elsewhere, but his new government needed all the credibility it could get. He distributed some of Washington's memorabilia throughout the main rooms, and the house, like European palaces

Jefferson had seen, was opened to the public in the spring of 1801. Except during wartime, it has been open to the public on a regular basis ever since, and today receives some million and a half visitors a year. Jefferson also commandeered the Marine Band to play for special White House occasions, a tradition that has continued through the years and has featured such notable band leaders as John Philip Sousa.

The Republican Jefferson also trimmed the august mansion down to republican size. He used only part of the house and added wings to the side to conceal the smokehouse, stables, and household workrooms under one roof. He ordered the outdoor privy torn down, and in 1801 two flush toilets were installed upstairs. What we know as the State Dining Room served as his office, and he usually worked there with very little help, dispatching letters to the appropriate departments for response and answering others himself. When at home, he often wore his housecoat, and this, along with the threadbare slippers he preferred, so miffed Britain's minister, Anthony Merry, that a controversy ensued. Jefferson often conferred with the architect of the Capitol, Benjamin Henry Latrobe, about building projects at the White House, but, with the exception of adding colonnades to the east and west wings, little change resulted.

On August 24, 1814, under President James Madison, Jefferson's successor, the White House became a victim of war when British forces invaded Washington and burned it to its stone walls. It was a dramatic moment. In an attempt to put on a happy face at the White House at this terrible time, Dolley Madison had sent out invitations to 40 people and had ordered the dining room set for dinner. Distant gunfire, rather than the rain of regrets from guests, finally caused her to flee, but not before ordering the removal to safety of Gilbert Stuart's portrait of George Washington. The British arrived at the White House at about 11 o'clock that night, to the accompaniment of thunder and lightening. They wandered through the vacant mansion, confiscating even such trifles as clean underwear, and then the officers sat down and ate Dolley Madison's dinner, complete with Madeira, while the house was prepared to be fired. Rear Admiral George Cockburn, less celebrated later as the jailer of Napoleon, was in charge, and it was he who gave the order to burn.

Fire was hurled into the White House by javelins at about one in the morning; by the rainy daybreak, the building was gutted. Madison and the Congress wanted the public buildings "repaired"—a word that was used to suggest economy, for if reconstruction was the issue perhaps another city would have contended successfully for capital of the victorious nation. The War of 1812 had been won, if not in fact then certainly in the emotions of Americans, by the Battle of New Orleans, on January 8, 1815. The White House was rebuilt in haste during the balance of Madison's Presidency and the first years of James Monroe's administration. At some point, a decision was made to build the two porticoes on the north and south. However, the house was occupied without the porticoes by New Year's Day 1818, when more than 3,000 people came to call on President Monroe.

In 1824, the year the Marquis de Lafayette stayed at the White House and thus became the first guest of state, the bow-like south portico, with its tall half-ring of Ionic columns, took

★ ★ ★ ★ ★

A servant stands in the middle of the rudimentary White House kitchen, below, photographed in 1890. Opposite, a White House chef collects herbs from the Jacqueline Kennedy Garden, which connects the residence's east wing with the mansion proper.

shape. Five years later, a few weeks after the arrival of Andrew Jackson, hero of New Orleans, construction of the north portico, a porte-cochère, commenced. James Hoban built both porticoes, just as he had rebuilt the burned-out White House. Hoban died at an old age in 1831, rich in real estate, in the legacy of clever children, in a position of prestige within his church, and in memories of his triumphant years building the White House.

With the completion of the north portico in September 1829, the look of the White House as we know it was complete. As the portico was going up, President Jackson ordered the decoration of the unfinished East Room. His comrade, Major William B. Lewis, contacted Philadelphia cabinetmaker and entrepreneur Louis Veron, and together they selected the yellow wallpaper, mahogany furniture, wall-to-wall carpeting, blue-and-yellow curtains, and some 20 spittoons. All these items—and more—were packed, shipped to Washington, and put into place. Perhaps most noteworthy were the three huge glass chandeliers of almost inconceivable splendor, each holding dozens of candles—which later were changed to lard-oil "peg" lamps because of the expense—that established the East Room's trademark look. The great chandeliers hanging there today are only the third generation from those first hung by President Jackson in 1829; the second were General Ulysses S. Grant's in 1874; and the present ones Theodore Roosevelt's, hung in 1902.

Thereafter the White House changed for the most part only in small ways. Martin Van Buren added central heating to some rooms in 1837 (Latrobe had installed a central-heat system for three rooms in 1809, but it was not replaced when the house was rebuilt). Running water, first installed by Andrew Jackson, was extended time and again, culminating in the 1850s in lavatories in all the upstairs rooms. James K. Polk replaced

candles and oil lamps with gaslight in 1848. This was accomplished by continuing the gas pipe from the Capitol down Pennsylvania Avenue to the White House. Not long after the connection was completed, crafty merchants along Pennsylvania Avenue tapped into the pipe, which was buried below the center of the street, to enjoy free gas until the trick was discovered.

Monroe created the Green Room in 1818. Van Buren painted the Blue Room blue in 1837, and in 1846 Mrs. Polk replaced the East Room's blue and yellow curtains with red damask. Polk, who was President during the war with Mexico (1846-1848), expanded the nation to the Pacific. To associate himself with an earlier expansionist in the public's mind, he ordered a statue of Thomas Jefferson, purchaser of the Louisiana Territory, to be set up on the north lawn. His shrewd wife, Sarah, must have seen her husband's military campaigns in a less flattering light, for she accepted a portrait of Mexico's conquistador, Hernan Cortés, from General William J. Worth, and had it hung in the Blue Room.

For most of the 19th century the President received a salary of $25,000 per year, and paid for everything except for the actual maintenance of the house himself. Today he makes eight times that amount, and pays for very little personally, although in fact he is billed for his own food and that of personal guests. Polk had the first government-paid secretary; he borrowed other staff from various departments. In his time, Presidents were responsible for paying the 14 to 20 servants who worked in the White House, but Chief Executives soon learned that the butler could be paid as a "laborer" (for blacks) or as a "clerk" (for whites) in the Departments of Treasury or War or Navy or State, and no one seemed to mind.

The Blue Room, depicted here in a 1903 painting by Charles Bittinger, has always served as a reception room. It was completely redecorated in 1972 during the administration of Richard Nixon.

By the 20th century the President usually paid only his valet, his wife's maid, and such nurses as he might need for his children. The other domestic staff was scattered over the federal payroll. This is no longer the case; the White House has its own appropriation from Congress, and the White House staff serves as federal employees, with the exception that they serve at the pleasure of the President, without the job protection of the civil service.

The White House to which Abraham Lincoln moved in March 1861 was still roomy, and it was a fine house, "better than any we ever had," he told his wife, Mary. It was on this stage that his dramatic Presidency would play out for just a month more than four years. In April 1865, his

read her newspaper and had her coffee in the Red Room, was the last to use the first floor in such a personal manner.

To alleviate the crowded White House, the Army Corps of Engineers presented a master plan for expansion, which would have provided useful space, although the final building projected was still only half of what L'Enfant and Washington had wanted. Nevertheless, the enlarged house would be vast and would resemble a public library. President William McKinley thought it a good solution to the problem of space: the Presidency was different now from what it had been in George Washington's time. The Spanish-American War of 1898 had revived the power and breadth of the office.

When McKinley was assassinated in 1901, it fell to his successor, 42-year-old Theodore Roosevelt, to dramatize the new Presidency. The Victorian White House, officially the "Executive Mansion," with its old-fashioned look of wall-to-wall flowered carpets, heavy gas chandeliers, and layers of wallpaper, was woefully out of style—certainly no setting for an international Presidency. Roosevelt cast aside the plans of the engineers, and turned instead to a full renovation by Charles McKim, partner in McKim, Mead & White, the leading architectural firm in the United States. Moreover, TR changed the residence's official name to the "White House."

corpse would lie in state in the East Room, the man of the age cut down at the peak of his triumphant career. Lincoln, indeed all the Lincolns—Abe, Mary, Willie, Tad, and even the eldest son, Robert Todd—cast a spell over the White House that perhaps has its least expression in the tall, lanky ghost that Harry Truman and Queen Juliana of Holland swore they saw wandering the lofty second-floor corridors. There probably would be no White House today had Lincoln not lived there. Already underway in 1866 was a move to relocate the President from the White House, then not much more than a half-century old, into a modern house on secluded grounds along Rock Creek. Andrew Johnson, Lincoln's successor, agreed to this plan, but Ulysses S. Grant put a stop to it in 1869 when he moved into a White House whose history he held in honor. By 1900 the White House was overcrowded and almost trembling from use. The President's office took up half the second floor, leaving the family with a mere seven rooms. It was no longer possible to use the first floor in an informal way. Mrs. Lincoln, who had

★ ★ ★ ★ ★

Photographer Frances Benjamin Johnston captured the unique mix of historic and personal fixtures at the White House in her 1890s photograph of the Lincoln bedroom, above. Lincoln's grand bed dwarfs a guest bed that features a specially crocheted pillowcase.

For more than four months in 1902, McKim pared away Victorian additions and restored the house in spirit to what he imagined it had been when it was "pure," just after the completion of the north portico 72 years earlier. He gave the interior a full remodeling, high in period panache, with two opulent beaux-arts state rooms—the East Room and the State Dining Room—flanking the simpler, "restored" state parlors, the Green, Blue, and Red rooms. Steam heat, a nickel-plated modern kitchen, and an abundance of shiny, white-tile bathrooms made the residence more comfortable than it had ever been. The President's office was moved to a separate building, and the rivers of social guests now flowed in through the east wing—instead of the north door. In the basement, convenient coat rooms and restrooms occupied areas that had once been dark, sooty, work- and storerooms. The house was born anew.

McKim's original west wing, which at first was only a staff office with a "President's room" included, was enlarged during President Howard Taft's administration, with the addition of the first Oval Office in 1909. Franklin D. Roosevelt put the now famous Oval Office in its present location in 1934, although no ceremonial business was conducted in the new executive office for some time. Woodrow Wilson was the first to use the new Oval Office for signing bills into acts. His first wife, Edith, connected the west wing to the White House with a rose garden, an instantly beloved addition.

Franklin D. Roosevelt added the east wing. Its construction was begun in 1942, a few months after Pearl Harbor, and it included a secret bomb shelter beneath it. Roosevelt loved remodeling, and made many small changes to the White House. As a diversion from the events of World War II, he worked nearly every day with government architect Lorenzo Winslow. Roosevelt refused to move out when the United States declared war in December 1941, and he would not allow the civil defense to paint the house with camouflage. Gas masks were permitted in the bedrooms, but even they were held in contempt by the President.

Fears about the vulnerability of the White House and its many rotting wooden parts did not subside after FDR was gone. President Harry S Truman paid little heed to such worries, until structural problems began to express themselves in the form of swaying chandeliers, snowfalls of plaster dust, and, at one point, the perilous collapse of Margaret Truman's piano through two shaky floor boards. Now Truman listened, and he and his household moved across the street to Blair House as engineers undertook structural analysis of the mansion. At first there was little interest in the residence's historical importance, but Truman ordered that, no matter what was done, the historic stone walls and the original general plan must be preserved.

Between 1948 and 1952 the stone shell of the White House was gutted and rebuilt with steel and concrete. Very few of the original materials were reused, although window sashes and frames survive. The paneling of the State Dining Room is from McKim's renovation of 1902, but it was so damaged during its removal that it had to be caulked and painted. And yet the White House still looked the same. In most respects, President Truman oversaw the remodeling job well, and thus assured that the Presidents would continue to live there. He knew that had the house been restored reusing its old parts, it eventually would have been abandoned to museum purposes. For

The President's helicopter prepares to land on the south lawn of the White House, above. English-born architect Benjamin Henry Latrobe designed the columned, semicircular portico, seen in the background, in 1807, although it wasn't completed until 1824. Opposite, President George Bush works in the Oval Office, located in the mansion's west wing. President William Howard Taft established the first Oval Office in 1909.

practical, structural reasons, a White House only technically restored would have been as unsuited for use as a President's house as, say, Mount Vernon.

Truman's new White House was larger by 30 or so more rooms and by many other spaces. There were mezzanines and sub-basements; and although the thick walls were restored, the trim new steel structure made the thickness unnecessary, and so room was found in the balance of space for air-conditioning ducts and many cabinets of hidden things. One might complain about a certain post-office monumentality that replaced McKim's elegant domestic beaux-arts design, but the house does not differ much in its main features from what McKim designed. The only alteration to the White House made by Truman that can be regretted is the unsightly balcony he added to the south portico in 1947, before his renovation. It was the only change to that facade since 1824. Had the balcony been cantilevered and set back even 20 inches from the columns—thus keeping them free—the results would have been better. As it is, no matter how spare in its lines it may be, the balcony bumps into the columns crudely and adds an

ugly horizontal to the once fine, airy verticality of the portico. Despite what may have been an architectural disaster, all subsequent First Families have loved the Truman balcony.

The White House did not feel historical to Truman's successors, however, and a series of efforts was undertaken to add more antiquated furnishings. This project actually predates Truman, going back as far as Rutherford B. Hayes in 1878, but it was initiated in the rebuilt White House by Mrs. Dwight D. Eisenhower in 1958. Mrs. John F. Kennedy took up the cause in 1961 and generated great popular interest in White House history and antiques. Hundreds, indeed thousands of historical furnishings were acquired during Richard Nixon's administration, with Mrs. Nixon taking a personal interest. The pace of acquisition has abated somewhat since Nixon, although the collecting of fine art has continued. During Ronald Reagan's administration the family quarters were redecorated and furnished completely, for what was really the first time. Meanwhile, the thrust of historical interest in the White House has centered on its old stone walls. Over the past decade they have been carefully stripped, extensively repaired by conservators, and repainted a yellowed white, which works better against the reflections of today's urban surroundings.

The White House has 134 rooms, about 32 of which are for the residential and private use of the President and his family. Of course, the President can use any of the 134 rooms in any way he chooses, right down to installing a television and lounge chair in the Blue Room. In fact, Taft put his Victrola there. No President, however, is likely to find such recourse necessary or even desirable: the state rooms work hard at their public duties and the private quarters, if perhaps less private than they might be, are wonderfully comfortable. Five state rooms on the main floor—the same number the White House has always had—are served by halls, pantries, bathrooms, coat rooms, offices, and other auxiliary spaces. Some 30 domestic employees work in the residence, presided over by the chief usher and his immediate staff.

The White House grounds and buildings are maintained with the assistance of the National Park Service, under the chief usher's direction. The rich historical collections are expanded, maintained, and researched by the curator in the Office of the Curator of the White House. The interpretation of the famous residence is sponsored through books and audio-visual materials created by the private, nonprofit White House Historical Association, itself created by Mrs. Kennedy in 1961. Offices for the First Lady are maintained in the east wing, and the "social office," where events are planned and from which invitations are issued, is located there also. The west wing holds the President's office, while the extended executive office— some 6,000 employees—are housed in the Old War and Navy Building, the New Executive Office Building on 17th Street, and other nearby buildings.

White House security is very tight, although still remarkably unobtrusive. If you walk from the northwest gate to the elevator inside, you'll encounter four or five guards at different stations along the way who may say hello or may call you by name, even though you've have never seen them before. Security was always an issue at the White House, and the first plainclothes men were stationed in the entrance hall in 1844. President Franklin Pierce had the first bodyguard in 1854. Lincoln was guarded by only a handful of men.

Up until World War II the White House was guarded only at its doors. One could leave a calling card in the butler's silver tray and expect an invitation of some sort in return. With the advent of war the security line moved to the fence, where it remains to this day. West Executive Avenue was closed to traffic during the Second World War and never reopened; East Executive Avenue recently followed suit, and is a delightful pedestrian way as well as both the social and tour approach to the White House. It may be only a matter of time until Pennsylvania Avenue and Lafayette Park's flanking streets also will be reserved for pedestrians. While the stated object may be better security, such an action would allow the White House to be enjoyed even more easily by passers-by.

From the time when it was referred to as George Washington's "palace" up until today, the White House has remained a symbol to the world, a timeless image that is as much a part of how we and the world perceive our culture as is the American flag or the American Eagle—perhaps more so. A real house, and not just a monument, it says "people" as well as "Presidency," for real people live in houses, but only visit monuments. Throughout our history the White House has been a great looking glass, mirroring and infinitely reflecting our culture in all its splendid drama. ★

At Home with the Presidents

BARBARA HOLLAND

WHATEVER YOU THOUGHT OF THEM POLITICALLY, YOU MIGHT FEEL YOU COULD POP OVER AND BORROW A LAWN MOWER FROM GERRY FORD OR JIMMY CARTER, BUT NOT FROM RICHARD NIXON. BEND A BLADE AND YOU'D GET ON HIS ENEMIES LIST. YOU COULD ASK FOR A RECIPE OR A CUP OF FLOUR FROM LADY BIRD JOHNSON OR DOLLEY MADISON,  BUT YOU WOULDN'T ASK ELIZABETH MONROE— SHE WOULDN'T LET YOU IN THE DOOR. AND NO USE ASKING SARAH POLK, A BUSY CO-PRESIDENT WHO WOULDN'T KNOW FLOUR IF SHE FELL INTO IT AND SOMETIMES FORGOT TO HAVE NAPKINS ON THE DINNER TABLE.

★ ★ ★ ★ ★

Top-hatted President Benjamin Harrison, left, watches grandchild Benjamin McKee take a ride in his goat cart. "Let the children have a good time," said Abraham Lincoln, shown above enjoying a quiet moment with son Tad in an 1864 miniature by Francis B. Carpenter.

As that big, white house next door keeps changing hands, Washington stays alert to its changing back-fence relationship. The town keeps a close eye on the First Neighbors as they go about their business beyond their 16-acre lawn. It's a dual vision: the well-informed public eye keeps sharpened on policies and politics; and the other, the private eye, watches and judges the private family.

Jokes, rumors, and downright gossip run flickering through the streets like comets. More than 100 years ago a columnist wrote, "In New York the chief talk is of money; in Washington gossip and great men are the leading subjects." This is still true today, and it's still a game everyone plays. Ronald Reagan—or his speechwriter—called Washington the only city where sound travels faster than light.

Sensible, dignified adults who otherwise wouldn't stoop to tittle-tattle, excuse themselves for gossiping on the grounds that such talk is important. This isn't just neighborly nosiness, this is national news. Does Pierce drink too much? Does Grant? Does Mamie? (It is a local custom to refer to the President by his last name and his wife by her first; no disrespect—or respect, for that matter—necessarily intended.) Lincoln took Tad to the theater again last night; that child doesn't get enough sleep. Lynda Johnson is dating a draft-dodger. Tricia Nixon is rude to the servants, and they caught Harrison's baby grandson stirring the contents of a spittoon with a roll of important state papers. Do the Hardings serve drinks upstairs to their friends, in defiance of Prohibition? If Ida McKinley is as ill as she looks, why doesn't she stay in her room? Is Nancy's fortuneteller running the country? Is Abigail Adams? Is Edith Wilson? Did Alice Roosevelt really jump in a pool with her clothes on? Do you know that Taft weighs 340

★ ★ ★ ★ ★

Easter-egg rolls, such as the one at right in 1929, have enlivened the south lawn of the White House since Rutherford Hayes' administration. The outings were originally held on Capitol Hill, but children were banned from playing there in 1879. Above, the crowded White House grounds on a recent Easter Monday.

Barbara Holland, who lives in the Blue Ridge mountains of Virginia, has written a number of books on subjects that range from cats to Presidents.

★ ★ ★ ★ ★

Visitors of every stripe, above, share a 1,400-pound cheese in 1837 at Andrew Jackson's last public levee. Jackson opened the White House to everyone. Seemingly natural-born hostess Dolley Madison, depicted at right in an 1804 portrait by Gilbert Stuart, virtually created Washington's social scene, even filling in at social affairs during Thomas Jefferson's Presidency.

pounds now and had to have an enormous new bathtub installed so he wouldn't get stuck? Did you hear Van Buren wears a corset and sprays French perfume on his whiskers? And why did Jackie plant those rhododendrons by the southwest gate? So we can't see what her kids are doing? Washington needs to know.

Every four years the rest of the country learns a mass of trivia about the would-be leaders and their relatives, and then sensibly forgets it. Washington keeps on learning. The town has been treasuring its insider nuggets ever since Abigail hung her wash in the East Room. It's rather like movie-star watching on the other coast, but there are plenty of stars in Hollywood to share the scrutiny. In Washington, there's only one First Family, living and working in a house once described by its head usher as a fishbowl made of magnifying glass.

No one else matters in the same way. However respected or controversial the Speaker of the House may be, nobody wants to know what he eats for dinner. The Vice President is vestigial, a kind of bureaucratic tonsil, important only for comedy routines. But unpublished news of the First Family wags Washington dinner parties year in and year out. Do Franklin and Eleanor Roosevelt look like the perfect team? Washington's been talking about his affair with Lucy Mercer since before he ran for Vice President in 1920. Does John Kennedy look like the picture of health and vigor? Washington knows how bad his back is; Washington has seen the crutches kept hidden from photographers.

White House staffers and servants go home and talk, hairdressers, caterers, and gardeners talk, but the major source of tidbits is the media, after hours. Washington reporters are numerous and energetic, and discover—or speculate on—a whole cookie jar of goodies. They're not for pub-lication, but "off-the-record" just means out of the papers and off the airwaves, not silence at parties.

Washington reporters always have been ingenious. John Quincy Adams wouldn't give reporter Ann Royall an interview, perhaps because he disapproved of women in such a public occupation. (According to his wife, Louisa, "As regards women, the Adams family are one and all peculiarly harsh and severe.") A pioneer fitness addict, John Quincy went every morning at dawn for a swim in the Potomac in the buff. Ann Royall tracked him down and, spotting his bald head bobbing above the ripples, sat on his clothes on the bank and refused to budge until she got the interview.

The more the First Family tries to protect its privacy, the more diligently the press digs. The Hoovers were uncooperative about sharing their private life, and the neighbors wanted to know how Christmas would be spent in the White House. All that was given out was that Girl Scouts, a particular interest of Lou Hoover's, would be there to sing carols. Desperate times call for desperate measures, and Bess Furman of the Washington Associated Press dressed as a Girl Scout and joined the carolers. Lip-synching, she gazed around greedily, memorizing all the visible details of the family's holiday.

In earlier days, Washington could find out

for itself, without help from the press. The White House was open from ten in the morning until two, and visitors wandered through it. A columnist in Grover Cleveland's time reported gazing over a railing at servants ironing the extra-large Presidential nightshirts and "other unmentionable garments." On frequent occasions the town simply combed its hair and went to the parties, the receptions, the teas, and the levees, where it inspected the First Family and speculated on how much Mrs. President had paid for her gown and what went into the punch. (One hundred years ago a proper Washington punch, suitable for the most delicate maiden, was made of whiskey, rum, claret, champagne, sugar, and lemon juice, with a dash of water. "Punch" seems the appropriate word.)

Dolley Madison first set the alarmingly high social standard at the White House and began Washington's fascination with its occupants. She was really the town's first First Lady; Abigail Adams barely had time to unpack and pack up again. Madison was Jefferson's Secretary of State, and since Jefferson was a widower, Dolley was his acting hostess for two terms. There had to be a hostess, for without one it was improper to invite ladies to White House functions, and for cheerless blanks in Washington history, Presidents without a presiding lady gave only stag parties.

Appropriately, Madison's was the first inaugural ball, with the whole town fighting furiously over a scant 400 tickets. Dolley was the undisputed star. Then she reigned over Madison's two terms, and afterwards continued for decades as Washington's queen and society arbiter, merry and dancing until the end.

By all reports she was a gem, and in the whole piranha tank of Washington she had no

★ ★ ★ ★ ★

Photographed, above, with one of her many pets, a raccoon named Rebecca, Grace Coolidge gained approval from Congress for White House acceptance of antique furnishings as gifts. At right, workmen mug for the camera in a bathtub custommade for President William Howard Taft.

The rambunctious Roosevelt boys appear in a rare sedate moment with their father, Theodore. T.R., who officially changed the name of the executive mansion to "the White House," oversaw the complete dismantling and renovation of the residence, beginning in 1902.

enemies. Even John Adams liked her, and he was a famously intolerant man. Her only recorded critic was a local preacher who thundered that God was going to burn the White House down if she didn't stop giving parties on Sunday. As it happened, it was the British who burned the White House down, and Dolley went right on giving parties seven days a week.

The year after Madison took office, a census counted just over 8,000 Washingtonians, and apparently they all came to see Dolley. She handed out punch and seedcake to everyone who dropped in, welcoming them with her famous dimples. One guest sniffed that the party was an odd mix of "greasy boots and silk stockings," including everyone "from the Minister from Russia to the under-clerks at the post office." Everyone had a ball, and foreign diplomats and dignitaries, who came to sneer at the American bumpkins, went away singing the praises of Dolley the queen.

In spite of her merry sociability, and an occasional kiss for a bachelor Congressman, no breath of scandal touched Dolley. The Madisons may have married for convenience: he was 43 and felt that it was time to get married, and she was a buxom widow of 26. Once married, however, they fell in love and lived happily ever

after. She called him "my darling little husband"—he was only five-six and didn't weigh 100 pounds with his boots on—and whenever he felt bothered or blue, Dolley would cheer him up.

She cheered everyone up. She was genuinely kind and generous, and politicked most successfully for her husband by inviting his enemies over and charming them shamelessly; some attribute his re-election to her charming personality. Washington's women copied everything Dolley did and wore. She took snuff, which wasn't quite respectable for ladies, but suddenly so did all of Washington. She had a pet macaw, and suddenly the entire town screeched with macaws. She made everyone learn to waltz, and they loved it.

After Dolley, Elizabeth Monroe was a terrible letdown. She didn't think anyone should come to her parties unless they were invited, and then she didn't invite them. Snubbed, the ladies decided to boycott and wouldn't show up even when asked. One woman wrote, "The drawing room of the President was opened last night to a beggarly row of empty chairs. . . .Only five females attended, three of whom were foreigners."

Luckily, Dolley was still around. After Madison's death she moved back to Washington and gave more parties, and advice about parties. When the widower Martin Van Buren came to the White House with four sons and no hostess, she sent for her pretty young relative Angelica Singleton to marry his eldest son. She advised John Tyler about his social life, played whist with John Quincy Adams, and was even friends with the Polks, who didn't have much time for friends. For as long as she lived—to about the age of 81—it was the custom for incoming Presidents to pay a call on Dolley.

She was a hard act to follow, and some Presidential wives, daunted by the critical eye

★ ★ ★ ★ ★

President Woodrow Wilson's daughter Eleanor was married to Secretary of the Treasury William Gibbs McAdoo in the Blue Room of the White House in May 1914.

and high expectations of Washington, didn't try. Anna Harrison hid out in Ohio and wouldn't even come to William Henry's inauguration. Letitia Tyler, who had had a stroke, stayed upstairs in her room. So did Margaret Taylor, who hadn't had a stroke; she just hated Washington. Abigail Fillmore stayed in her room and said she was sick, which wasn't true. She was perfectly all right in private, and was rumored to be witty and attractive. She just didn't feel up to the role of First Lady.

In the 19th century, it was easy for women to slip out of unpleasant jobs on the grounds of ill health; no one asked what exactly ailed them, since simply being female was considered an unhealthy condition in itself. Jane Pierce played it to the hilt all her life, and as First Lady she, too, stayed in her room, dressed in black, and whined. When the city heard that her husband had been arrested for running down an old lady

★　★　★　★

The joy of White House babies: First Lady Frances Cleveland, above, holds her second child, Esther, in September 1893, while President Wilson cradles his first granddaughter, Ellen Wilson McAdoo, in 1915.

113

with his horse, it speculated that he must have been drunk—he'd been called "the hero of many a well-fought bottle"—and who could blame him? Jane was dismal.

The arrival of Harriet Lane, the niece of bachelor President James Buchanan, was greeted with cries of relief. She was 27, energetic, and charming, with violet eyes and a passion for gardening. She actually liked giving parties, and never had nerves or migraines. Washington fell in love with her. "Listen to the Mockingbird" was dedicated to her, and a flower, a racehorse, and a warship were named after her, as well as most of the girl babies in town.

Alas, she was followed by Mary Lincoln, who, like Ida McKinley, really should have sulked in her room, but wouldn't. She wanted to play the Southern belle and have tantrums in public. Even with the Civil War rattling around their heads, everyone gossiped about Mary's jealousy, her compulsive shopping, and the way she interrupted President Lincoln at work whenever she wanted attention. Her unpaid bills were enormous and all over the town—and don't think Washington didn't know.

Eliza Johnson was so invisible that after her four years in the White House the local papers described her as "almost a myth." She showed up only twice: once for a dinner, where she started to cough and left; and once for a children's party, where she told the little guests that she was an invalid.

Her husband was no great shakes as President, but Julia Grant, though slightly cross-

eyed, was healthy and cheerful, and brightened the atmosphere. She liked feeding people in the White House, and served dinners with 29 courses and plenty of excellent French wine. With the arrival of the Hayeses, the wine glasses went back to the basement; Washington called Mrs. Hayes "Lemonade Lucy." Everyone said that at her parties "the water flowed like wine," and the sophisticated sneered at the family hymn-singing that was the Hayeses' idea of a rousing good time. It was highly respectable, of course, but not much fun.

Nor did things look up under the Garfields. Lucretia was rather a bluestocking, and there were stories about her handsome husband's love life. In any case, she spent most of her time in town nursing the poor man after he was shot. Social life at the White House languished.

Chester Arthur, though a widower, was an improvement. The official White House line was that he grieved constantly for his departed wife, Nell. The rest of the country believed it, but Washington knew about the streams of women who stopped by his office to offer themselves in marriage. Washington knew him as a generous host and a bit of a flirt. Indeed, there was so much talk about the British Minister's illegitimate daughter that the White House had to issue a formal denial. Arthur gave gluttonous dinner parties and ran up terrific bills with the florist and the tailor, but he wouldn't marry. Perhaps he was having too much fun.

Still, the city longed for a really satisfactory Presidential wife, someone to spice up the December-to-Lent social season and bring back the glory days of Dolley. No wonder the local mood was glum at the inauguration of Grover Cleveland. He was a bachelor and likely to remain so; his friends said he hadn't much use for women, in spite of the child he had admitted fathering. Besides, he was 49, looked like a walrus, and was sometimes called "the Beast of Buffalo."

Astonished rejoicing greeted his marriage to the pretty, 21-year-old Frances Folsom. She was the daughter of his late law partner, and he had

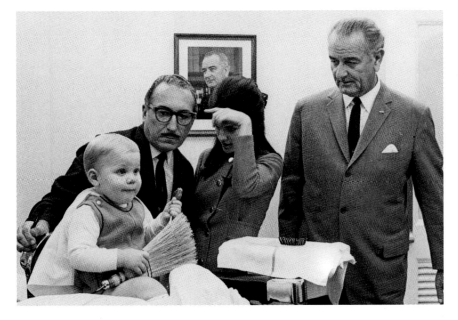

been her acting guardian since she was 11. Theirs was the first Presidential marriage ceremony to have taken place in the White House, and reporters tried to bribe the caterers and musicians for a chance to sneak in, but security held. The public had to be content with peering in the windows. The papers were reduced to inventing details, and the reporters had to hide in the bushes around the honeymoon cottage in their efforts to eavesdrop.

Frances was an instant hit in Washington. She was a natural-born celebrity and was having the time of her life. In addition to the usual whirl of parties, she added her own noontime receptions to accommodate the hordes of people who wanted to get a look at her. Her New Year's Day open house was a smash.

The White House was open to all on New Year's Day until the Hoovers put an end to this custom in 1930. By the 1880s the city had grown to 200,000, and it was a gallant gesture to invite them all, but Frances loved it. A visitor called the party "gorgeous, gay, and giddy," and said "the dear people come by the thousands. Of all classes, ages, and sizes, of all colors, sexes, and conditions, they formed long lines reaching from the White House door . . . to the War Department." John Philip Sousa conducted the Marine Band, and Frances was described as having "a fresh smile for every newcomer, and I can assure you it is no easy matter to produce five thousand new smiles and no two alike." All the diplomats were there, encrusted in gold braid, and so was a shabby old lady with a black veil and a tin ear-trumpet a yard long.

There would never be another First Lady as popular as Dolley, but Frances came close. Seven out of ten Washington women wore their hair "à la Cleveland," in a bun fastened low on the neck. During the Clevelands' two disconnected terms she produced three First Daughters, one of whom actually was born in the White House, to

the city's delight. (At first she tried to protect them from the relentless public eye, but she gave up when rumors promptly flew that they were ill or possibly deformed.) They were sweet little girls, and the White House servants remembered them fondly after Teddy Roosevelt's wild horde moved in to throw spitballs at portraits of past Presidents and take their pony, Algonquin, up and down in the elevator.

Washington is a transient town, created artificially for a single purpose, and its style sways to the First Family's style. The old European capitals have their established ways and their solid social structure, but Washington's tune changes with the administration. When the new neighbors move in, the town goes over a noticeable bump in the road, like the overnight passage from the sleepy, canasta-playing Eisenhowers to the cultural dash and style of the Kennedys. The barometric pressure changes. Information still leaks out through the walls, even if the ordinary citizen can no longer watch the President's underwear being ironed.

The neighbors who used to jostle the First Family's privacy have been replaced by the Secret Service, who dog the footsteps of the Presidential family with the irritating persistence of tag-along kid brothers. Security isolates them, and they can no longer hop on an uptown bus as Eleanor Roosevelt frequently did. The First Lady no longer is required to invite the whole town for a visit, and the townsfolk no longer wander the grounds the way they did when Taylor's old warhorse, Whitey, grazed there and let them pluck souvenir hairs from his tail. No longer on summer Saturdays do the citizens picnic at free Marine Band concerts on the lawn. Except for the Easter Monday egg-rolling, a pretty custom begun by Lucy Hayes, Washington now has to wait for an invitation to the house next door—wait and continue to talk. ★

First Lady Barbara Bush enjoys time in the Rose Garden with spaniel Millie and one of Millie's puppies. In addition to being Millie's amanuensis, Mrs. Bush is an avid flower gardener.

Capital Delights

Monuments and Memorials

Frank Getlein

Washington is the country's most monumental city in the most basic way. It has more major monuments than anyplace else. As you move through the city, you are passing the people and events memorialized in the monuments; and you are also passing by the moment and mode of the memorialization. Something of the past is always close at hand.

★ ★ ★ ★

As Union Station rises in the background, Christopher Columbus gazes south from his fountain memorial by Lorado Taft, 1921. A detail, called "Discovery," stands on the prow of a Greek trireme directly below the man for whom the District of Columbia was named.

A tall man who cast a giant shadow: Thomas Jefferson's portrait statue, below, by Rudolph Evans, 1943, resides in his memorial, opposite. It reposes amid Japanese flowering-cherry trees and tulip beds beside the Potomac's Tidal Basin.

While no one planned it that way, the city's three most visible monuments, the Washington Monument and the memorials to Lincoln and Jefferson, compose a perfectly coherent and fitting statement about the history and the purposes of the United States of America. Washington, first in war, first in peace, and first in the hearts of his countrymen, is represented by the tallest obelisk ever built. This ancient form can be regarded as a giant "Number One" for all those firsts, but there is much more. It stands alone, straight and true, clean and uncluttered. The

Egyptian shaft goes back to the first great Western civilization, which happened also to be a great African civilization, thus architecturally uniting the two elements of our mixed society that have proved so resistant to the melting pot.

Jefferson's and Lincoln's involvement in that American challenge live on in their own words carved into the walls of their temples. "I tremble for my country," said Jefferson, "when I reflect that God is just." Lincoln's Gettysburg Address reflects the burden of the war that resolved the conflict Jefferson had foreseen. And his monu-

ment fittingly formed the backdrop to two of the most significant events in the 20th century's continuation of the struggle for human rights: the 1939 open-air concert by the great contralto Marian Anderson after she had been denied the use of Constitution Hall because she was an African-American; and, in 1963, the intensely moving "I have a dream" speech by the Reverend Martin Luther King, Jr., at the March on Washington. Like much official Washington architecture, both the Jefferson and the Lincoln memorials recall the model for the American republic consciously held by most of the signers of the Declaration and framers of the Constitution, the republic of ancient Rome. Another such Roman recollection is the White House, which for many Americans is the heart of the republic. Just across the street from the Presidential mansion is Lafayette Square, which in its corner statuary continues the story of the Revolution begun with Washington and Jefferson. The square's center, however, is firmly occupied by General Andrew Jackson, "Old Hickory," the Hero of New Orleans, which battle, though it occurred after peace was made with the British, gave Jackson's countrymen a substitute for victory in the War of 1812.

Jackson's down-home, not to say raucous, style permanently changed the way things work across the street. His first inaugural open house featured bourbon by the barrel, spurs that ripped upholstery and scratched parquet floors, broken windows and broken heads, and probably the most monumental hangover this monumental city has ever had. But the party and the party-giver ended forever John Adams's decorous dream of a monarchical Presidency, and laid bare the realities of Jefferson's nation of yeoman philosophers. Suddenly, with the addition of Jackson's West to the original mix of North and South, it was an all new country, which it has continued to become quite regularly.

A Washington-based critic of the arts, Frank Getlein is a frequent contributor to *Smithsonian* magazine. He is author of *Art Treasures of the World, The Bite of the Print, Jack Levine,* and numerous other works.

The Jackson statue is important in itself. The General salutes the current occupant of his former home and does so in his own flamboyant style, doffing his hat and simultaneously rearing his horse. This, in 1853, was the first equestrian statue cast in the United States. The almost occult balance of horse and rider drew instant admiration, and still does. At a stroke, sculptor Clark Mills also stated the Americanness of his subject. The horse descends from those noble bronze steeds of Rome, Venice, and Padua, and points the way to Remington and Russell in a West even more Western than Jackson's.

As if in counterpoint to Jackson's fierce Americanism, the square's corners are devoted to some of the Europeans who came here to help us gain our freedom from the British. The foreign volunteer the square is named for stands pedestaled on the southeast corner, arm outstretched in his plea to the French Assembly to support the Revolution in America. Below him are his countrymen in the American adventure, Rochambeau and Portail, commanders in ground combat, and the commanders of sea forces, the Comtes d'Estaing and de Grasse. Rochambeau, fittingly enough, has his own statue in the southwest corner of the square, depicting him in active command of the 3,500-man French Expeditionary Force. Besides rallying the support of the French government, Lafayette contributed $200,000 of his own money to the American cause, as well as his personal, distinguished military service from Valley Forge to Yorktown.

Baron von Steuben, on the north side of the square, was a Prussian veteran of the Seven Years' War, in which his country was allied with England. Looking for work in Paris, he fell under the persuasive powers of Benjamin Franklin and got over here in time for that mythic winter at Valley Forge, where he introduced professional drill to the Army. The results showed themselves immediately at the Battle of Monmonth, where von Steuben rallied troops in full retreat to gain an important and unlikely victory.

General Thaddeus Kosciuszko, in the northeast corner, came to our Revolution out of love for liberty everywhere, especially in his native Poland, threatened then and until quite recently by one or more of three aggressive neighbors, Prussia, Russia, and Austria. A military engineer, his fortifications on the Delaware River, at Saratoga, and at West Point were of inestimable value in repelling British advances by land and water. After the war, he and his Poles were less successful in turning back the Russian invasion of Poland, but he persisted until his death and remains a hero to both nations. Before returning to Poland's endless struggle for freedom, he sold his Congressional land grant in Ohio and gave the proceeds to found the Colored School in Newark, New Jersey, one of the first educational institutions for blacks in America. After his stunning success with the Andrew Jackson, Clark Mills returned to the charge, as it were, with the equestrian bronze statue of George Washington on Pennsylvania Avenue west of Lafayette Square in Washington Circle. Shortly after Washington's resignation from the Army in 1783, the Continental Congress proposed that an equestrian statue of the general be erected, but it took until 1860 for the Father of his Country to get mounted in the city bearing his name. The work is based on an incident of the Revolution. At the Battle of Princeton, Washington's horse froze in fright at the sudden eruption of shot and shell. The commander in chief calmly asserted his authority and carried the day. The importance of the victory in New Jersey lay in holding the Army together at a crucial moment in the war. In Mills's sculpture, the

incident of the horse becomes a metaphor for what Washington did for the Continental Army and indeed for the American nation aborning.

There was, of course, a Continental Army before Washington took command. New Englander Nathanael Greene joined the Rhode Island militia as a private in 1774, but became a brigadier general within the year. He more than lived up to that early promise. He led the Rhode Island campaign, planned the defense of New York City, conducted the trial of the British spy,

Here, and on the opposite page, four Union generals, cast in bronze, appear in equestrian statuary. Below, Philip H. Sheridan, memorialized by Gutzon Borglum, was dedicated in 1908. In 1864, Sheridan commanded the cavalry of the Army of the Potomac. The George H. Thomas Memorial, right, celebrates the Civil War hero known as "the Rock of Chickamauga."

Major André, fought in all the battles of the Mid-Atlantic, reorganized the supply system of the Army, conducted the successful Carolina campaign, and occasionally acted as commander in chief. His bronze equestrian monument stands at Massachusetts and Maryland avenues, Northeast, in Stanton Square. Horse and rider seem perfectly united in a resolute summons to action.

Two more men complete this bronze pantheon of the Revolution in Washington, one on either end of the Treasury Building. On the south side stands Alexander Hamilton. A native of Jamaica and thus a reminder that in 1776 there was some thought of bringing the British West Indies with us into independence, Hamilton served in the War as Washington's aide-de-camp, became the first Secretary of the Treasury, and, sadly, is best remembered for having died in a duel with Jefferson's Vice-President, Aaron Burr. Hamilton was much more important than that. He got the new country on a sound financial footing by paying off the debts of the Continental Congress. In a modest way he began the now bipartisan favorite fiscal finagle, deficit financing. He left the new

republic with a $14,000,000 debt.

The man on the north end of the building is Albert Gallatin, Secretary of the Treasury under Jefferson, whose great accomplishment was paying off the $14,000,000 in only six years while also financing such Jeffersonian expansionist exploits as the Lewis and Clark expedition to the Louisiana Purchase and the Pacific. Gallatin then went on to amass a small surplus!

The two statues are masterpieces of portraiture and personification by the man who was perhaps the greatest of the classical, realistic sculptors in America, James Earle Fraser. Fraser's forte was the ability to see and to let others see nobility expressed in what are indubitably authentic details of face and form, even of fashion, as in the exposure of those well-turned calves.

Washington's public sculpture is in low public repute thanks to cartoonists and the belief that it is all unknown Civil War generals on horseback. They do indeed exist, but there is much more to the city's monuments than all that top brass in bronze. Those generals have inspired a few works of first-rate sculpture by any

standard, and one equestrian ensemble that must be the best in the country, and possibly in the world, the Grant Memorial.

The Civil War also had its civilian heroes. The earliest in oratory was Daniel Webster, of Massachusetts, who, in a fiery Senate debate, put into imperishable words the view that made the war unavoidable: Liberty and Union, Now and Forever, One and Inseparable. Those words and others of Webster's are engraved on his monument in Scott Circle.

Abraham Lincoln, the great civilian of the

Atop its pedestal, George B. McClellan's statue, right, by Frederick MacMonnies, honors the Union general who led the Army of the Potomac during the early years of the Civil War. The John A. Logan Memorial, below right, reveals the Union officer and politician noted for service in the West and particularly for the siege of Vicksburg.

war, was memorialized twice in the city before the great temple overlooking the river was built. In front of the U.S. Courthouse on Judiciary Square stands Lincoln the lawyer, in marble, carved in 1868 by a local "gravestone maker," Lot Flannery, as the city's first expression of grief for the lost leader. Not great sculpture, the work is touching and somehow meet and right. In Lincoln Park, on East Capitol Street at 12th Street, Northeast, is the Emancipation Monument, erected in 1876, the centennial year of the republic that Lincoln preserved. He is shown making a gesture of freedom over the head of a kneeling slave, taken from a photograph of Archer Alexander, the last runaway returned to slavery under the Fugitive Slave Act. The $18,000 for the bronze group was given entirely by emancipated slaves.

Major General John A. Logan is distinguished by the all-bronze base for his bronze statue in Logan Circle at 12th and P streets, Northwest. He helped significantly at the Battle of Vicksburg, but his constant meddling in civilian politics led to his being relieved by Sherman. His most lasting contribution was the postwar invention of Memorial Day, first celebrated in 1868.

Like Logan, Lieutenant General Winfield Scott has his own circle, at Massachusetts and Rhode Island avenues, Northwest. His statue there was cast from cannon he captured in the Mexican War. Scott was perhaps the longest serving officer in our history, beginning in 1808 and fighting in the War of 1812 and Mexico, but also serving from the Canadian border to the Indian

Civil War commander Ulysses S. Grant sits on his mount, below, between two statuary groups—one cavalry and one artillery—at the base of Capitol Hill. A vista of the memorial appears opposite, and detail below. The gun crew struggles at bottom, and cavalrymen charge directly above it. Sculptor Merwin Shrady worked with architect Edward Pearce Casey to complete the three-part memorial.

borders. Loyal to the Union despite his Virginia birth, Scott finally resigned his commission early in the Civil War.

Another Union officer from Virginia, Major General George H. Thomas, became a national hero as "the Rock of Chickamauga" for his superb performance in the critical Chattanooga campaign. The bronze statue by John Quincy Adams Ward is in Thomas Circle at Massachusetts Avenue and 14th Street, Northwest.

Brigadier General James Birdseye McPherson had a short but brilliant career, moving swiftly up through the ranks for his work in the Tennessee Campaign, the Battle of Vicksburg and elsewhere. He commanded a Corps in Sherman's relentless March to the Sea, and was killed in the Battle of Atlanta at age 36. His loss was keenly felt by Grant and Sherman, who regarded him as one of the best officers in the army. His statue in the city square named for him was cast from cannon captured at Atlanta.

It is rare for a staff officer to be memorialized in bronze or any other way, which may be why Major General John A. Rawlins is presented on foot. He owed his entire career to the accident of being the neighbor of Ulysses S. Grant in Galena, Illinois. When the war began and Grant returned to the Army, he asked young Rawlins to

be his aide. Step by step, Rawlins followed Grant up the military stairway of rank and through the geography of the war. In spite of Lincoln's famous endorsement of whatever brand of whiskey Grant used, Rawlins is credited for cutting down his old neighbor's intake on campaign. His statue presides over one of the loveliest little retreats in Washington, Rawlins Park at 18th and E streets, Northwest.

With General Philip H. Sheridan, on Sheridan Circle, 23rd Street at Massachusetts Avenue, Northwest, we arrive at a much more widely known hero and a very much livelier statue. Sheridan seemed to be all over the place, fighting tenaciously, often brilliantly, in battle after battle, beating one Confederate general after another. His most famous feat, immortalized in a poem once memorized by Northern schoolchildren, was "Sheridan's Ride," with the stirring refrain, "And Sheridan twenty miles away!" What he was 20 miles away from was the Battle of Winchester, which the Union was losing. Sheridan raced his horse, Rienzi (afterwards renamed Winchester), down the Shenandoah Valley, stopped the retreat, and turned it into victory. He then withdrew very slowly, burning or

seizing all possible resources until, as he reported, even a crow flying down the valley would have to take his rations with him. The sculptor, Gutzon Borglum, caught the critical moment of Sheridan meeting the retreat, waving his hat and heartening the troops by his very presence. Borglum performed heroically himself in creating the gigantic Presidential heads on Mount Rushmore.

General William Tecumseh Sherman was second only to Grant in winning the war. In the South for decades afterwards his name was even more opprobrious than his superior's, but he knew better than anyone that war is hell, and making it so helped to end it.

His monument, south of the Treasury, on the spot where he reviewed the victory march of the Union Army, was designed by Carl Rohl-Smith but completed after the sculptor's death by other hands under the supervision of his widow, Sara. There are bronze sentinels representing infantry, cavalry, artillery, and engineers; portrait medallions; inscriptions; bas-reliefs; figures for War and Peace; even mosaics around

Sculptor Daniel Chester French paces at the base of his famous statue of Abraham Lincoln as its final pieces are fitted together by workmen in 1920. Opposite, the memorial itself, raised on its foundation awaiting its broad steps, undergoes construction in 1916; also, a modern photo of Lincoln's head.

the base listing Sherman's battles. The sculptor-designer and his wife insured that there is ample space for all these elements with no crowding. Really examining the details—and then again the whole ensemble—gives the visitor some metaphoric sense of the duration of the war and its complexity, as well as a deep respect for the mind that could deal with it all.

All that is true in a higher power of the General Ulysses S. Grant Memorial at the foot of Capitol Hill, on the east end of the Mall. The sculptor, Henry Merwin Shrady, immersed himself in a study of his subject, enlisting in New York's National Guard, dissecting horses, observing combat drills at West Point, obtaining authentic uniforms, and talking to his own father, a doctor who had attended Grant in his final illness. Yet all of this study shows only on close examination. The great ensemble consists of a wide marble plaza supporting freestanding artillery and cavalry groups in action on either side of the high pedestal that bears the general on horseback, watching the progress of battle. The base of the pedestal has low-relief bronze plaques of marching infantry on either side and in front the only word in the ensemble, "GRANT." Grant's watchful calm contrasts with the intense activity of the two mounted groups; it is almost a lesson in the conduct of war: keep aware and calm no matter what. In this grand climax of the bronze apotheosis of Civil War generals, Grant is clearly no god. He is a human like the rest of us, out in the rain, eyes peeled, working, hoping for the best. Finally, the presence of those enlisted men and their company-grade officers is something new in military monuments, a note of democracy pointing the way to the flag raisers of Iwo Jima and the classless society of the dead of Vietnam.

The Navy and seafarers in general have been of incalculable importance to this country. The first, Christopher Columbus, has lately been subject to the ravages of revisionism, but he did find the place as far as Europe was concerned and does deserve notice. He has it handsomely in the Columbus Fountain, planned by architect Daniel Burnham and executed in marble by sculptor Lorenzo Taft as the centerpiece of Union Station, Burnham's monumental gateway to the monumental city. The discoverer stands erect, arms folded, on the stylized prow of a ship, flanked on either side of the pedestal behind him by figures representing Old World ancients and New World Indians. There are flagpoles and eagles, and, on top of all, the great globe itself, turned to show the Western Hemisphere. It is hard to think of an airport anywhere with that grand an entry to its city.

John Paul Jones was a maritime adventurer more than anything else, but he was a gifted sea fighter and the hero of America's first legendary victory at sea. In reply to a surrender demand, he said, "I have not yet begun to fight!" He took and boarded the enemy, HMS *Serapis,* from which he watched his own *Bon Homme Richard* sink. After the Revolution he became one of a series of foreign military men recruited by Catherine the Great for Russia, but died in Paris

in poverty. His body, preserved in rum, was found in Paris in 1905 and reinterred at the United States Naval Academy at Annapolis, Maryland. His monument, commissioned by Congress the following year, stands at 17th Street and Independence Avenue, Southwest, in West Potomac Park. The sculptor, Charles Niehaus, collaborated with the distinguished architect Thomas Hastings for an effect well above that of the bronze figure alone.

It took the Civil War to raise our top sea dogs to the rank of admiral. David Glasgow Farragut was first to be vice admiral and then first to be full admiral. Both honors were richly deserved. Farragut was by far the most successful and the most famous naval officer of the war. After capturing New Orleans, he aided Grant in the crucial Vicksburg campaign, and ended blockade running in the Gulf of Mexico with a bold attack on Mobile Bay, where he issued the order, "Damn the torpedoes! Full speed ahead!" His local fame is burnished by two separate Metro stations bearing his name.

His statue in Farragut Square between 16th and 17th on K Street, Northwest, the work of Vinnie Ream Hoxie, is a perfect likeness, and shows him on deck, telescope in hand, watching the action. The statue and the four chopped mortars at the corners of the base were cast from the propeller of Farragut's flagship at Mobile Bay, the U.S.S. *Hartford.*

Rear Admiral Samuel F. Dupont has become much more widely and favorably known through his memorial than he was himself in life. Dupont Circle and its broad-based central fountain constitute the city's most popular place for pausing or slow sauntering, sunning or reading through an idle hour, casual conversation, water watching and walker watching. The central fountain was made by Daniel Chester French working with Henry Bacon, architect, the partnership that produced the Lincoln Memorial. Against a cen-

Enigmatic faces and forms peer out from Washington's buildings and parks: "Sky," the 1921 sculpture, above, by Daniel Chester French, at Dupont Circle, is part of the Samuel F. Dupont Memorial. Below, "Man Controlling Trade" was sculpted in 1942 by Michael Lantz for the Federal Trade Commission. Opposite top, "Sphinx," at the Scottish Rite Masonic Temple, was created by Adolph Weinman in 1915. "Guardianship," a male figure at the National Archives, by James Earle Fraser and Sidney Waugh, symbolizes the necessity of eternal vigilance to maintain freedom.

tral plinth, three allegorical figures, Sea, Wind, and Stars, support the upper basin, from which three streams flow to the lower.

Across the Potomac, between the Memorial and the 14th Street bridges, in Lady Bird Johnson Park, near the water, stands the Navy-Marine Memorial to the servicemen who died at sea in World War I. It is one of the most immediately evocative monuments we have—and there is parking. Seven sea gulls are poised in flight above a breaking wave, and that simple arrangement can clutch your throat. The sculptor, Ernesto del Piatta, made the memorial of cast aluminum, a highly experimental medium at the time, and used some color: green on the undersides for the reflected surface of the sea, yellow for the glint of sunlight on wing tips and crest.

The Marine Corps War Memorial, universally known as the Iwo Jima memorial, located farther north on the same side of the river as those sea gulls, became the city's most visited and admired war memorial from the moment of its dedication in 1954 and remains very popular, although the Vietnam Memorial now attracts even more visitors. The figure group records an incident in World War II. In the long and bloody war for island after island in the Pacific, Iwo Jima was an especially tough fight. With victory in sight but far from secure, six Marines, all enlisted men, took a flag and a length of pipe to the island's highest point, the peak of Mount Suribachi, and there

raised Old Glory. Associated Press combat photographer Joe Rosenthal caught the action at its keenest moment and sculptor Felix W. de Weldon, a long established master of classical realism, successfully translated Rosenthal's paper image into three-dimensional bronze, an accomplishment by no means as simple as it sounds. The statue is six times life size, and the faces are portraits of the real men. The crowds of visitors testify to its power. With the actual flag moving in the wind, the group seems intensely real.

More quietly but still movingly, the bronze figure of the single sailor, sea bag at his side, outside the new Navy Museum at Pennsylvania Avenue and 7th Street, Northwest, embodies another maritime virtue. The young seaman seems to scan the skies for any sign, as, with all his world in the bag at his feet, he waits to ship out to ports unknown.

Besides the great ones already seen, the city has a somewhat mixed bag of Presidents. James A. Garfield, elected in 1880, didn't do much as President because he was shot three months into office and died three months after that. Yet on the Mall, at the foot of Capitol Hill, there he stands in bronze on a pedestal bearing symbolic figures of his prior successes as a scholar, a soldier, and a statesman. Garfield's true monument is the civil service, which came into being in national shock over his death at the hands of a disappointed office-seeker.

If Garfield did little, Buchanan did worse. He was Lincoln's immediate predecessor, and the Civil War actually began in the last days of his administration, due in no small part to his

four years of indecision and inaction, right down to reinforcing the garrison at Fort Sumter just too late. Yet he sits today in imperishable bronze in Meridian Park at 16th Street and Florida Avenue, Northwest, the gift to the nation of his niece, Harriet Lane Johnston, who was his White House hostess and whose art collection is an important part of what is now the National Museum of American Art. Flanked by great marble benches and symbolic figures representing Law and Diplomacy, Buchanan looks worried, as well he might.

There is a vivid contrast between the memorials to those two do-nothing 19th-century Presidents and that of the 20th century's do-everything President, Franklin Delano Roosevelt. FDR is visibly remembered in the capital of the country he presided over longer than anyone else has or will in a simple block of stone in front of the National Archives building at Pennsylvania and Constitution avenues, Northwest. It gives his name and his dates.

FDR's distant cousin, Theodore Roosevelt, inherited the office from the assassinated President William McKinley. A vigorous "trust buster," TR was also an advocate of preserving the wilderness, and that aspect of his many-faceted Presidency and personality sets the scene for his memorial on Roosevelt Island in the Potomac, just above Theodore Roosevelt Bridge. TR, in bronze, by Paul Manship, has his arm raised in a typical oratorical gesture, palm open, fingers bent. Surrounding him is a controlled wilderness of nature trails and some remnants of the farm the island used to be. The combination

of urban orator and bosky setting is exactly right for the police commissioner, governor, and President who was also a lover of the American West, a big-game hunter of note, and canal builder in Panama's jungle.

The John F. Kennedy Memorial is as simple to the eye as FDR's, though rather more complicated below ground. Washingtonians have always called it "the eternal flame," and many of them still recall their shock when Mrs. Kennedy lighted it at the grave of her slain husband at the end of a day of sad ceremony. The grave and its flame are in Arlington National Cemetery, at what looks like halfway up the hill from the parkway to the Custis-Lee Mansion. It is almost always visible to one going west across Memorial Bridge, and is best seen from the rear platform of the Lincoln Memorial at night, when the flame seems indeed a kindly light amid the encircling gloom, as John F. Kennedy did to so many Americans.

Downstream, directly across the parkway from the Navy-Marine Memorial—those sea gulls—is the entrance to what is probably the quietest, most soothing, restful, and restorative Presidential memorial, that of

Kennedy's Vice-President and successor, Lyndon B. Johnson. No one of those adjectives would have been used about LBJ by anyone who knew him or even read about him, yet they all apply to this lightly wooded area, full of rambling paths, the smell of foliage, and a sturdy wooden bridge across a narrow branch of the Potomac, all centered on the memorial proper. This is a great vertical slab of rough-cut pink granite glittering with a thousand points of light. That's it: there is no image of Johnson, only quotations in the pavement, all stressing his devotion to equal rights for all, which he proved in action, or to his childhood values learned in Texas.

Joseph Henry is certainly the most influential private person memorialized. He was the first Secretary of the Smithsonian Institution, and, in his term, from its founding in 1846 to his death in 1878, he set the new establishment on the path that has so enriched this nation and the world. At the time of his appointment, Henry was the most distinguished scientist in the country, with a long string of basic discoveries and laws to his credit, especially in the field of electromagnetism. His statue stands where it should, on the Mall outside the main entrance to the original Smithsonian building, the "Castle." The sculptor, William Wetmore Story, clothed Henry in a scholar's robe, and, on the side of his stand, modeled an electromagnet. The statue now faces outward from the Institution, signifying both the increase and the diffusion of knowledge.

The increase and diffusion of a different knowledge is memorialized in the statue of Thomas Hopkins Gallaudet, on the grounds of Gallaudet College, named for the inventor of the sign language used by millions of the deaf. The little girl is Alice Cogswell, his first student, who is seen in the act of learning the letter A in sign. The group, by Daniel Chester French, shows a charming informality in contrast to the classical invocations of his Lincoln and the Dupont fountain.

Another teacher is seen in the Mary McLeod Bethune Memorial in Lincoln Park, East Capitol and 12th streets, Northeast. She was born the child of freed slaves in 1875 and died in 1955, having been friend and adviser to President Franklin D. Roosevelt and chief of the Negro Affairs Division of his National Youth Administration. It is impossible even to estimate the number of young black people who benefited from her efforts. The statue has a pleasant openness, measured by the arms of the three figures. The teacher is portrayed as passing her legacy to the little girl. Excerpts appear on the base: "I leave you love. I leave you hope. . . . I leave you racial dignity."

The Samuel Gompers Memorial, 10th Street and Pennsylvania Avenue, Northwest, is New Deal sculpture simultaneously at its loftiest and its most pedestrian, by no means an uncommon combination in the arts. The man and the movement here memorialized have been essential to the still evolving nature of American society. Gompers was the founder of the American Federation of Labor, which bettered the lot of American working men and women in ways beyond measure. The AFL-CIO was an enormous political force throughout the mid-20th century, and that "was" is perfectly embodied in the sculpture.

There are three poets among the capital's memorial sculptures. From very different countries, they share a significance in the growth of

nationalism in Europe and America. The first, and assuredly the greatest, is Dante Alighieri, whose heroic size statue adorns Meridian Hill Park, 16th Street and Florida Avenue, Northwest. Dante's monumental work, *Divine Comedy,* summed up medieval theology in an epic journey through Hell and Purgatory to Heaven. But he used his Florentine Tuscan in place of the traditional Latin and his guide through the Christian afterlife was the pagan poet Virgil. A national language, perfected or revived, is basic to nationalism. And Virgil was vital to the Renaissance, or rebirth of classic antiquity. The poet's face is grim, but so was the Inferno.

Henry Wadsworth Longfellow was America's best loved writer throughout the end of the 19th century and into the 20th. Robed in bronze, he sits at the busy intersection of M Street and Connecticut Avenue, Northwest, surrounded by an urban life he could not have imagined when he died in 1882. Read and recited in home and school, his verses celebrated America as America liked it. Hiawatha, Paul Revere, Miles Standish, and other heroes live only or chiefly by dint of Longfellow's effort. At his death, he became the first American to be honored in the Poets' Corner of Westminster Abbey.

Taras Shevchenko was a 19th-century Ukrainian poet who wrote and worked for his country's liberation from Czarist Russia. For this he was sentenced to 10 years in prison. Paradoxically, he was widely popular throughout the Soviet Union, which, from a Ukrainian point of view, was the Russian Empire come again. When Ukrainian-Americans proposed erecting the statue, on P Street between 22nd and 23rd, Northwest, there were violent objections from some Washingtonians, but it was unveiled by President Eisenhower before 100,000 who liked it. When the USSR imploded and Ukraine became free, the statue became a sisterly gesture to newly achieved independence.

Memorials come wholesale, as it were, in cemeteries. Several in Washington are unusually well-supplied. The Congressional Cemetery, at 18th and E streets, Southeast, is especially rich in sepulchral sculpture. The name no longer applies but the monuments erected when it did offer a fascinating view of funerary fashions. The most original shape is that of the Lieutenant John T. McLaughlin Monument, 1847. It is a cannon, pointing straight up, resting on four cannon balls, all carved from a single block of stone. John Philip Sousa, the March King, is buried here with enough family members to suggest the audience at a small concert, a view strengthened by the bench and the bar of music on his stone.

Another repository for sepulchral sculpture is the Rock Creek Cemetery, at the end of North Capitol Street at Rock Creek Church Road and Webster Street, Northwest. One work there so far transcends the category as to have entered the class of truly great American sculpture. Some would call it the greatest we have produced. This is the Adams Memorial, popularly and inaccurately known as "Grief." It was made in 1892, by Augustus Saint-Gaudens, in a setting by Stanford White, for their friend Henry Adams, novelist, historian, and the intellectual giant of the family that entered our history with John Adams. Henry Adams's wife, Marian Hooper Adams, an invalid in deep melancholy following the death of her father, committed suicide. Adams's happiest years were those of his marriage, and he commissioned his two friends to make a fitting memorial. The power of the piece is instantly perceived and deepens with further viewing. Usually thought female, the completely and loosely draped figure is actually of neither sex,

or of both. It sits rapt in contemplation of life and death, of eternity and the fleeting moment. That visitor is hurried indeed who can fail to sit, too, and join the process.

Instead of generals, symbolic figures and forms and anonymous soldiers characterize memorials for 20th-century wars. Thus, the First Division Monument, immediately south of the Old State, War, and Navy building on State Place at 17th Street, Northwest, is a simple 80-foot-high column, in one piece of pink granite, surmounted by the Greek goddess of Victory, winged, with flag and outstretched hand. The lithely proportioned form is by Daniel Chester French, the architectural design by Cass Gilbert, with the names of the Yankee Division dead in the Great War and the division's battle honors and campaigns inscribed on bronze plaques and on the column itself, respectively. Later, Cass Gilbert, Jr., expanded the design to include the dead and the campaigns of World War II.

The Memorial of the Second Division was created by an equally distinguished team, James Earle Fraser, sculptor, and John Russell Pope, architect. Pope's great granite doors, facing Constitution Avenue at 17th Street, Northwest, stand for the gate to Paris, defended successfully by the division's great golden sword of flame. Again, wings were added for the dead of World War II and Korea.

The names of the dead are the point of war memorials. That has never been clearer than in the latest, the Vietnam Veterans Memorial, in Constitution Gardens along Constitution Avenue at 22nd Street, Northwest. The controversy that swirled around the memorial from its beginning through its magnificent realization now seems distant and unimportant. What dominates are the names—more than 58,000—of those killed or missing in the Vietnam War, arranged in the

order of their dying. They are on two triangular walls of dark granite that reflect their surroundings, especially the intent faces of families looking for their dead. The triangular walls are almost 500 feet long overall, and 10 feet high where they meet at the center. The ends point to the Washington Monument and the Lincoln Memorial.

The creator of this was Maya Ying Lin, at the time a 21-year-old architectural student at Yale University who entered and won a national competition. The whole enterprise was initiated and carried out by a group of Vietnam veterans

appalled at and resentful of the imposed invisibility both of them and of their war to the people they had fought for. The memorial has changed that completely.

At the strongly expressed wish of some Vietnam veterans, a bronze, life-size figure group has been added: three infantrymen, or "grunts," as they called themselves, the work of Frederick Hart, a long established Washington sculptor, in the tradition of Fraser and French. The men, clearly of different ethnic origins, are a kind of pendant to the wall, adding, not distracting. Not heroic, even anti- heroic, they seem to be just coming out of combat, beat up, exhausted, hanging in there.

In writing about our century's first war of independence, the Irish Rebellion, William Butler Yeats said, "Too long a sacrifice/ Can make a stone of the heart./ O when may it suffice?/ That is Heaven's part, our part/ To murmur name upon name/ As a mother names her child/ When sleep at last has come/ On limbs that had run wild." ★

The National Mall

John Hoke

WASHINGTON, D.C., IS OFTEN CALLED THE MOST IMPORTANT CITY IN THE WORLD, AND TO THE EXTENT THAT THIS IS TRUE, THE NATIONAL MALL AND NEIGHBORING PUBLIC SPACES MIGHT BE THOUGHT OF AS BELONGING TO ALL THE WORLD. THE NATIONAL MALL, THIS SIMPLE, ELEGANT EXPANSE OF COMMON, IS ONE OF THE SINGLE MOST CELEBRATED FEATURES OF ANY CAPITAL CITY IN THE WORLD. AND IT MAY BE THOUGHT

OF AS A MIRROR TO REFLECT THE UNITED STATES OF AMERICA, ITS GOVERNMENT, ITS PEOPLE AND THEIR SPIRIT. FROM JUST ABOUT ANY POINT YOU CAN CATCH GLIMPSES OF OUR NATIONAL EDIFICES—FROM THE CAPITOL, WITH ITS TWO HOUSES OF CONGRESS, TO THE WHITE HOUSE. OUT OF THE WINDOWS OF THE WASHINGTON MONUMENT—AT THE 500-FOOT LEVEL—YOU CAN SEE THE SUPREME COURT BUILDING, WHICH HOUSES THE THIRD BRANCH OF GOVERNMENT, AS WELL AS, SWEEPING AWAY IN EVERY DIRECTION, THE REST OF THE CITY OF WASHINGTON.

The west-side promenades of the Capitol also provide magnificent vantage points. Here the unique openness of the capital area can be appreciated, one that is as yet uncluttered and unoverwhelmed by the skyscrapers, in their pipe-organ clusters, that so often accompany urban progress. In its restraint, the National Mall still expresses the inspiring vision of planner Pierre L'Enfant and the founding fathers.

There is nothing accidental about the design: this vista was specified by Pierre L'Enfant. It didn't just happen, and certainly not in a day, and it will not endure without help.

While there are many opinions regarding the origin of the concept of the Mall, National Park Service staff members John G. Parsons and Glen DeMarr have written that ". . .the Mall provides a formal work of landscape architecture. . .which virtually and symbolically links the Legislative and Executive Branches of our government. This grand and dignified green avenue provides the unifying element for the carefully placed, but diversified, architectural symbols, repositories, and shrines of the heritage of our democracy which are on and along its length. Above all, the Mall, as a design element, is the centerpiece of the Nation's Capital, providing continuity and stability, and symbolizing to the world the strength of this democracy. It is the Nation's front yard which belongs to all Americans."

When L'Enfant stood on Jenkins Hill looking westward, back in our country's early years, his view was unlike anything we see today. The Mall is largely manmade land. From Jenkins Hill, George Washington and Pierre L'Enfant looked out over lowland that was boggy and became progressively more swampy as it approached the Potomac River. In fact, the line formed by today's Constitution Avenue was Washington Town's southern edge.

Then the land was much, much lower, and malaria a major bane of a city that today is better known for Potomac Fever, another kind of local malady altogether. Waterways such as Tiber Creek slid through sandy marshes. "Foggy Bottom," they called it, a name that survives today for the area around the nearby State Department.

Loads of fill dirt raised the land from its original elevation of about eight feet (above mean high tide) to its current elevation of about 22 feet. Construction of all sorts came and went, little of it taking root. One exception was the original Smithsonian Institution Building, the red sandstone "Castle" that was largely completed by 1855 and that would become the hallmark of the National Mall. A railway station can be seen in some early pictures. During the Civil War, the Mall was a staging area, with troop encampments and a vast stable for horses, and even a slaughterhouse. Streets crossed it, some horticultural gardens were placed here and there: it became something of a hodgepodge extension of the city. Certainly it afforded nothing like the unobstructed vistas of today.

Democracy's thunder and lightning storm across the Mall on various occasions, including visits from foreign dignitaries, military triumphs, and the glorious Fourth. Below right, a lone celebrant adds her own shimmer of delight to festivities on the 4th of July.

sores thrown up during World War I, were razed, and the uncluttered view to the west began to take shape. Stately groves of American elm trees were planted. Streets and rail lines still criss-crossed the Mall, but it was at last taking the shape of the "grand avenue" planned more than a century before.

Then World War II arrived. Again, "temporary" buildings went up to house instant government offices that would manage instant mobilization. Sleepy Washington grew at an astonishing rate; stories are legion about how hard it was just to find a room to rent. Plans for the National Mall were not high priorities, but, except for new tempos—still wooden but no less massive and durable than their predecessors—it still retained the openness that is so much a part of its basic character.

And, heedless of war, the elm trees quietly grew and began to take on their characteristically graceful shape. Early pictures of them, from the air or from the Washington Monument, show that they were assuming the delightful "muffins-in-a-baking-tin" aspect that can result from the regimented planting of such trees on a vast scale.

Although the Smithsonian's Castle, Arts and Industries Building, and Natural History Museum, and the National Gallery of Art all pre-dated World War II, a vast, postwar cultural legacy was further assembled along the Mall. Perhaps nowhere else can one wander and stroll amid such a diversity of great museums and galleries. And in Washington, most major collections are free. The Mall is a portal to education; Smithsonian scholars often call it the campus.

Over the years, several agencies were created to see to it that all construction was tasteful and to safeguard the character of the National Mall. Among these agencies are the Fine Arts Commission and the National Capital Planning Commission. All plans affecting the Mall come

At the turn of the century, the 57th Congress produced the McMillan plan, a major review of plans for the National Mall. While this plan described and illustrated some grandiose monumental elements, including modifications to the Washington Monument, it called for the completion of the National Mall along the "openness" lines that we see today.

Only in the mid-1930s, however, was the plan made reality. The shabby wooden temporary buildings, the first of the famed "tempos," eye-

before these committees for examination and final approval. With very few exceptions, no new structures are permitted to rise higher than 12 stories in order to avoid eclipsing the National Mall and surrounding edifices and monuments—and thus diminish their stature and prominence. Wisely, certain areas—Lafayette Park's surroundings, most notably—were restricted from modernization. Their historic flavor must be maintained. When such structures as the current Old Executive Office Building (once the War Department building), just across the street from the White House, were modernized internally, the exteriors of the buildings were preserved with all the design details that fixed their places in architectural time.

Early on, the Department of Interior's National Park Service was given responsibility for the care of the National Mall. While much of this involves the simple task of meeting the horticultural needs of the "resource" (bureaucrat-ese for such facilities), the job isn't all that simple.

★ ★ ★ ★ ★

The National Mall, a bully pulpit, is also a big farm whose main crops are turf, elm trees, and cherry blossoms. Sodding operations go on near the Capitol, above. Below, Japanese performers delight visitors to America's 200th-anniversary party on the Mall in 1976, the National Folklife Festival, an event jointly sponsored by the Smithsonian Institution and the National Park Service.

As Washington became a national and even global Mecca of sorts, it fell to the Park Service to clean up after celebrations and "happenings." Some of these attracted as many as a million visitors. A notable annual event is the celebration of Independence Day, on July 4th, which nowadays includes concerts on a number of sound stages up and down the Mall, and which always ends with a thrilling display of fireworks as darkness falls.

As they "ooh" and "ahh," the enthralled crowd, presumably absent-mindedly, deposits truly heroic expanses of trash the length and breadth of the National Mall. And yet the Park Service usually has the place swept up by dawn's early light! As the last celebrants of the nation's birthday wander home, workers arrive in the middle of the night. They corral paper and other light trash with giant blowers while others with gunny sacks round up the bottles and heavier stuff that the blowers miss.

The National Mall has also become increasingly a site for people—in their hundreds, thousands, and hundreds of thousands—who wish to focus legislative attention on their concerns and causes. Many gatherings protest the government's handling of their interests. This is not a

new phenomenon: the women's suffrage movement included protests on the National Mall. Later, in the early 1930s, the Bonus Marchers—jobless World War I veterans—camped on the National Mall while they demanded payment of veterans' bonuses. Initially peaceful, the affair turned sour and left a lasting scar on the nation's soul

★ ★ ★ ★ ★

The addition of Constitution Gardens, above, at the time of the country's Bicentennial, provided the Mall with a curving lake and islands to the north of the long, formal Reflecting Pool, and the oval Rainbow Pool, east of the Reflecting Pool, where helicopters land dignitaries going to the White House.

when mounted troops under the personal command of General Douglas MacArthur charged the petitioners.

The results of these gatherings are sometimes damaging to the "resource" for the simple reason that all those feet, trampling the site, leave a wasteland where green grass once flourished. The Park Service sets things right, makes it all green again, and all in a hurry—sometimes just in time for it to be all torn up again by another large-scale event.

The Park Service can find itself in quite a dilemma. The care of the resource is important; like our own front yards, the National Mall looks best when green and uncluttered. Yet a funda-

mental aspect of the American way of governing is also involved: a basic American right is to petition and seek redress of the Congress and, in the main, that is what is behind many of the increasing numbers of public demonstrations that take place in Washington.

Any effort to police certain events—to prevent them or try to move them elsewhere—may run afoul of the basic right of petition, and the courts in recent times have often taken the position that the right of petition comes first. In the case of the Mall resource, "it's only grass that you can replant." Such conflicting requirements must be kept in balance; the Park Service does its part by patiently repairing the Mall. And so, today, the visitor to certain monuments may find conspicuous evidence of the right to petition—stands displaying brochures and other things—that would otherwise be considered out of harmony with the original intent of the designers, but the grass will usually be green and neat.

The National Park Service now confronts a dilemma of a more conventional kind. It concerns the care—the survival—of the American elm trees that are such an important living architectural component of the National Mall. Shortly after World War II, it was discovered that the elm

trees were suffering from an affliction known as
Dutch elm disease. This malady was soon to
become a worldwide environmental disaster. A
particularly virulent form of it erupted in
Europe, killing, for instance, every elm in
London's Hyde Park by the early 1970s.

While scientists of the National Park Service
explored every strategy open to them to arrest
or at least ameliorate the impact of this disease
on the Mall's American elms, a simple, practical
consideration was to make their efforts even
more difficult. When the extent of the disease in
North America reached epidemic proportions,
tree farms and nurseries stopped raising and
selling elms. America's blighted home-town tree
had become too hot to handle. In recent years,
in response, the National Park Service has created a greenhouse to husband cuttings from those
precious few American elms that show the greatest resistance to Dutch elm disease. Healthy
saplings can replace trees lost to the blight and
other causes.

The "other causes" actually create significant
problems of their own for grass as well as trees.
The increasing use of the National Mall for celebrations as well as protests means more facilities
to handle crowds, and more important, more
feet. All are destructive to both the elm trees
and the central turf areas. The summer 1991
Desert Storm military hardware exhibit was followed almost immediately by that year's July 4th
celebration, and the central grass panels were
all but obliterated. The landscape resembled a
corner of the African Sahel.

The elm trees suffered unexpected damage.
The rotor wash from military helicopters blew
the tops out of a few of them as the choppers
landed and took off. Then a freak Washington
wind storm blew out of nowhere to slash and
shred the leaves and branches.

Perhaps the trees suffer the most damage,
however, from the heavy foot traffic of the hundreds of thousands of visitors who gather to witness these events. The original idea of the
"grand green avenue" was to offer visitors a place
to stroll and perhaps picnic on the grounds—
"passive" visitor use, in Park Service terminology.
With today's increasingly intense use of the
National Mall for what are often very active purposes, the elm trees suffer from the compacting
of the soil around them that turns the dirt into
something like concrete.

Tree growth suffers, studies indicate. And,
remember, the Mall is covered by only the
thinnest layer of viable topsoil. Right under it is
all that rubble—bricks, shards, slabs of metal—
left by long-ago Washingtonians. As a result, the
root systems of these trees are restricted to a
surface mat. Just imagine what it would take to
provide a proper, deep bed of soil for every elm
on the Mall!

Solid evidence indicates that the elm-tree
groves are in a state of decline. If the Park
Service, with all the skills at its disposal, cannot
reverse this trend, the future for this beautiful
and most harmonious feature of the National
Mall may gradually diminish and be lost.

Scientists, both in and out of the Park
Service, are constantly trying new tricks—and
continuing to nurture cuttings and seed stock
from disease-resistant trees. So, with a little bit of
luck and perhaps some changes in public sentiment, we may yet put things right. As the 200th
anniversary of the L'Enfant plan passes, let's be
sure that we don't love our dear old National
Mall to death. We need to support efforts to
restore it to health so that folks 200 years from
now will still be able to enjoy its grassy vistas and
to lounge in the shade of the elms. ★

Treasures of the Smithsonian

EDWARDS PARK

"SMITHSONIAN," I SAID BRISKLY AS I SCRAMBLED INTO A TAXI OUTSIDE THE NATIONAL PRESS BUILDING. USUALLY I WOULD HAVE BEEN MORE SPECIFIC: "THE MUSEUM WITH A DOME, ON CONSTITUTION AVENUE," I WOULD HAVE STIPULATED, OR "THE FUNNY OLD RED-BRICK ONE." BUT, MY MIND ASTRAY, I JUST LEFT IT TO THE CABBIE. I COULD STOP HIM IF HE HOMED IN ON THE NATIONAL AIR AND SPACE MUSEUM, AS MOST WASHINGTON TAXIS USED TO DO IF YOU MURMURED "MUSEUM."

★ ★ ★ ★ ★

A statue of Joseph Henry, the Smithsonian's first Secretary, stands at the edge of the Mall in front of the Institution's Castle building. Above right, architectural detail over the Castle's arched entrance.

149

Beautifully patterned plantings of seasonal flowers beckon visitors into the Smithsonian's Enid A. Haupt Garden and its flagship Castle beyond. Originally used for exhibits, the Castle recently became the Institution's main visitors' center, its Great Hall outfitted with user-friendly, computerized information services, opposite.

Instead, my driver swung off 14th Street onto Jefferson Drive, the south side of the Mall, and creaked to a stop outside the old Smithsonian Castle—exactly what he should have done without further direction. I realized that times have changed. A decade ago I covered the Smithsonian meticulously, day after day. Now, retired, working at home, I'd obviously let the place get away from me. It was time to catch up.

Since 1989, when a new visitors' center, pulsing with electronics, took over the Castle's Great Hall, even taxi drivers have come to know that this original Smithsonian building serves to welcome and inform the weary and bemused. Among its many video guides are maps and models of the Mall area to help people plan citywide expeditions. Those visitors who wish only to drop in before speeding off to the White House, Capitol, and great monuments will benefit from this briefing. I usually pass through the Great Hall, admiring the confident way that small children assail the interactive TVs, then enter the little South Tower Room—set aside in 1902 as a place for children—and step out into the four-acre Enid A. Haupt Garden. The floral carpet of its parterre stretches before me, in line with its distant gates, and I pause among the grassy berms and flowering trees in the center of the garden, turn, and look back at the looming Castle.

A sprawling mass of ruddy sandstone, it peaks into nine varied towers, some crenelated, some capped by curving pyramids. James Renwick designed it in the Romanesque style of the 1840s, strenuously avoiding symmetry, and for a century and a half critics have either applauded or decried his work, depending on the changing fads that have washed around its immutable stones. The Castle has survived war,

A founding member of *Smithsonian* magazine's Board of Editors, Edwards Park is also author of the best-selling *Treasures of the Smithsonian*. Retired, he still writes his *Smithsonian* column, "Around the Mall and Beyond," from Annapolis, Maryland, where he lives with his wife.

fire, politics, and habitation by bats, owls, and a few eccentric scientists. Today, sirens wail beyond its walls and airliners howl above its snapping flags. I find it comforting that it doesn't give an inch.

Fortunately, the Haupt garden doesn't give an inch, either, for its rich loam is only a few feet deep. The bright flower beds, serene walks, and splashing pools form the roof for two magnificent new underground museums and the S. Dillon Ripley Center, a small village of offices, meeting rooms, and special-exhibition areas some 60 feet down.

Twin pavilions, rising amid the garden greenery, mark the museum entrances. The eastern one, with round windows, rounded arches, and hemispheric domes, is a 90-foot-long "vestibule" for the National Museum of African Art. Enter and descend a grand stairway that circles down past three underground levels to a round pool reflecting light from far above. I'm sure I could lose a weekend or two amid the African displays. Many symbolic icons, carved by village artisans, are as deliciously abstract as a multi-million-dollar Picasso. Household objects capture the essence of design—pleasure in utility.

The western pavilion is all angles—diamond-shaped windows, pyramidal caps on its roof, and an angular staircase taking you into the exhibition rooms of the Arthur M. Sackler Gallery, with its non-pareil collection of Asian and Near Eastern art. Dr. Sackler collected a trove of jades and bronzes, to which I pay dutiful homage. Some of the jades, delicately carved, bring me back

often. But it's the endless parade of temporary exhibits and shows—Sumatran dancing, Korean concerts, Sri Lankan sculpture, and many more—that enthrall many Sackler watchers. Miss one, and the next is soon on the way.

Though the Ripley Center, entered from a copper-domed kiosk in the garden, was designed primarily for activities of the Smithsonian Associates, many of its temporary shows have been open to everyone. The delights of this entire underground complex are still new, and quite different from the traditional Smithsonian

★ ★ ★ ★ ★

Pyramidal rooflines delineate the Arthur M. Sackler Gallery, above, which, along with the National Museum of African Art and the S. Dillon Ripley Center, comprises the Smithsonian's newest complex, much of which is underground. Right, a 15-and-1/4-inch-high Chokwe mask from southern Africa, exhibited today at the African Art Museum.

museums up there at ground level along the Mall.

There's the Freer Gallery of Art, for example, next door to the Sackler and now connected to it by a tunnel. This discreet Florentine building opened in 1923 to house the Oriental art collection of the 19th-century manufacturer Charles Freer. In 1988 it closed, partly for the building of that tunnel, partly for a general revamping of its displays.

One great treasure here is the Peacock Room, a British industrialist's dining room completely decorated by James McNeill Whistler. Art experts have studied the much restored blue-green décor of this room and other experts have

analyzed microscopic corings of paint from its walls. Result: the room has been returned to Whistler's original colors—bright, distinct greens and blues.

East of the Castle, the second oldest Smithsonian building, Arts and Industries, is gradually being readied as the home of a new African-American museum. The building is a wondrous Victorian folly of multi-colored brick in which President James Garfield had his inaugural ball. I hope the place lasts forever.

Its next-door neighbor along the Mall is about 180 degrees removed, architecturally. The ultra-modern Hirshhorn Gallery and Sculpture Garden is not only round in plan and hollow in the middle, but eccentric as well, a lopsided doughnut of flat, gray stone in which modern art resides comfortably.

Joseph H. Hirshhorn was no systematic collector of paintings; it's hard for art scholars (and impossible for me) to find a clear-cut path through his purchases, which range from Thomas Eakins through the Philadelphia Five and the Ashcan School to cubism and surrealism. But the great moderns—Sloan, Hartley, Davis, Miró, Hopper, Benton, Pollock, de Kooning, and many others—are displayed effectively in this building.

The sculptures, from Rodin's massive group, *The Burghers of Calais,* to works of Lachaise, Epstein, Giacometti, Moore, and others, show the

progress from realism to abstraction more clearly. They reside in the sculpture garden, a small, sunken patch, green with lawn and soft with leaves, that juts into the Mall.

Modernity in all the arts blossomed in the early 20th century—and in the sciences, too. So the Hirshhorn's neighbor toward Capitol Hill is, aptly enough, the National Air and Space Museum. Cabbies may not head for it with blind instinct as they once did, but its jam of tourists is thicker than just about any other Washington museum can boast.

Actually coming face to face with the true icons of flight—the Wrights' plane, Lindbergh's Spirit of St. Louis, Yeager's X-1, the X-15, the Apollo 11 spacecraft Columbia, and, upstairs, Earhart's Lockheed Vega and Doolittle's Curtiss R3C-2 racer—still packs a wallop. I've seen busy curators of this museum hurry through the entrance hall, "Milestones of Flight," and despite its familiarity pause for a moment to look up and around at these treasures as though checking the weather—almost as though saluting.

Most visitors to "NASM," as we call it, seem to know exactly where to go. Often that's because they're being towed around by small boys. As every parent learns, small boys communicate by bush telegraph, and so know instantly what to see. Here they can hardly miss, because every gallery fascinates, every large-screen IMAX film at the Langley Theater is a winner, and every star show at the Einstein Planetarium sparkles.

The flight-technology gallery, on the second floor, has changed its mission from an explanation of aeronautical design to one of computers. Overhead hangs a full-scale model of the X-29, an experimental fighter with forward swept wings. Such futuristic designs are too dicey for human pilots to keep in the air. Only computers, or "black boxes," can handle them—a humbling revelation.

153

So, in a way, is the new World War I gallery. It's not just about Sopwiths and Fokkers sputtering over the trenches of 1914-1918. It's a thoughtful and moving visual essay about that whole murderous, senseless world event; about lessons it taught, and others it failed to teach; about the end of an age of innocence.

Across the Mall, great things have happened, and are happening, to the National Museum of Natural History. As that grand, domed building sidles closer to its 100th year— it will reach it in 2011—its exhibits are gradually being wrenched up to date, in step with new knowledge. Popular Dinosaur Hall has expanded, becoming one spectacular episode in the whole drama of early life. Entering this Mall-level area, you can keep left and explore ancient life in the sea, then pay homage to the age of dinosaurs, then, moving to the right, give a nod to the origin of us mammals.

Great plans are in store for the Hall of Minerals, upstairs. The glorious Hope diamond, ever a star attraction, will have a different environment, being presented near the entrance to the minerals display so that visitors who want to see only it, and nothing else, can do so—and get out of the way of those who wish to learn a little mineralogy.

Completion of this project depends (like everything else at the Smithsonian) on available money. We may own the Hope diamond and the glittering trove of other great gems on display, but we can't hock 'em—a sometimes frustrating irony in the running of a museum.

The Hall of Anthropology is also undergoing modernization at time of writing. And by the time of reading, a new Insect Zoo should be receiving callers. This live display has been a "must see" since it started in 1976. At the rate of a million a year, viewers, mostly kids, have crammed that small room, where the tweeps and chitters of live insects resound through an amplifier. Now the space—still, unfortunately, only 3,600 square feet—has been redesigned with distinct areas for display and learning. Interactive TVs and monitors supplement demonstrations. Those youngsters who can't get close to the orange-legged tarantula at feeding time can watch the proceedings on TV.

The idea of this living exhibit is to help us accept the huge success of our tiny fellow creatures, to feel a bit awed by being so vastly outnumbered by them, and to note their relatively rapid evolution, which allows them to adapt to the changing world much faster than we can. Putting it bluntly, they'll probably out-survive us.

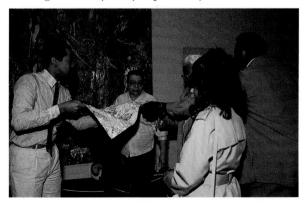

★ ★ ★ ★ ★

A huge African elephant, the world's largest stuffed specimen of this species, greets visitors to the National Museum of Natural History, in the rotunda, just off the Mall entrance. The museum's new Dinosaur Hall features a special area depicting life in the ancient seas, right.

When I was last in this grandly bewildering old museum, I wandered down the corridor that leads past dioramas of North American mammals. It was quiet and uncrowded, and I stopped before each one and really looked. What marvelous scenes—caribou crossing a vast Alaskan valley; mountain goats among British Columbian peaks; elk at Yellowstone; bear, deer, moose, cougar, each mounted in its niche with a painted background of pristine American wilderness. These displays, and those in the similar bird corridor, are due for some upgrading. But I'm assured that those painted habitats, all the more haunting as we nibble away at the real ones, will not be altered.

Other major changes are underway at the National Museum of American History, the great, white rectangle west of Natural History. Here the huge old flag of Fort McHenry is revealed every hour on the half-hour to a tinkling, jumpy, early-19th-century rendition of the "Star-Spangled Banner." The museum was built in 1964, but not, as originally suggested, erected around the 200-ton Southern Railway locomotive that still crouches on its scrap of track on the lower floor, its endless tape spinning the antique sounds of a train.

All of the transportation section, extending inward from that engine, contains the right stuff for displays. Carriages, early bikes, old-timey cars, and one long, sinuous drag racer from today—all these and the trolleys and engines make wonderful viewing.

But social and political history is also the meat of this museum, as the generations that trooped by the First Ladies attest. After a hiatus

for rejuvenation, a new First-Ladies exhibit has arrived at the same area (turn right at the Foucault Pendulum), with an emphasis on the lives and times of Presidential families. You won't see all the White House hostesses modeling their gowns, only the recent ones. Time took too much toll on the oldies. But you'll learn far more about these extraordinary women—a unique mix of politics and manners— than the original fashion parade could reveal.

"American Encounters" is the newest major exhibition at "MAH." Inspired by the Columbus Quincentennial, it looks at the oldest region in our country where the 16th-century clash of cultures—Indian versus Spanish—still echoes: the American Southwest. We probe the Upper Rio Grande Valley in New Mexico and find a vital, colorful interplay of hyphenated Americans: Native, Spanish, African, and Anglo. The story pours out: four and a half centuries of subjuga-

★ ★ ★ ★ ★

Touching is believing, in the Natural History Museum's hands-on Discovery Room; here, a child closely inspects the head of a crocodile. At right, a perennial favorite at Natural History, the fabled, deep-blue Hope diamond.

tion and rebellion, of art forms adapting and mingling, of diverse religions and bitter racism, of shared struggles against climate and land, of getting along, somehow. This exhibit, and "From Field to Factory," well described by its title, offer realistic and telling statements about the thrusts of American life.

I like to go back further, to the exhibit called "After the Revolution," which evokes a time when we had to cope with our independence and survive the land's rigors; when we somehow prospered. There is a "hands-on" section in this exhibition where children and confident adults actually can handle and work with the devices of early times. I spent a frustrating hour trying to

put together a small wooden pail called a piggin with ready-made hoops and staves. Badly deflated by my 20th-century ineptitude, I tried on stiff 18th-century clothing and found I could "make a leg" before a mirror.

I also like to touch base with our great leaders: Washington, always impatient, often ill-tempered, mercilessly self-driven; Jefferson, enviably creative; and then Lincoln. . . . His base is best touched at the National Portrait Gallery, housed in the historic Old Patent Office between 7th and 9th streets, where he held his 1865 inaugural ball. Here in the Meserve Collection is the cracked-plate photograph of Lincoln that Alexander Gardner took just a few days before the President was shot. People—including me—have tried to describe its gripping, moving realism dozens of times, and I've resolved not to try again. I just go over there and look at it every so often.

I find that the NPG doesn't change much, except to add a new portrait to its Gallery of Presidents at proper political intervals. Carter, Reagan, and Bush have moved in since my days of close coverage. But the other galleries, formulating shows from the collection, are endlessly interesting, and the building is a delight, with its open courtyard luring you to eat a sandwich under a tree on a spring day.

★ ★ ★ ★ ★

A group of visitors rest their weary feet and limbs in front of the National Museum of American History. As with all Smithsonian museums, there is much inside to see and enjoy, including exquisitely crafted American quilts, at right, and the gowns and other dresses of "First Ladies: Political Role and Public Image." Featured opposite are the inaugural gown and accessories of the young Mrs. Grover Cleveland.

Preceding pages: a school group takes in Robert McCall's 75-foot-wide space mural—this section memorializing the landing of the first astronauts on the moon in July 1969—at the National Air and Space Museum. At left, a detail of Auguste Rodin's powerful *Burghers of Calais* (1886) in the outdoor sculpture garden of the Hirshhorn Museum and Sculpture Garden, and at right, Willem de Kooning's *Woman, Sag Harbor* (1964) in the museum's interior.

The courtyard is a good way to travel between the NPG and the National Museum of American Art, co-resident of the building. Here is a diversion of American painting, going back to Colonial portraiture (which took the place of today's family photographs), including a fine collection of George Catlin's Indian paintings and continuing to works of a few American moderns—Clifford Still, Helen Frankenthaler, Robert Rauschenberg, and others—that overlap the Hirshhorn's field. Most impressive to me have always been the landscapes, leading you from the gentle Hudson River School to the mighty impact of the Western scene in huge paintings by Albert Bierstadt and Thomas Moran.

The beautiful Renwick Gallery, an offshoot of MAA, stands opposite the White House. Temporary shows of paintings and design visit here for the delectation of Washingtonians. But the beautifully restored building itself gives every harried motorist on Pennsylvania Avenue a matchless glimpse of Victorian architecture.

Finally, the National Zoo, out on Connecticut Avenue, remains one of the country's best, largely because of the important breeding programs it fosters for endangered species. The exhibits delight children up to the age of 95. One new and notable one is the invertebrate exhibit in the basement of the old Reptile House. Here the world's largest—and possibly ugliest—invertebrates, Japanese giant spider crabs, stride very slowly about a huge tank.

The giant pandas? Oh, yes. They're still frustrating would-be panda breeders. The Zoo experts have persuaded orangs, gorillas, golden-maned tamarins, and other endangered species to produce young. But Ling-Ling and Hsing-Hsing just smile wisely and munch bamboo sprouts. ★

Capital Arts

BENNETT SCHIFF

IF YOU WERE TO PLACE YOURSELF IN FRONT OF THE SMITHSONIAN CASTLE, MIDWAY BETWEEN THE CAPITOL AND THE LINCOLN MEMORIAL ON THE NATION'S MALL, THAT HANDSOME, AIRY, AND SWEEPINGLY DISTIN-GUISHED PLACE, YOU  COULD WALK TO SOME OF THE WORLD'S PRE-EMINENT PUBLIC AND PRIVATE COLLECTIONS OF ART—NO FEWER, IN FACT, THAN A ROUND DOZEN OF THEM. YOU COULD SPEND A FULL DAY AND MANAGE TO SET FOOT IN EACH OF THEM, OR YOU COULD DEVOTE A LIFETIME TO THEM AND STILL NOT TAKE IN ALL THEY HAVE TO OFFER.

★ ★ ★ ★ ★

Smithsonian art galleries line the south side of the Mall, left. Above, Alexander Calder's *Effect of Red* mobile in the East Building of the National Gallery of Art.

★ ★ ★ ★ ★

The Chinese Moon Gate sculpture in the Smithsonian's Enid A. Haupt Garden frames the ornate architecture of the Arts and Industries Building. Below right, Alexander Calder's *Two Discs* stands sentinel outside the Hirshhorn Museum and Sculpture Garden. Opposite, a seventh-century, limestone representation of the head of Buddha highlights the Sackler Gallery's diamond-shaped stairway.

Formerly art editor and member of the Board of Editors, *Smithsonian* magazine, Bennett Schiff still frequently contributes articles on the arts from retirement. He lives in Washington, D. C.

Right there with you on the south side of the Mall you would find the Freer Gallery of Art; the National Museum of African Art, the only one of its kind in the world; the Arthur M. Sackler Gallery; and the Hirshhorn Museum and Sculpture Garden. Across the Mall to the north are the National Gallery of Art, that neoclassic temple of roseate marble, and its East Building, a glory of geometric architectural dynamism. A five-minute walk from these superlative collections will take you to the National Museum of American Art, which shares the same magisterial building, across a common courtyard, with the National Portrait Gallery, only the second of its kind in the world, the other being in London.

You would be closer now to downtown Washington, and you could walk to the National Museum of Women in the Arts, and from there to the Corcoran Gallery of Art, which would put you just another five-minute walk from the Renwick Gallery. From there, still on foot, you could head north for 20 minutes or so to the Phillips Collection, whose treasures are worth a far more arduous pilgrimage. And, if you were still game, another 20- or 30-minute walk would bring you to Dumbarton Oaks, which is a wonderful place to finish up—or, for that matter, to begin.

Altogether you would have walked a good five miles or so, not counting—how could you?— the ground covered within the museums and galleries and collections themselves. Of course, you could string this sparkling necklace together with public transportation. However you did it, it would be one of the most unforgettable and enriching journeys you'd ever made.

What is there to see? Well, what there is to see is entirely beyond the size and scale of the physical city. Washington's art collections have nothing to do with proportionate equity. In terms of its population and size, Washington is a middling cosmopolis. Culturally speaking, however, Washington boasts a proportion of masterpieces to population that would be remarkable on any scale of universality and that very well may be unprecedented in the contemporary world. What about Florence? you ask, but Florence, glorious as it is, features Italian art created during two centuries or so. Washington offers the art of all times and all places, and all of it is easily accessible in one small city.

Here is just a hint of what there is to see:

We are, you remember, standing on the Mall in front of the Castle. It is a simple matter to turn and enter that grand structure, built in the style of a Norman castle, and to walk straight through, taking a moment to enjoy the stately Great Hall, and thence out into the ordered pleasantry of the Enid A. Haupt Garden. On the left is the National Museum of African Art; on the right, the Sackler Gallery. To the right of the

Columns of green Tennessee marble encircle a visitor to the nearly spherical rotunda of the National Gallery of Art, right. Below, *The Knock Down*, a 1928 work by artist Mahonri Sharp Young.

Sackler, outside the garden proper, is the Freer Gallery of Art. The setting is spectacular in a quiet way, and intimately inviting. Spring is a very good time to be here.

The Museum of African Art, on the left, and the Sackler Gallery, to the right, stand at the southern corners of the Haupt quadrangle, equidistant from the central, flower-bedded, parterred lawn, the centerpiece of the garden. These museums are a study in harmonious contrasts, African Art topped with six domes, dressed in pink granite and curvilinear in general motif, and the Sackler, on the other hand, crowned with six perfect pyramids of gray granite and angular and pointed in its windows and decorative devices. The work of architect Jean Paul Carlihan, these two museums form an architectural counterpoint that strikes a distinct visual chord. Furthermore, the greater part of each of these lovely buildings is underground. The treasure here, and it is bounteous, is buried. And this buried treasure is for everyone, at no charge.

The Museum of African Art came about through the singular efforts of Warren Robbins, an ex-Foreign Service officer who housed his collection in a row house on Capitol Hill, and, in 1964, opened it to the public. Robbins continued to build his collection through the years, and, in 1979, he generously entrusted it to the Smithsonian Institution.

There are more than 6,000 objects in the collection of the Museum of African Art, the first and only museum in the country dedicated to the exhibition and study of the traditional arts of

★ ★ ★ ★ ★

The opening of the East Building of the National Gallery of Art in 1978 featured sculptures from the David Smith collection, above. Architect I.M. Pei's glass prisms, right (foreground), bring light to the underground passageway that connects the classical West Building with its modern counterpart. Below right, the interior of the East Building.

sub-Saharan Africa in all their richly imaginative, vivid, and spiritual vitality and color. Included in the permanent collection are sculptures in metal and wood, textiles, jewelry, architectural pieces, decorative arts, and utilitarian objects, which, in African art, frequently are invested with a rare beauty that takes them out of the commonplace. A permanent installation showcases 100 master works that are grouped according to major geographical and cultural regions and are designed to display diverse cultures and styles. In 1985 the Hirshhorn Museum and Sculpture Garden gave the African Art Museum its collection of 21 invaluable Royal Benin cast-metal sculptures, outstanding examples of an art that dates from the 15th to the 19th centuries. To see them there, displayed brilliantly in one gallery, is a rare treat.

Only a few yards away, in the Arthur M. Sackler Gallery, you are in a different world. Put simply, it is a museum of Asian art, a complex universe in itself. And yet here you can gain access to this universe in all its complexity, its staggering weight of history, its overwhelming grace and simplicity, its sheer beauty, and its magical power of entrancement.

In 1982 Dr. Arthur M. Sackler invited Thomas Lawton, who was then director of the Freer Gallery, to choose $50 million worth of objects from Sackler's superlative collection to launch the proposed gallery. Lawton, a noted scholar of Chinese art, reached that dizzying figure all too soon, and still had far to go to list all that he wanted for the gallery. "Oh, forget about the $50 million; take what you want," said Dr. Sackler airily. In the end, Lawton acquired for the American public some 1,000 pieces of superb art of inestimable value today: Chinese, Japanese, and Southeast Asian ceramics, paintings, jades, bronzes, and lacquer works, as well as

a large number of pieces from the Middle East. In addition, the Sackler owns the Vever collection, an assemblage of 11th- to 19th-century Indian and Persian arts of the book, including paintings, bookbindings, and calligraphy. It is indeed an enchanted world down there.

When it opened in 1923, the Freer Gallery of Art, the gift of industrialist Charles Lang Freer, was the first Smithsonian building designed exclusively to be a museum for the preservation

and display of works of art. Before that time, art that came to the Institution was placed here and there throughout its buildings, wherever a likely space appeared.

The Freer building is a beauty, a meticulously refined adaption of a Florentine Renaissance palazzo done up in granite from Stony Creek, Connecticut. With an interior court of Tennessee white marble, it houses some 27,000 works of Asian art, in addition to its American-art holdings, which include the world's largest collection of works by James Abbott McNeill Whistler.

The Asian collection spans at least 5,000 years, ranging from the third millennium B.C. to the early-20th century. It includes Far and Near Eastern painting and works of bronze, ceramics and porcelain, jade, sculpture, calligraphy and manuscripts, glass and crystal, gold, lacquer, and carved bamboo. And, because Freer was an inveterate and eclectic collector, it also includes late-l9th and early-20th century paintings, watercolors, drawings, pastels, and prints by American artists such as Thomas Wilmer Dewing, Childe Hassam, Winslow Homer, Gari Melchers, John Francis Murphy, Charles A. Platt (the Freer's original architect), Albert Pinkham Ryder, John Singer Sargent, Abbott Handerson Thayer, John Henry Twachtman, and others.

The handsome Renaissance Revival building, right, on the corner of 13th and H streets and New York Avenue, in Northwest Washington, houses the National Museum of Women in the Arts. Founded in 1981, the museum features the work of female artists from around the world, including Mexican artist Frida Kahlo's oil painting *Between the Curtains* (1937), opposite, a self-portrait dedicated to Leon Trotsky.

Just down the street from the Castle resides the Hirshhorn Museum and Sculpture Garden, a museum-in-the-round set on the edge of the Mall. Referred to as a "doughnut" and a "bagel," among other descriptions far less complimentary, when it opened in 1974, it holds forth between its architecturally highly disparate neighbors, the Arts and Industries Building and the National Air and Space Museum.

By now the Hirshhorn is settled comfortably into its position, both physically, seeming always to have been there, a sure sign that something belongs where it is; and in stature, as a collection of modern and contemporary art that is equally stimulating and enlightening. There is a brightness and liveliness here, and a depth of expressiveness and energy that is immediately enlivening.

Joseph H. Hirshhorn, who immigrated to the United States as a child, gave the nation 12,378 works of art, including about 5,000 paintings and 4,500 works on paper. There are more than 3,000 sculptures and mixed-media pieces, forming one of the most comprehensive collections of modern sculpture in the world. The collection features a strong representation of European painting since World War II and American painting from the late-19th century to the present day; as well as significant works by sculptors such as Constantin Brancusi, Alexander Calder, Edgar Degas, Alberto Giacometti, Henri Matisse, Henry Moore, Auguste Rodin, David Smith, and many more. Also represented are painters Francis Bacon, Balthus, Willem de Kooning, Richard Diebenkorn, Jean Dubuffet, Thomas Eakins, Arshile Gorky, Edward Hopper, Anselm Kiefer, and Frank Stella.

When Joseph Hirshhorn donated his collection to the United States, he said, simply, that it was "a small repayment for what this nation has

done for me and others like me who arrived here as immigrants." How immeasurably we benefit from this exquisite "small repayment."

If you now strike out across the Mall from the sunken Sculpture Garden, in only a few hundred yards you will arrive at the luminous, pink-marble-sheathed National Gallery of Art, whose gently rounded dome swells so naturally against the sky. There is something elusive about this great place. Although it is one of a handful of the world's truly monumental museums—it is larger, for example, than London's National Gallery—it is at the same time a remarkably intimate place to visit. It is imposing, to be sure, but in spite of its dignity and scale it is an instantly welcoming sort of place, a home for beautiful art, respectfully and pridefully displayed, all of it for your pleasure.

In his introduction to a volume published in 1991 to commemorate the 50th anniversary of the National Gallery's West Building, President George Bush noted that "it may well be the largest single gift ever given to a government by a private citizen." That citizen was Andrew Mellon, the Pittsburgh industrialist who served three Presidents as Secretary of the Treasury and who was also ambassador to Great Britain. Over the years Mellon avidly collected Old Masters, choosing carefully from the works of 16th-, 17th-, and early-18th-century European giants, including Rembrandt and Vandyck. In 1931, for $7,000,000, he bought a treasure trove of paintings from the Russian government, then, as now, in desperate need of hard cash. Included were world masterpieces, priceless today, such as Botticelli's *Adoration of the Magi* and Raphael's *The Alba Madonna* and *St. George and the Dragon.* Mellon paid more than $1 million for the Madonna, marking the first time in history that anyone had gone over the million mark for a painting.

Mellon's gift to the nation amounted to 121 paintings of impeccable quality, and architect John Russell Pope's magnificent pantheon to house them. Today the collection numbers 82,000 works of art—paintings, sculpture, drawings, decorative arts, and photography—and includes the great collections of Samuel A. Kress, Chester Dale, Joseph Widener, and Lessing Rosenwald, as well as many other princely gifts through the years.

If you enter from the Mall and turn left from the museum's marbled rotunda, you will find, about 50 yards down the hall, a roomful of Rembrandts—eight of them. In the very next room you will find six more! Farther along you will come across Leonardo da Vinci's luminous portrait of Ginevra de' Benci, one of only three portraits from that master's hand and the only one on this continent.

One thousand people work there in the West Building, but you would never know it. And the halls generally are not crowded, except during the special blockbuster shows that bring crowds in Super-Bowl proportions. On an average day you will find yourself in uncrowded galleries, wandering around at leisure, stopping here and there at whatever great artwork happens to catch your eye; or standing still, dumbfounded, and thankful, before a painting that hangs on the wall and captures your mind and heart. You might be the seven-millionth visitor of the year, but it's unlikely you would ever know it.

Andrew Mellon died in 1937, four years before his museum opened, and yet he had the foresight to ensure that the site directly to the east of his proposed building be reserved for future expansion. As it turned out, the nine-acre site marked for expansion could not have been more awkward. To begin with, it was trapezoidal (critic Russell Lynes likened the space to an ill-folded napkin), presenting a daunting challenge to any designer, who had also to consider the adjacent West Building and the location of the proposed structure on the Mall.

Architect I.M. Pei met the challenge head-on by boldly slicing through the trapezoid to create two interlocking triangles—one an isosceles and the other a right—and aligning the two both with each other and with the central axis of

the older building. It is a brilliant piece of architecture, sheathed in the same pink marble as its parent building, all angles and geometry but at the same time graceful and welcoming—and very popular. The entire cost, some $94 million, was borne by Paul Mellon and Ailsa Mellon Bruce and the family foundation.

The East Building houses a notable and growing collection of American and international contemporary art, and also serves as the locale for temporary exhibitions of all places and of all times, many of them extraordinary for their range, and acuity, and pertinence. In its various galleries you will find examples of sculpture and painting and prints and drawings of the outstanding artists of this century. There is scarcely any point in mentioning the names; they're just about all there.

A 10-minute walk away, in what once was the U.S. Patent Office Building, one of the finest examples of Greek Revival architecture in the country, are the National Museum of American Art and the National Portrait Gallery, and they, too, are outstanding. Since 1968, when the handsomely renovated building was turned over to the Smithsonian's museums, the National Museum of American Art's collection has quadrupled. Today, with 35,000 works in its possession, it embodies the world's largest representation of American art, spanning 200 years and featuring works by masters of the Colonial era, such as the Peales and Benjamin West; luminaries of the 19th century, including 16 paintings by Albert Pinkham Ryder; and the American Impressionists Mary Cassatt, Childe Hassam, and John Twachtman. Once again, all the great names are here: Bierstadt, Cole, Inness, Church, Moran,

and Homer. The "moderns" include Helen Frankenthaler, Robert Rauschenberg, Jackson Pollock, Franz Kline, Clyfford Still, Morris Louis, Kenneth Noland, and a great many more.

Then, across the courtyard, a visit to the Portrait Gallery awaits. Primarily an archival collection maintained and kept up-to-date for historical purposes, the Portrait Gallery offers a printed and painted record of people who influenced or were prominent in the nation's experience. Many of these portraits are fine art as well. There are more than 11,000 objects in the permanent collection: paintings, posters, photographs, prints, sculptures, and drawings. And, as you might expect, subjects range from American Presidents to Hollywood moguls in their prime, from diplomats and statesmen to prizefighters and composers of popular songs. There is also always something that you didn't expect and that may come as either a pleasure or a disappointment, depending on what your expectations are. You'll find villains here as well as heroes: the Sundance Kid, whose real name was Harry Longbaugh, and Butch Cassidy, who was Robert Leroy Parker; as well as George Herman "Babe" Ruth and Jack Dempsey.

While you're still in the downtown area, the privately founded and funded National Museum of Women in the Arts, the only one of its kind in the world, is but a 10-minute walk away. Its collection is housed in a handsome Renaissance Revival building that was completed in 1911 as a Masonic temple and completely renovated in 1983 as the new museum. The museum was founded mainly through the efforts of Wilhelmina Holladay, a collector who discovered that many of the basic art histories of women artists in whose work she was interested were inadequate.

The collection of the Museum of Women in the Arts ranges from the 16th century to the present and features more than 500 paintings,

Pierre Renoir's *The Luncheon of the Boating Party* (1881), below, is one of the masterpieces of Washington's Phillips Collection, which resides in the neo-Georgian mansion at right. Once the childhood home of Duncan Phillips, the elegant house—and its collections—were opened to the public in 1921.

sculptures, prints, drawings, and even pottery by some 250 artists from 25 countries. Many of the paintings are by such well-known artists as Mary Cassatt, Berthe Morisot, Lilla Cabot Perry (who studied with Monet), Cecilia Beaux, Joan Mitchell, Anne Truitt, Elaine de Kooning, and Nancy Graves. Others are by artists whose work you are not likely to see in other museums; these pieces are more than worth your while.

Another 10-minute walk—you are now dipping into the city's mid-town section—will bring you to the imposingly grand, white-marble, beaux-arts Corcoran Gallery of Art. Frank Lloyd Wright called it the best designed building in Washington, which is an extraordinary tribute by the acclaimed modernist. The Corcoran is the oldest museum in the city and one of the three oldest in the nation, the other two being New York's Metropolitan and the Boston Museum of Fine Arts. (All three were founded in the same year, 1870.) Its founder, W.W. Corcoran, was a financially successful, public-spirited private citizen who became interested in art, collected it, housed it magnificently, and gave it all to the United States. Altogether, it is really one of the nation's finest artistic assemblages.

The Corcoran collection, which makes this gallery a major center for the study of American art, contains 11,000 paintings, prints, drawings, and sculpture. Included are two major individual collections: the William A. Clark, noted for its Dutch, Flemish, and French Romantic works;

and the Walker, which has outstanding examples of French painting from the late-19th and 20th centuries, including works by Renoir, Monet, Courbet, and Pissarro. Its contemporary collection includes many major artists: Frank Stella, Mark Rothko, Helen Frankenthaler, Willem de Kooning, Joan Mitchell, Gene Davis, and Andy Warhol. Its biennial surveys of contemporary art are famous for the controversy they engender and for the work they bring together, displaying every aspect of what is being done by living artists. Some dozen special exhibits are mounted each year, ranging from historical surveys to individual retrospectives of major contemporary artists and group shows featuring the efforts of young and relatively unknown artists. To round things out, the Corcoran is also the center of a four-year art college that offers a Bachelor of Fine Arts.

Five minutes on by foot, a stone's throw from the White House, is the Renwick Gallery. Administered by the National Museum of American

A young child stands transfixed by the statues that greet visitors to the Children's Museum, right, on Capitol Hill. Crafted by Indian folk artist Nek Chend from discarded materials, the statues came to the museum in 1983. Below, detail from the 1,200-foot-long frieze depicting Union forces that rings the mammoth Building Museum, far right. Originally the Pension Building, the structure was designed in classical Italian Renaissance style by architect Montgomery C. Meigs, and built in 1883.

Art, the Renwick specializes in crafts and design. The building itself is an exhibit: two of the gallery's great rooms, the Octagon Room and the Grand Salon, are furnished in the styles of the 1860s and '70s. With their 20- and 30-foot ceilings and authentic decorative details and rich colors, they evoke the period better perhaps than any other rooms in the country, providing an instant trip back through time. But it is the Renwick's ongoing special exhibits, displaying the latest and the best in craft and design, that keep the splendid old place alive and vital.

A few miles uptown, near Dupont Circle, you come upon the Phillips Collection, which must be, for very good reasons, one of the most beloved privately collected and endowed small museums in all the world. When it opened to the public, in 1921, Duncan Phillips called it "a public gallery with its main stress on living painters." But, he added, it also would feature works of previous periods that "would be forever modern." So, in addition to the work of Phillips' contemporaries, such as Milton Avery, Ben Nicholson, Paul Klee, Arthur Dove, Adolph Gottlieb, and Georgia O'Keeffe, among many others, you will find key works by van Gogh, Gauguin, Goya, El Greco, Cézanne, Braque, Matisse, and Bonnard—and Renoir's life-

The fountain terrace at left is but one of the myriad treasures to be found in the extensive gardens of the Dumbarton Oaks estate in Georgetown. The gardens were designed by American landscape architect Beatrix Ferrand. The estate's mansion, above, dates to the 1800s, and features a library of early Christian and Byzantine art as well as an impressive collection of pre-Columbian art.

enhancing *Luncheon of the Boating Party,* which seems to have gathered up all of the pleasure of feeling alive and happy in life.

The collection of more than 2,000 works is housed in the neo-Georgian mansion at 21st and Q streets, N.W., in which Duncan Phillips lived as a boy, and in two adjoining annexes, the latest of which was added in 1989 as the collection continued to grow.

Phillips wrote in his inventory of 1921, when the collection was made public: "It has been my policy, and I recommend it to my successors, to purchase spontaneously and thus to make mistakes, but to correct them as time goes on. All new pictures in the Collection are on trial, and must prove their powers of endurance." He made very few mistakes; you will be making one if you don't spend a good bit of time here.

Finally, you now are not too far—a 20-minute walk through Georgetown—from the estate of Dumbarton Oaks, whose treasures were gathered here by Robert Woods Bliss and his wife, Mildred. The Blisses bought the historic, beautifully proportioned Georgian mansion in 1920. They deeded it to Harvard University 20 years later, but only after they had established it as one of the country's most distinguished and felicitous estates. You could spend one of your most memorable days here, wandering about its 16 acres of magnificent gardens, taking in the Byzantine collection in the mansion, and marveling at the pre-Columbian art displayed in the linked pavilions designed by Philip Johnson.

Dumbarton Oaks is administered by Harvard as a center for Byzantine studies, and is the only library and museum devoted exclusively to early Christian and Byzantine art. The library—some 90,000 volumes strong—is the largest in the world devoted to Byzantium, the Greek-speaking Christian civilization that lasted from A.D. 330 to 1453. The collection of Byzantine art—silver, metal, ivories, jewelry, coins, enamels, textiles, and lead seals—is renowned throughout the world for its quality and catholicity.

The mansion's music room, a reincarnation of one you might find in a Renaissance palazzo, complete with Flemish tapestries, oak-parquet floors made in 18th-century France, and other similar adornments, was the site of private Bliss concerts performed by the likes of Igor Stravinsky, Aaron Copeland, Joan Sutherland, Leontyne Price, Wanda Landowska, and Rudolph Serkin. The pre-Columbian art collection is of similar eminence. Bliss began to collect it in Paris in 1914, and kept collecting for the next 50 years. It includes objects of great rarity in stone, jade, and gold from the cultures of Mexico and Central and South America. Johnson's eight pavilions are jewel cases of glass strung together with a connecting passageway around a fountain—all of this set in a lovely woods. Think of it!

It is, let us say, approaching evening now. You have had your day, or week, or whatever time you could manage, in the art museums of Washington. And what did you discover?

Washington, it turns out, is a museum in itself.

What, you haven't had enough? Well, count your blessings, soak your feet, and come on back. ★

The Nation's Reading Rooms

JOHN Y. COLE

"OF COURSE YOU CAN. JUST WANDER AROUND AND LOOK AT THE BOOKS," THE LIBRARIAN BEHIND THE DESK TOLD THE TIMID 13-YEAR-OLD IN THE CARNEGIE LIBRARY IN ELLENSBURG, A SMALL TOWN IN THE MIDDLE OF WASHINGTON STATE. THIS IS UNBELIEVABLE, I REMEMBER THINKING, AS I QUICKLY SCURRIED INTO THE ADULT-FICTION ROOM BEFORE SHE COULD CHANGE HER MIND.

★ ★ ★ ★ ★

Beneath the copper dome of the Library of Congress, or LC, above, alcoves cradle researchers, as at left. Reference books in the Main Reading Room can be taken from the shelves by readers.

Several decades later, in the mid-1960s, I stepped into the Main Reading Room of the Library of Congress for the first time. It was filled with scaffolding, undergoing its first renovation since the doors had opened in 1897. I had that unbelievable feeling again. Soon I joined the Library's staff. I was hooked on Washington, D.C., and, especially, on the Library of Congress. One of the reasons, I now realize, was because our nation's political capital is also the library and research capital of the country.

We come by it honestly. The majority of our founding fathers, and perhaps most conspicuously John Adams, Thomas Jefferson, and James Madison, were readers— avid readers, in fact, who were well-acquainted with classical works in history, political philosophy, law, and literature. Not only did the founding fathers take education seriously, they actively used their knowledge of the past to shape the new American nation. Their exercise of the "science of politics" in the development of a self-governing republic was based on books and ideas of the past.

Jefferson, in particular, believed that democracy was not possible without knowledge; that self-government depended on the free and unhampered pursuit of truth by an informed and involved citizenry. This Jeffersonian spirit of enlightenment ("to give information to the people is the most certain and the most legitimate engine of government") is the connection between Washington as a political capital and as a city of learning—for tourists as well as scholars, for citizens as well as policy researchers. It is what makes Washington itself a reading room for the nation.

There are more than 900 libraries in the Washington, D.C., metropolitan area. It is estimated that perhaps one-sixth of the library resources—collections and professional librarians—in the United States are here; so are dozens of large research organizations and hundreds of smaller research institutes and offices. The Library of Congress; the Archives of the United States of America, commonly known as the National Archives; the Smithsonian Institution; the National Library of Medicine; and the National Agricultural Library are the big names, but Washington, D.C., is also the home of the Folger Shakespeare Library, the National Gallery of Art, the Woodrow Wilson International Center for Scholars, the National Institutes of Health, more than five dozen small federal libraries—and 12 universities. The American Historical Association, the Association of Research Libraries, and the Special Libraries Association have their headquarters here, and every few years the American Library Association thinks about moving east from Chicago. The pull is a strong one. I think it's idealistic as well as practical.

The magnetism is particularly intense in the case of the Library of Congress and the National Archives: they are the public memory of what is still a young nation. The treasures and documents of these institutions are a unique part of our heritage, but their shared purpose—to inform, enlighten, and inspire—is more important. These two great repositories are educational institutions rooted in the democratic experience: each is open to the public and each makes its collections accessible and useful to all who are interested. Taken together, in a real sense they have become the national university that Jefferson and Madison, in their Presidential messages to Congress, advocated in the early years of the republic.

John Y. Cole, a librarian and student of American civilization, is founding Director of the Center for the Book in the Library of Congress. The center was established in 1977 to stimulate public interest in books, reading, and libraries.

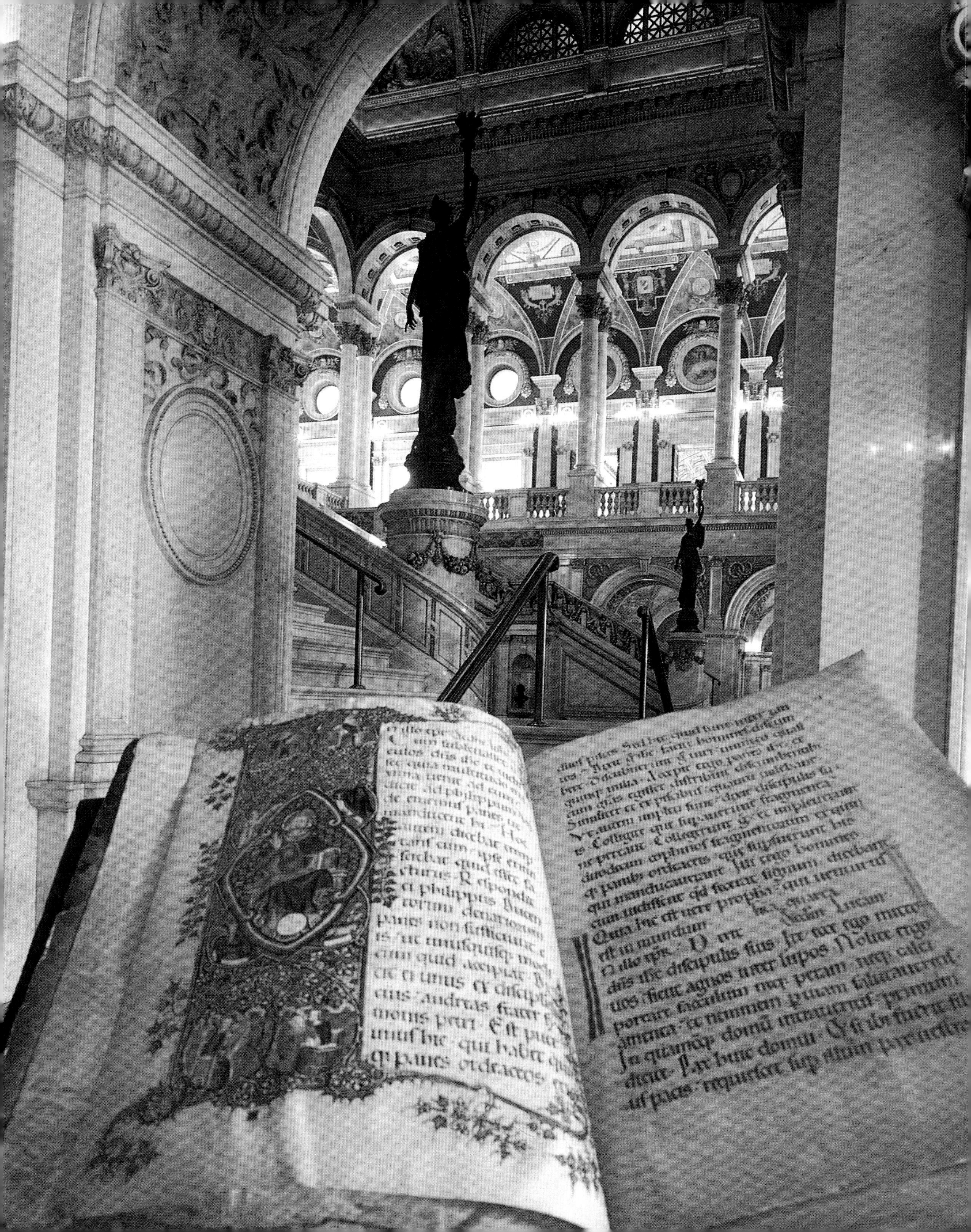

Enlighten the people generally, and tyranny and oppression of the body and mind will vanish like evil spirits at the dawn of day.
                              -THOMAS JEFFERSON

The Library of Congress is the largest single repository of recorded knowledge in the world, and the most open and accessible of all the great national libraries. Its diversity is startling; I am still making discoveries after 25 years of studying the institution. It is, among other things, the major research arm of the U.S. Congress; this country's copyright agency; one of the world's largest providers of bibliographic data and products; a world center for scholarship that collects research materials of all kinds (from papyrus to videodisc) in most subjects and in more than 450 languages; and a public institution that admits anyone 18 years or older for research, and serves readers in no less than 22 reading rooms. Its collections total more than 100 million items. Each day about 31,000 new pieces arrive at the Library; approximately 7,000 of them will become part of the permanent collections.

The reader visiting the Library sees three massive structures on Capitol Hill, directly across from the U.S. Capitol. They are a dramatic symbol of culture in a political setting. The Jefferson Building, opened in 1897, is a grand monument to civilization, culture, and American achievement. It is the home of nine of the Library's

reading rooms, including the spectacular and inspiring Main Reading Room, one of the best-known reading places in America. The functional Adams Building, named for President John Adams, who signed the legislation creating the Library in 1800, was opened in 1939. Both the Jefferson and the Adams buildings currently are being renovated. When work is completed in 1995, the Jefferson Building will house the Library's area-studies divisions and reading rooms—African and Middle East, Asian, European, Hispanic—thus becoming a center for the humanistic study of world culture. The Adams Building will become the focal point for collections and reference service in science, technology, and business.

When I arrived at the Library in the 1960s, staff and collections were wedged into the Jefferson and Adams buildings. Temporary offices even filled the Great Hall and the exhibit halls now being restored on the Jefferson Building's second floor. This space crisis eased, at least temporarily, with the opening in 1980 of the James Madison Memorial Building, which serves as both the Library's third major structure and this nation's official memorial to James Madison, the "father" of the Constitution and the Bill of Rights and the fourth President of the United States. With its two million square feet of space, the Madison Building is the third largest structure in Washington, exceeded only by the Pentagon and the F.B.I. Building. Here are many of the Library's reading rooms for special collections: manuscripts, maps, newspapers, motion pictures and television, music and performing arts (another branch for these sources is located in the John F. Kennedy Center for the Performing Arts), and prints and photographs. The Madison Building is also the home of the Congressional Research Service, the Copyright Office, and the Law Library.

How did the Library of Congress grow into

★ ★ ★ ★ ★

An elaborate builder's plan shows the location of stonework in the cellar of the Library of Congress, below. At the center, opposite, surrounding the building's bull's eye, rings of desks accommodate readers. Books that readers may request from distant stacks, even from annexes, arrive swiftly by pneumatic tube.

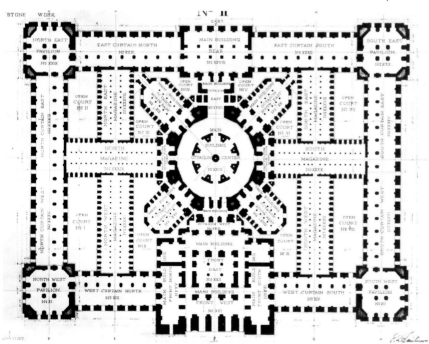

such a large, diverse, and multi-purpose institution? Several developments permanently established its national roots. First, it was created by the national legislature in 1800 as it prepared to move from Philadelphia to the new capital city of Washington. Thus it became the first cultural institution in Washington, D.C., and the first library of the government itself: the President and Vice President could borrow books, along with members of Congress. And, in 1815, the scope of the Library's collection was permanently expanded, thanks to Thomas Jefferson.

As a man who, by his own description, could not live without books, Jefferson took a keen interest in the fledgling library while he was President, from 1801 to 1809. He personally recommended books and appointed the first two Librarians of Congress. In 1814, the British army

invaded the city of Washington and burned the Capitol, including the 3,000-volume Library of Congress. Jefferson, who had retired to Monticello, offered to sell his personal library, the largest and finest in the country, to Congress in order to "recommence" its library. Approval for the purchase of Jefferson's 6,487 volumes for $23,940 was given in 1815.

Jefferson's library not only included more than twice the number of volumes that had been in the destroyed Library of Congress, but also expanded the scope of the Library far beyond the bounds of a legislative library devoted primarily to legal, economic, and historical works. Jefferson was a man of encyclopedic interests, and his library included works on architecture, the arts, science, literature, and geography. It contained books in foreign languages as well. Anticipating the argument that his collection might be too comprehensive, he argued that there was "no subject to which a Member of Congress may not have occasion to refer." Jefferson's library provided the base for the expansion of the Library's functions, and his concept of universality is the rationale for the comprehensive collecting policies of today's Library of Congress.

Ainsworth Rand Spofford, Librarian of Congress from 1864-1897, successfully convinced Congress that the Library of Congress was also the national library. He emphasized that the Library's collection should be shared with all citizens, for the United States was "a great Republic which rests upon the popular intelligence." The centralization of all U.S. copyright activities at the Library of Congress in 1870 was Spofford's most impressive collection-building feat. It ensured the continuing development of the Americana collections, stipulating that two copies of every book, pamphlet, map, print, photograph, and piece of music registered for copyright must be deposited in the Library.

The copyright law in 1870 had another major effect: it forced the construction of a separate building for the Library. Copyright deposits immediately began flooding the Library's rooms in the west front of the Capitol, and, in 1872, the Librarian presented a plan for a new building. In it he envisioned the Main Reading Room of today's Jefferson Building, which he described as a central "circular apartment" which would be "surmounted by a dome of iron and glass." When the reading room, then called the Rotunda, was completed in 1897, its 160-foot-high dome overlooked one of the most impressive rooms in the city, a symbolic tribute in sculpture and design to the evolution of knowledge in all fields of endeavor. As described in a contemporary guidebook, the character of the room is "warm and rich in ornament as befits a room where people remain to read."

Knowledge will forever govern ignorance, and a people who mean to be their own governors must arm themselves with the power which knowledge gives.
-JAMES MADISON

The National Archives and the Library of Congress are, in many ways, sister institutions, even though they are in separate branches of the government. Their functions differ, but each is a public agency that presents our government and citizens with unparalleled opportunities to explore the past. Less than a mile apart, their combined resources often satisfy the lifetime needs of individual researchers and historians.

Known formally as the National Archives and Records Administration (NARA), the National Archives was established in 1934 to identify and ensure the preservation of those records of the United States government that have continuing historical value. Each year the government creates millions of cubic feet of records, of which only one to three percent are worth preserving.

A small portion are kept in the colossal National Archives Building on Pennsylvania Avenue, which was designed by architect John Russell Pope. Other records are kept in 12 regional archives and, at least temporarily, in 14 federal-records centers throughout the country. The National Archives also administers nine Presidential libraries across the nation that contain the papers of Presidents Herbert Hoover, Franklin D. Roosevelt, Harry Truman, Dwight Eisenhower, John F. Kennedy, Lyndon B. Johnson, Gerald Ford, Jimmy Carter, and Ronald Reagan. The Archives also hold the Presidential papers of Richard Nixon. (It does not, however, administer the Nixon Library in San Clemente, California.)

To millions of tourists, the National Archives is best known as the home of America's "charters of freedom": the Declaration of Independence, the Constitution, and the Bill of Rights, which are on permanent display in the Exhibition Hall. The research collections are enormous and include many different formats. The Archives contains about three billion pages of textual material; six million still photographs; 91 million feet of motion-picture film reaching back to the inauguration of President William McKinley in 1897 and including documentaries, combat footage, and newsreels; 70,000 sound recordings, including Congressional hearings, Supreme Court arguments, and the Nuremberg trials; two-million cartographic items; and nine-million aerial photographs. This documentary record of the American people includes the always popular census records (the 1920 census was made available on microfilm early in 1992), military service and pension records, ship-passenger lists recording the arrival of immigrants, and diplomatic records. Many of the people who use the Archives are doing genealogical research about their personal family histories.

My first visit to the National Archives many

years ago was to the Central Research Room, but my search for some early records of Congress soon led me—thanks to a helpful curator—up into a crowded "attic" where I spent a day happily searching through documents in manuscript boxes. Today a reader would find that, in addition to the Central Research Room, the Archives has six reading rooms in the metropolitan Washington, D.C., area. The regional archives and Presidential libraries also have their own reading rooms. The big news is the plan for Archives II, a badly needed new National Archives building that is being constructed on the University of Maryland campus in College Park, Maryland. This 1.7-million-square-foot-building, situated on a 33-acre site, is scheduled for occupancy in 1994. The most heavily used materials, including genealogy and legislative and judicial records, will remain in the original Archives Building.

In a public institution, especially in Washington, D.C., an exhibit hall can be a special kind of "reading room." The common purposes of the Library of Congress and the National Archives are linked historically through a pair of shrines in their respective monumental buildings. An interesting tale illustrates the point.

In 1907, and again in 1917, J. Franklin Jameson, a historian at the Carnegie Institution and the driving force behind the movement for a national archives or "hall of records," solicited and received an endorsement of the idea from Librarian of Congress Herbert Putnam. The Library would continue to collect historical materials, but governmental documents and papers would go to the new Archives. (This understanding eventually was carried out regarding Presidential papers. The Library of Congress holds Presidential collections from George Washington through Calvin Coolidge, but a separate system of Presidential libraries under the jurisdiction of the National Archives developed after the Archives was established.)

Putnam's enthusiasm for the "hall of records" idea began to wane, however, after 1921, when the State Department transferred the Declaration of Independence and the Constitution, America's "founding documents," to the Library of Congress. In 1924 they went on public display in a special "shrine" installed in the Library's Great Hall.

In the meantime, through the work of Jameson and others, the National Archives was becoming a reality. Congress made the first

★ ★ ★ ★ ★

Banners and bunting celebrating the 200th anniversary of the United States in 1976 welcome visitors to the National Archives' downtown building, a part of the Federal Triangle. Through the center door, within the Exhibition Room, reside many documents associated with this nation's conception and birth.

appropriation for its building in 1926, and, at the laying of the cornerstone in 1933, President Herbert Hoover dedicated the structure to the people of the United States. He also stated that the Archives would house the Declaration of Independence and the Constitution in the great interior exhibition space then being planned. As if to accentuate the point, later that year architect Pope commissioned two huge mural paintings for the new Archives Exhibition Hall. One depicts Thomas Jefferson presenting the Declaration of Independence to the Continental Congress, and the other shows James Madison submitting the final draft of the Constitution to George Washington. Then, in 1938, the Bill of Rights was transferred to the Archives from the Department of State.

Librarian Putnam refused to give up the documents, however, and everyone decided to wait until he retired. Putnam did not depart until 1938, and then World War II intervened. Finally, in 1952, the Library of Congress reluctantly but gracefully relinquished the two treasures. On a sunny December 13, the sacred parchments—carefully encased, crated, and placed on mattresses—were carried in an armored Marine Corps personnel carrier down Constitution and Pennsylvania avenues to their new home. The vehicle was accompanied by tanks, a motorcycle escort, a color guard, two military bands, and four servicemen carrying submachine guns.

The careful bureaucratic sparring between the National Archives and the Library of Congress over the Declaration of Independence and the Constitution is testimony to the symbolic importance of the American past and its icons. The elaborate procession down Constitution and Pennsylvania avenues in 1952 was simply a shift of exhibition halls or "reading rooms" for the American public.

The location of the documents was not as important as the democratic tradition they represented. Today the National Archives and the Library of Congress still perform this national function together. "Litera Scripta Manet," or "the written word endures," is the motto of the Archives; the same phrase is inscribed in the ceiling of the Librarian's office in the Library's Jefferson Building.

Yet reading rooms and the tradition of print culture which have nurtured the Library of Congress and the National Archives through their formative years are changing in significant ways. And both institutions are adapting, just as library users are adapting to the realities of the new "information age."

When the renovated Main Reading Room in the Library's Jefferson Building reopened in June 1991, it combined 19th-century elegance with 21st-century technology. Four reference-desk computers and 44 new readers' desks wired for work stations replaced the card-catalog cabinets. Sixteen personal computers for reference librarians and 70 for the public were installed. Readers are now able to conduct their own electronic searches in 12 alcoves off the Main Reading Room and in a new Computer Catalog Center. Within the Library, this new capability is supplemented by other reading rooms that take advantage of developing technologies. In 1988 the Library established a Machine Readable Collection Reading Room to service materials in machine readable formats, including microcomputer software programs and information or data files issued on microcomputer, compact, or videodiscs. In April 1992 the Library opened its National Demonstration Laboratory (NDL) for Interactive Information Technology, a futuristic multi-media center that contains examples of powerful information storage, transmission, and computer technology.

What does this mean for the old-fashioned reading room? Is it a goner? I don't think so. This spring I finally succumbed and bought a home computer. The possibilities, of course, seem endless, but they are very time-consuming. Today there is much talk about home electronic-retrieval and document-retrieval systems or "virtual libraries" replacing today's libraries and their separate buildings. Yet my home library of just plain books seems to fit nicely alongside my new home computer. Sometimes I feel like James Madison, "arming" myself with all "the power that knowledge gives."

Libraries and reading rooms are changing, but the meanings they symbolize and the useful functions they perform are essential to a free people. The great public reading rooms of the Library of Congress and the National Archives embody the American experience. Whatever happens to reading rooms in the future, through its ownership of these two institutions the American public will be both a witness and a participant. ★

Washington Itself

Hail to the Redskins

Jake Page
Carl Hoffman

Through the years they come and go, fueling the engines of government: attorneys, lobbyists, ambassadors, bankers, job seekers, think-tank eggheads, bureaucrats, power-brokers, Presidents. Even long incumbent U.S. Representatives and Senators eventually leave. The nation's capital is, in part, a city of transients. What remains are monuments to our great political heroes, and institutions—such dependable fixtures of the oldest democracy on the planet as the beloved Smithsonian Institution . . . and the Washington Redskins. Yes, the Redskins.

★ ★ ★ ★ ★

A sampling of Redskins memorabilia, left, hints at Washington's love of its football team. Above right, the Hogettes, Redskins cheerleaders extraordinaire.

Players huddle for warmth under piles of straw on the sidelines of the 1945 National Football League championship between the Redskins and the Cleveland Rams, a contest the 'Skins lost, 15-14.

It is noon at Duke Zeibert's, the consummate Washington power-lunch center. Dressed in pin-stripes, men and women take their seats and look out through plate-glass windows at the intersection of Connecticut Avenue and L Street, where then Soviet President Mikhail Gorbachev upstaged George Bush by leaping out of his limo to engage in some good, old-fashioned flesh-pressing. The famous photograph of the scene was shot from Zeibert's balcony; after all, Duke says casually, the two luminaries were on their way to his place for lunch. Over the 50 years Zeibert has been in business, six Presidents and anyone else who is anyone at all has dined on his crab cakes. But Duke knows what flows through the aorta and nourishes the heart of the nation's capital.

"Football," he says, "is the most important thing in the whole city. Politics isn't even close.

From the shoeshine man to the White House, when it's football season, that's the topic of conversation. People digest the sports pages like there was a new world being discovered." And the movers and shakers won't find pictures of themselves or of Duke's Presidential visitors on his walls. Instead, one sees the likes of coach Joe Gibbs, team owner Jack Kent Cooke, former owner the late Edward Bennett Williams, and former coach the late George ("The future is now") Allen. Moreover, just inside the door is a shrine and testament to the true excellence, the lasting pride, and the mother- meaning in the hearts—as well as in the AP bulletins—of this

Jake Page, presently a New Mexican, lived in the Washington area for 20 years while he was an editor of *Smithsonian* magazine and founding director of Smithsonian Books. He is co-author of *Lords of the Air: the Smithsonian Book of Birds*. His son-in-law, Carl Hoffman, is a magazine journalist and travel writer based in Washington. Both root, in a dignified manner, for the Redskins.

Some 30,000 fans at old Griffith Stadium watch the home-town Redskins defeat the Green Bay Packers on November 28, 1937, the first year the Redskins played in Washington.

most powerful city on the globe: three burnished mahogany stands bearing the Redskins' three gleaming Super-Bowl trophies.

Other teams have won more—Pittsburgh won four sometime back in the Pleistocene—but as of 1992 there had been 26 Super Bowls and the Redskins had appeared in five and won three, making them overall perhaps the most consistently good team in the NFL over the past two decades. But even that honor hardly can explain the almost mystical hold the Redskins have over the entire metropolitan area, considered by many to be the power center of the Earth. Of the nearly four million people in the region, well over a third watch every game, home or away. They needn't give a passing thought (no pun intended) to the rule that a game will be blacked out locally if the stadium isn't sold out: Robert F. Kennedy Memorial Stadium, or RFK, has been sold out to season-ticket holders since October 9, 1966, and there are currently some 44,000 people on the waiting list to get tickets, more than in any other NFL city.

People organize their time around the games. Playwright Larry L. King, author of The Best Little Whorehouse in Texas, considered putting off a cataract operation until the doctor guaranteed that the bandages would be off by the next opening kick off. It has been said that the best time for a coup or any attempt at a takeover of the U.S. government would be during the third period of a tightly contested Redskins game. During the season the gauges that measure water pressure in the reservoirs of two populous Maryland counties that abut the capital take a noticeable dip about one and a half hours into each game. "If you're a Redskins fan," explains the lab director of the Suburban Sanitary Commission, "you don't get a real break until halftime."

Highway traffic eases, shops empty, Washington nears ghost-town status. In the words of a local TV executive, "When the game is on, I could walk down 14th Street nude and no one would notice." Officer Ed Wilson of the D.C. police's public-information branch reports that the cops "have noticed a decrease in the number of calls during Redskins games, even more of a decrease during play-off games." But there is a down side to such partisan support. After a loss, domestic violence tends to rise. And, according to Michael O'Harro, who runs the area's two most popular sports bars, both named Champions, the Monday after a loss is no time to be looking for comfort. "I certainly hate to do business with the U.S. government or the city after the 'Skins lose because everyone's in a bad mood the next day."

The Redskins are typically good enough to win any game but always capable as well of some inexplicable loss, some failure to pay attention to what the fans seem to take as the nation's busi-

30,000 see Redskins stop Packers, 14-6. Griffith Stadium, November 28, 1937

ness. Part of the Redskins' aura, locally, may derive from the fact that Washington feels a certain responsibility for global affairs: everything in Washington takes on a heightened importance that outsiders find silly, if not presumptuous. The Redskins reside and struggle in the mud at the nexus of the world. And so more than a million fans watch the pre-game show on TV with the same butterflies in their stomachs that the players have when they line up for the opening kick off. In Redskins country, you don't just love the team, you hate Dallas, New York, and Philadelphia—generally in that descending order. This animosity predates biblical prejudices, so far as anyone knows.

To help the team in these primordial competitions, many fans develop strange rites, such as sitting in the same seat at home every week, plastering themselves with paint, wearing outlandish burgundy-and-gold boxer shorts, drinking certain drinks. (It goes without saying that no two-million-dollar-a-year lawyer from Yale would be caught dead wearing a maroon jacket and yellow slacks, but if you call that tacky color scheme burgundy and gold, it's as legit as Brooks Brothers—at least on autumnal Sundays.) Once, when the Redskins were losing, a fan went into the kitchen and the Redskins scored: the fan was told to stay in the kitchen until the game was over. Truth be known, the men and women of reason who run the government, fine tune the economy, and seek to maintain world peace are capable of the most pagan superstition when game time arrives. Some forgiving psychologists say that anyone can believe in a totem or a prayer if it works more than half the time (which in recent decades all have with the Redskins).

How does all this love focused on the Redskins (and hate focused on the opponent) translate on the playing field? Football's most

★ ★ ★ ★ ★

Redskins quarterback Doug Williams uncorks a winner in the 'Skins 42-10 shellacking of the Denver Broncos in Super Bowl XXII, in San Diego, on January 31, 1988.

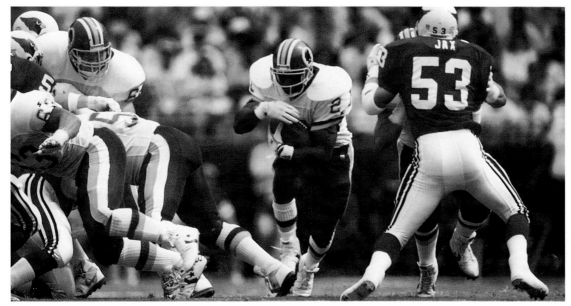

The importance of being Earnest is clear on this autumnal Sunday in 1991 as Redskins running back Earnest Byner rushes through a hole in the Phoenix Cardinals' line opened up by his blockers. Below, a cartoonist's view of how most Washington Redskins fans think the U.S. Capitol *ought* to look.

enthusiastic scholar, TV commentator and former NFL coach John Madden says flatly: "The best scene is Washington, RFK Stadium, the Redskins. You get in there, and it's real grass, and they're playing that great fight song, 'Hail to the Redskins,' and the whole place kind of rocks. From October on, that's just a great scene!" And Bill Walsh, coach and commentator, adds, "When the fans at RFK stomp their feet, you can't hear yourself . . . you can't think."

"You feel it when you're landing at the airport," says New York Giant Everson Walls. "When I played for the Cowboys and we played in Washington, you couldn't get in and out of the hotel without security." Giant guard William Roberts agrees that there is nothing like playing in Washington because "you are so hated."

Washington is as polyglot, ethnically diverse, and divisive a city as can be found. It is based, at its core, on controversy and disagreement—Republican vs. Democrat, the executive vs. the legislature, environmental vs. industrial lobbies—and it also has the common ills of most

cities—rich vs. poor, neighborhood vs. neighborhood . . . on and on. And, almost self-consciously, as if they felt a bit guilty about being so divisive and divided a community, people proclaim that they can put aside their differences and pull together on at least one topic: the Redskins.

They are "the tie that binds," the entire area's "unifying passion," warbles the Washington Post. Champions' Michael O'Harro says they are "the one thing in this town that everybody loves. You can be a Democrat or a Republican. You can be Irish or you can be from Nairobi. You can be black. You can be white—rich, poor, Catholic, Protestant." Indeed, O'Harro echoes Washingtonians' widespread local pride in themselves for being so fanatic about the Redskins. "I'm from L.A.," he says, "and people there could care less about the Raiders. It's a city of 10 million people and they can't even sell out the stadium. I came to D.C. in 1963 and the Redskins have always been the hot ticket."

Well, not quite. When George Preston Marshall brought the Boston Redskins to Washington in 1936, professional football was still in its infancy and the nation's capital was definitely a Southern city. While Marshall was an innovator—he was the first to produce his own radio network to boost the team, the first to put

A sunny day at RFK—Robert F. Kennedy Memorial Stadium—shows off the sweeping lines of the ballpark, a place other teams dread visiting. Below, quarterback Mark Rypien and teammate Earnest Byner hold the Vince Lombardi trophy on high after defeating the Buffalo Bills 37- 24 in Super Bowl XXVI, in (brrrr!) Minneapolis.

on a half-time show, and also the first to propose the Pro Bowl—he was also the last owner in the league to let an African-American athlete play on his team . . . in 1962. That player, Bobby Mitchell, is now the team's general manager. In 1988 the Redskins became the first team ever to play a black quarterback (Doug Williams) in the Super Bowl, and today, while about 26 percent of the metropolitan area's population is black, almost 30 percent of the fans in RFK every game are black. (Forty percent are female.)

"The Redskins," Duke Zeibert says, "have been adopted by the city and the people and, hey, even when they didn't have a good team, they used to sell out. You couldn't get a ticket."

For many people in the city—newcomers, or those who feel alien for one reason or another—this football team and its associated

mania seem to serve as a focus for the universal human need for a sense of community. For example, in the Addis Ababa restaurant in the capital's polyglot Adams-Morgan neighborhood, some 40 Ethiopians from every social stratum gather each week for the game, cheering the team in their native Amharic. One, an accountant, declares, "This is my RFK, this is my stadium." Another, a cab driver, says, "Whenever people get in my cab, we end up talking about the Redskins. With all the diversity in Washington, it's the one thing that binds us together." For the Ethiopians, the opportunity to gather in such a way provides them a time not only to hoot and holler but also to share their common heritage, necessary for surviving in an adopted country.

So the claims may be true. The team may be, along with the Metro, as Washington calls its subway, the only thing that keeps this fractious region together. (There are some Native Americans who strenuously object to the team's name and mascotry: it probably will not relieve their feelings to know that the coach of the team when it took on the monicker "Redskins" was a full-blooded Indian named William "Lone Star" Dietz.)

In any event, hail to the community-building Redskins. But what have they done for the rest of the nation? In a town of spin doctors and legend-makers, one is tempted to look to the Redskins for some symbolic meaning, some analogue to the course of the republic. For example, didn't the regime of George Allen in some way bespeak the national mood, or at least that of his greatest fan, Richard Nixon. Allen was relentless, his philosophy being to win at any cost. He was secretive. He held ostentatious prayer meetings. He traded off draft choice after draft choice for veteran players and coined the phrase "The future is now." Did that herald the S&L scandal a decade or so later?

In any event, there is something a bit more tangible that the Redskins have given the nation. It is the Hogs. Yes, the Hogs, the team's celebrated offensive linemen, the titans of the turf, revered by all and impersonated—in a sense—by the Hogettes, that group of gentlemen fans one sees on TV, sitting in the stands in frumpy dresses and wearing hog noses. Until Joe Bugel, then the Redskins line coach, coined that term, no one—no one—paid any attention to offensive linemen, those nameless toilers in the trench. Great defensive players got noticed, even defensive linemen, but the true glitz was accorded to running backs and quarterbacks. These were the Lochinvars of football, the aristocrats. Now even the most inattentive fan anywhere in the nation knows that the offensive line is the key. Linemen, too, are now stars, celebrities. And this celebrity extends beyond the gridiron, even into what might be thought of as the world of "culture." In a review of the film "Final Analysis" for People magazine, Leah Rozen complained bitterly of a series of plot twists, "each more ridiculous and far-fetched than the last and each with a hole so big you would think the script had been worked over by the Washington Redskins' offensive line."

How 'bout them Hogs?

And thus, in a tradition stretching back to Thomas Jefferson, have the Washington Redskins celebrated and elevated the common man. ★

★ ★ ★ ★ ★

Tubas and other instruments at the ready, the famous Redskins Marching Band enjoys a game, ever prepared to launch into a rousing rendition of "Hail to the Redskins."

Washington Architecture

Tony P. Wrenn

THE UNITED STATES CAPITOL IS THE BEST EXAMPLE IN WASHINGTON OF HOW

BUILDINGS GROW AND EXIST IN SETTINGS OR SURROUNDS. THERE ARE FEW

APPROACHES TO THE CITY IN WHICH IT IS NOT ONE OF THE MOST, IF NOT THE

MOST, VISIBLE BUILDING ON THE SKYLINE. NOW NESTLED

AMONG OTHER BUILDINGS, SOME WITH LESSER TOWERS AND

DOMES, IT DOMINATES ITS SURROUNDINGS, BECKONING AND

GIVING DIRECTION TO THE VIEWER, MAKING ONE AWARE OF

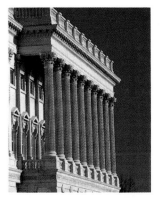

ITS IMPORTANCE. THE FEATURE ONE SEES ON EVERY

APPROACH, THE GREAT DOME OF CAST IRON DESIGNED BY THOMAS U. WALTER, IS

NOT THE OLDEST PART OF THE BUILDING, NOR EVEN ONE OF ITS ORIGINAL PARTS.

IT WAS FINISHED DURING THE CIVIL WAR, SUPPLANTING A LESSER DOME OF THE

1820S DESIGNED BY CHARLES BULFINCH. THE TWO SMALLER BULFINCH DOMES AT

EITHER SIDE OF THE GREAT DOME WERE BOTH COMPLETED BY 1807, AND THE

★ ★ ★ ★ ★

Installed atop the dome of
the Capitol in 1863, Thomas
Crawford's "Freedom," left,
faces east across Capitol
Square. Above, Corinthian
colonnade on the west
facade of the House of Representatives.

★ ★ ★ ★ ★

Perched atop one of the
loftiest spots in Washington,
the National Cathedral,
above right, whose official
name is the Cathedral
Church of Saint Peter and
Saint Paul, was finally completed on September 29,
1990. The soaring structure,
built of Indiana limestone, is
the sixth largest cathedral in
the world. The gargoyle
above was sculpted by Con-
stantine Seferlis in 1987.

House wing to the south and the Senate wing to
the north, also by Walter, were completed,
respectively, in 1857 and 1859. From the east
one sees less of the older building, for both the
center section and hyphens to the wings were
extended eastward and refaced in 1961. After a
prolonged fight, the same fate for the west front
was averted in the early 1980s, and there one
sees, above the great terraces and landscaping of
Frederick Law Olmsted, much of the original
building. It is Classical Revival and Neo-Classical
Revival, visibly spanning a 161-year construction
period. The Capitol stylistically foreshadowed
most of the other public buildings of Washington until almost World War II.

It is of some interest that the Capitol's competition for most prominent building on the
Washington skyline is the National Cathedral,
the great Gothic mass whose construction spans
most of the 20th century. It is on ground even
higher than the Capitol and seems to hover over
its surroundings, appearing almost totally visible,
while the Capitol shows its dome for public viewing from afar. The wag may note that these two

great architectural symbols, one of men and
women, the other of God, are the coequal landmarks one sees on the horizon in most
approaches to Washington, with lesser buildings
and monuments rising here and there.

On any passage down Pennsylvania Avenue
from the Capitol, it is the Treasury Building, in a
Greek style, that faces one at the end of the
street. One of the largest of Washington's Classical Revival buildings, its earlier parts are the
work of Robert Mills, who was architect from the
1830s to 1851 when Thomas U. Walter took over,
finishing the work by 1869.

In the center of Washington, midway between
the Capitol and the White House, built astride
8th Street, Northwest, between 7th and 9th, is the
other great Greek Revival building of the early
city, sometimes still known as the Old Patent
Office. It is the building that houses the National
Museum of American Art and the National Portrait Gallery, but once it was home to the Patent
Office, the Department of the Interior, and,

Tony P. Wrenn, Archivist,
the American Institute of
Architects, lives in
Fredricksburg, Virginia.
His works include *Walking
Tours, Washington, D. C.;
America's Forgotten Architec-
ture,* with Elizabeth D.
Mulloy; *Wilmington, North
Carolina;* and contribu-
tions to *The Best of
Washington.*

prior to the establishment of a National Archives and National Gallery of Art, many of the nation's archival and cultural treasures, from the Declaration of Independence to Gilbert Stuart portraits. Walt Whitman once worked here for the Bureau of Indian Affairs, and Abraham Lincoln's second inaugural was held here. During the Civil War it served, among other uses, as a hospital where Clara Barton helped care for the wounded. Actually the third federal building completed, after the original parts of the Capitol and the White House, its original architect was William P. Elliott, beginning in 1836. Robert Mills and T. U. Walter also worked on this building, but it was Edward Clark who completed it in 1867, just after the Civil War.

Across the street from the Old Patent Office is the smaller and more sedate Post Office Building, another of the Mills and Walter classical masterpieces. Mills designed the section nearest Pennsylvania Avenue, completed in 1844, and although Walter began the section closest to the Patent Office only a decade later, it was not completed until after the Civil War.

It is the White House, occupied, as was the Capitol, in 1800, that is in many ways the most important government building, culturally and historically. Since John and Abigail Adams moved into this grand, elegant Georgian mansion in that year, it has been the home of American Presidents. James Hoban designed the house, producing his plans in 1792, and Benjamin H. Latrobe, who also supervised construction of the Capitol, worked here until 1824. The White House was burned by the British in 1814, rebuilt by Latrobe, renovated by the New York architectural firm of McKim, Mead and White in 1902, and gutted by Lorenzo Winslow between 1948 and 1952, when the interior was rebuilt and detail replicated. It was also during this era, when Harry Truman

★ ★ ★ ★ ★

Frederick Hart's relief sculpture *The Creation*, above right, originally called *Ex Nihilo* (1975-1982), crowns the central portal of the National Cathedral's west entrance. Below, this capital detail is one of more than 3,000 hand-carved stone sculptures that distinguish the Gothic-style Cathedral.

was President, that the famous "Truman Balcony" was built on the Ellipse or south side of the White House.

Across Lafayette Square from the White House, at H and 16th streets, is St. John's Church, the "Church of the Presidents." It was built after designs of Benjamin Latrobe in 1816. The tower and present entrance were added later, so that one must step back and look behind them to see the Greek Cross, Federal-era church by Latrobe. Soon after the church was completed, President and First Lady James and Dolley Madison attended church here, as have all Presidents since, regardless of their religion.

Other pre-Civil War structures survive in the White House area, many of them residences. Decatur House, on Lafayette Square, is one of these. The third building on the Square, after the White House and St. John's, it was also designed by Latrobe. An almost casebook example of Federal era design, it is avant-garde as well, since both interior-window and door lintels terminate in corner blocks. Later, in the Greek Revival era, the device would be refined, while in the Victorian era it deteriorated into the bull's eye that framed almost every opening. The use of the device at Decatur House is very early; interior detail elsewhere that uses the corner block can safely be said to have been designed after around 1820.

Several other houses around the square are

★ ★ ★ ★ ★
Built to accommodate 60 railroad-freight cars' worth of exhibit material from the 1876 Centennial in Philadelphia, the "modernized Romanesque" Arts and Industries Building was inaugurated on March 4, 1881, at the inaugural ball of James A. Garfield and Chester A. Arthur. The National Museum, as it was then called, was the second Smithsonian structure on the Mall.

pre-Civil War, as is Blair House, the President's guest house, on Pennsylvania Avenue. Robert E. Lee was offered command of the Federal forces here in 1861; Andrew Johnson lived here after Lincoln's assassination until Mrs. Lincoln vacated the White House; and Harry Truman and his family lived here in the late 1940s while the White House was being redone.

Next door is the 1859 building known as the Renwick Gallery, today part of the Smithsonian Institution. Designed by James Renwick, it was an early American example of the French Second Empire or Mansard style and a most impressive one. Passing up its steps and through the

massive Victorian doors, one enters an opulent interior where a grand staircase invites one to climb to the galleries.

Nearby at 18th and New York is the Octagon House, designed by William Thornton and built around 1800. Occupying a triangular site, the structure has multiple facades with entrance through a circular bay at the corner rather than from either street. The house is red brick and decidedly Georgian in character, an appropriate style for John Tayloe, the Virginia aristocrat for whom it was built. President and Mrs. Madison occupied the Octagon House after the White House was burned by the British in 1814, and the Treaty of Ghent, ending the War of 1812, was signed here by President Madison in 1815. Since 1898 the Octagon has been associated with the American Institute of Architects, which, through its American Architectural Foundation, operates the house today as a historic house and architectural museum.

Several buildings of the Civil War era exist in the Old Patent Office area, midway between the Capitol and the White House. Notable among them is Ford's Theater, with its plain brick facade and gable end to the street. Built in 1862 by John T. Ford, its Italianate exterior is relieved by dropped lintels, a broad unadorned cornice frieze, and closed pediment gable. It was soon a popular theater. Abraham Lincoln was shot here on April 14, 1865. He was taken across the street to the Greek Revival Petersen House of 1849, where he died the next morning.

Also in the area, at 604 H Street, is the Surratt House, where in 1864 and 1865 Mary Surratt operated a boarding house. Although the simple Greek Revival exteriors are no longer obvious, their form can be spotted elsewhere in the neighborhood. It was here that John Wilkes

Booth and some of the other conspirators planned first the kidnapping and ultimately the assassination of President Lincoln.

Notable among the neighborhood's churches of this era is Calvary Baptist, at 8th and H streets, Northwest. Built on a site exactly midway between the Capitol and the White House, it was designed by Adolf Cluss and begun in the fall of 1864. The congregation came together in opposition to slavery; since then the church has been a powerful force in ministering to the hearing impaired, to minorities, and to the homeless. A

★ ★ ★ ★ ★

A statue of Alexander Hamilton, the first U.S. Secretary of the Treasury, stands at the south entrance to the Treasury Building. Construction of this Greek Revival edifice spanned more than 30 years (1836-1869), and in the end the immense structure blocked the vista from the Capitol to the White House.

major Gothic presence on a major downtown corner, its tower was the tallest structure between the White House and the Capitol when completed, displaying handsome clocks on its four faces, an open-work iron tower above, and colorfully patterned slate, along with pressed brick, iron, wood, and stained glass.

On the Mall stands the Washington Monument, designed by Robert Mills. The site originally approved by Pierre L'Enfant proved too swampy, so much so that a site marker placed by Thomas Jefferson in 1804 soon sank out of sight. When construction began in 1848, the monument was sited on higher ground and nearer the

Capitol than L'Enfant had planned. A simple obelisk of stone, it is the tallest masonry structure in the world, at slightly over 555 feet. It, too, is one of the true landmarks of the Washington skyline.

On the Mall, not too far from the Washington Monument, stands the Castle, the first Smithsonian building. Begun in 1847 after designs by James Renwick, it is Washington's premier Gothic Revival monument, completed in 1855, though rebuilt and enlarged just after the Civil War by Adolf Cluss.

On Capitol Hill, flocking around the Capitol, were the generally smaller and less pretentious houses of government workers. Rows of houses remain here in Federal, Greek, Italianate, and later Victorian styles. Philadelphia Row, in the 100 block of 11th Street, Southeast, is a block-long row of three-story brick dwellings built in the 1850s in a late Greek Revival style. Another Greek Revival row, smaller and less pretentious, is just behind the Madison Building of the Library of Congress, on D Street, Southeast. Uniform, three bays wide, and three stories high, these houses step down the hill from 2nd to 1st Street in military precision, displaying fine doorways, marble steps, and simple Greek detail. In the early years the steps certainly were washed and polished regularly and the row must have been even more handsome than it is today.

Alleys from the Victorian and earlier eras still exist, and off them one can spot the carriage houses and stables necessary to life in the horse-drawn era. In the alleys, paving materials of many types survive. Cobblestone, Belgian paving block, brick, terra-cotta of many types, asphalt block, and other materials give the texture and feel of the era when the alleys were actively used.

In the interiors of buildings there is also
much to see. Ford's Theater has been restored to
its Civil War-era form, and the Presidential Box
appears as it did on the night of the Lincoln
assassination. The Petersen House where Lincoln died displays a sitting room and bedroom
appearing much as they did that night. Furniture of the era is used, and one exits through the
rear past a view of the garden and service structures of the house.

Calvary Baptist Church retains its great Victorian interior of 1895, designed by Washington
architect James G. Hill, while nearby St. Mary's
Church, at 727 5th Street, Northwest, still has its
1891 E. F. Baldwin interiors, almost totally free of
the changes made in most Catholic church interiors since Vatican II.

The Library of Congress offers its poly-
chromed entrance and great, domed reading
room, while the Pension Building (now the
National Building Museum) maintains its mas-
sively columned atrium. The Smithsonian Castle
is a bit more sedate and human in form, though
the Arts and Industries Building next door
exudes 19th-century Victorian taste.

There are a great many other wonderful Victorian interiors, but these are all readily accessible, as is perhaps the finest of them all, Patent
Hall, in the National Portrait Gallery section of
the Old Patent Office building. Within a Classical Revival envelope, Patent Hall replaces space
damaged by fire in 1877. Tile, stained glass, and
polychroming survive, with all the iron and wood
to complement them. It is an interior worth
making a special effort to see.

Mills, Latrobe, Walter, and others responsible
for Washington buildings up to the Civil War
were architects who had earned their reputation
elsewhere before coming to Washington to fash-

ion a new federal city. By 1865, though, an increasing number of important designers made the city their base, where they created some of Washington's most important buildings.

One of these, built beside the Smithsonian Castle from 1879 to 1881, is the Smithsonian Arts and Industries Building. Designed by Adolf Cluss and his firm, Cluss and Schulze, it was constructed to house and display permanent exhibits from the 1876 Centennial Exposition in Philadelphia. Its high Victorian towers, domes, complex roofs, and colored and patterned brick and slate are unmatched elsewhere in Washington. Like a pavilion in brick, patterned after exhibition structures of the era, it has itself become an exhibit. The interior of its center court retains both the engineering and architectural and interior design elements of the era, while outside plantings in a Victorian design are maintained. The complex is a satisfying and unique Washington design experience.

Although Montgomery Meigs worked on plans for the Arts and Industries Building perfected by Cluss and Schulze, the Pension Building, between 4th and 5th and F and G streets, Northwest, was his alone. A massive Italian pallazo of brick and terra-cotta tile, it features a wonderfully detailed frieze of Civil War units that march, ride, and row around the building between the first and second levels. The interior court, with its gaudily gilded columns stretching to the roof, is one of the city's most magnificent interior spaces, not surpassed by any of the atria which began to appear in hotels and office and government buildings in the 1980s. Now the

National Building Museum, the Old Pension Building retains intact tile floors, and these and the terra-cotta steps leading to upper stories exhibit the wear of long use.

The old State, War, and Navy Building (now the old Executive Office Building), is at 17th and Pennsylvania, adjacent to the White House. Built from 1875 to 1888 from designs by Alfred B. Mullett, it is a later version of the 30-year-older Renwick Gallery across the street. Massive and robust, French Second Empire-style in stone, cast iron, and slate, it features different design elements for each level, from basement to roof. Although at first glance it is difficult to relate this building to the Greek Revival Treasury Building on the other side of the White House, it mimics both the plan and size of the earlier Treasury. Never a building to stir gentle passions, it has, from time to time, brought forth from its detractors threats varying from plans to remake it into a Treasury Building twin to outright demolition (during the Eisenhower Administration). It is said that the bids for demolition of the fortress structure were so high that the decision on its future was left to the following administration. It was John F. Kennedy who reversed the plan to demolish almost everything around Lafayette Square, including this

★ ★ ★ ★ ★

The south facade of the Old Executive Office Building exhibits some of the 900 freestanding columns that support this French Empire-style structure, which stands just west of the White House.

Row houses built about 1870 line a street on Capitol Hill. Anticipating a compact city, Washington's residential investors adopted the row-house architectural style of Philadelphia, Georgetown, and Alexandria.

building, so that today the square retains its residential character and depth and heterogeneity of area styles.

Perhaps the greatest of these late-19th-century architectural behemoths sits on Capitol Hill. It is the Library of Congress, completed in 1897 from the designs of Smithmeyer and Pelz and Edward Pearce Casey. Patterned after the Paris Opera, it offers visual feasts almost everywhere one looks, from the Neptune Fountain, by R. Hinto Perry, out front, to the great keystone heads above the second-level windows and the dome that tries to compete with the dome of the Capitol. The dome, with its broad expanse featuring color in tile, fresco, and glass, can best be enjoyed from the interior.

In a city that has many fine bridges, at least one deserves special attention. Glenn and Bedford Brown's Buffalo Bridge, also known as the Dumbarton or Q Street Bridge, over Rock Creek Park, owes its arches and general design to Roman models. What is unusual about the bridge, other than that it curves to join two streets that do not quite meet in a straight line, is that it is consciously designed to be seen both from above and below, and that it features distinctly American design motifs. The corbels are representations of the Minneconjou Sioux Chief

Kicking Bear, and were modeled from a life mask, while the buffalo at each end were modeled by sculptor A. Phinmister Proctor after animals in the nearby National Zoo.

The Old Post Office on Pennsylvania Avenue, W. J. Edbrooke's 1899 pile that nods to the Richardsonian Romanesque, and the Willard Hotel, at 14th and Pennsylvania, a massive, block-long, Second Empire hostelry of 1901 by Henry Hardenbergh, are among the last gasps of Victorian opulence in downtown Washington. Washington's next mood was decidedly Neo-Classical Revival, much of it produced not by architects who lived in Washington, as did Latrobe, Mills, Walter, and Cluss and Brown, but by well-known architects from elsewhere. After 1900, official Washington harked back to and stylistically copied the Washington of 1800.

Such well-known, out-of-town architects were always present, of course, doing a building here and another there, but after 1900, and the production of the McMillan commission plan, they led the way. Charles Follen McKim, of the New York firm of McKim, Mead, and White, did work at the White House for Theodore Roosevelt in 1902, beginning a tradition continued by Daniel Burnham. His Union Station of 1908 and City Post Office of 1914 are two of the most noticeable of the turn-of-the-century, Neo-Classical Revivals. Roman rather than Greek, and in the best beaux-arts tradition, Union Station served, and serves again today, as a ceremonial introduction and entry point to Washington. It was designed to set the mood, to establish an expectation of grandeur, and to acclimate one to the spaces and detail of a national capital. Beside it, the Post Office offered a grand display of Ionic columns flanked by projecting entrances.

Nearer the Capitol, at Constitution and Delaware, the Old Senate Office Building (today the Richard Brevard Russell Office Building) of 1909, by New Yorkers Carrere and Hastings, does not deviate from the style of McKim and Burnham, nor does their Old House Office Building (the Cannon House Office Building) of 1908, across Capitol Square at Independence and New Jersey. The Treasury Annex of 1919 and the Chamber of Commerce Building of 1925, both on Lafayette Square across from the White House, and both by Cass Gilbert of New York, follow the trend with classical street colonnades in stone.

It is in the Federal Triangle, along Pennsylvania Avenue between the White House and the Capitol, that the Neo-Classical Revival reached its zenith. The National Archives Building of 1937 is by John Russell Pope, of New York. Oriented at an angle to Pennsylvania Avenue, it faces via an 8th Street vista the great Classical Revival Patent Office Building of a century

earlier. The Department of Justice building of 1934 is by Zantzinger, Borie, and Medary, of Philadelphia. The Department of Commerce building, of 1932, is by York and Sawyer, and was, when completed, the largest office building in the world. Nearer the center of the Federal Triangle is the Post Office Department building by Delano and Aldrich, of New York. It, too, is unabashedly Neo-Classical Revival.

On the Mall at the eastern end of the Triangle is John Russell Pope's National Gallery of Art, completed in 1941. Its classicism is as Roman as Cass Gilbert's 1935 Supreme Court building is Greek. Gilbert, a New Yorker, as was Pope, chose to emulate the Capitol rather than the Library of Congress across the street. Pope's 1943 Jefferson Memorial, south of the Tidal Basin, was the last major Neo-Classical gasp in a city trying to move in other directions.

Perhaps the greatest of the Neo-Classical Revival structures is New Yorker Henry Bacon's Lincoln Memorial, part of the cross axis of Mall structures consisting of the White House, Washington Monument, and Jefferson Memorial in the north-south axis; and the Capitol, Washington Monument, and Lincoln Memorial in the east-west axis. Begun in 1912 and completed in 1922 on filled-in land, the Lincoln Memorial's massive columns surround a ceremonial room that projects above them as an attic bearing the names of the states during Lincoln's Presidency. The memorial is approached by multiple runs of massive steps leading to the chamber containing Daniel Chester French's seated Lincoln and Jules Guerin's murals of Lincoln's speeches. The columned promenade around the memorial, elevated as it is, is designed to offer views down the Mall and across, as well as up and down the Potomac. It was at the Lincoln Memorial that Marian Anderson sang in 1939 when the Daughters of the American Revolution refused to allow her to sing at its Constitution Hall facility; and here that Martin Luther King, Jr., gave his "I Have a Dream" speech in 1963. The memorial has become a part of the national conscience and was long the most visited site in Washington, though absolutely nothing happens there. Maya Lin's recessed, reflective Vietnam Veterans

Memorial of 1980 now receives more visitors, though the Lincoln follows closely. One can scarcely imagine two structures that more successfully memorialize, in both design and in visitor response.

Modernism never quite came to Washington, nor did the skyscraper. In 1894, architect Thomas Franklin Schneider built the Cairo Hotel on Q Street at 17th. It was a steel-frame building 160 feet high, and it so concerned its neighbors and the city as a whole that nothing like it ever happened again. The city adopted height limitations, and although the Cairo still stands, it has no peers of such a shocking height.

Paul Cret's 1937 Federal Reserve Bank building at Constitution and 17th did give a nod toward modernism and is certainly one of the better government-modern structures of the 1930s, but it still preserved classical forms. Its cleanliness and unadorned surfaces were enough to shock some, however.

Mies van der Rohe's horizontal skyscraper of 1972 for the Martin Luther King Memorial Library, at 901 G Street, has worn well. Only four stories tall, but a block long, it is sheathed in black and is far more successful than were the myriad Miesian buildings that sprang up along streets such as K. They formed canyons of buildings all of the same height and facade line, all without ornamentation. Unfortunately, they seemed to set the style for Washington.

When President Kennedy halted the proposed demolition of structures around Lafayette Square in 1963 and set in motion a study of how

the square's residential character could be maintained, the result spawned a series of follow ups that continue today. Around the square, John Carl Warnecke restored existing older buildings while demolishing newer buildings whose scale was not residential, and replacing the torn-down structures with new ones of appropriate scale and character. Behind these, and divorced from them, he built new multi-story buildings of brick in the interior of the blocks. The result was a happy one, completed in 1968 and still working.

During this era the American Institute of Architects had mounted a design competition for a new headquarters building to wrap around the historic Octagon House, at 17th and New York. Neither the winning competition design nor a modification of it could win design approval, and the competition winner withdrew. After some delay, a new building was approved and built, opening in 1973, some nine years after the initial competition. The multi-story headquarters building echoes the corner site of the Octagon in its shape, respects the Octagon's building line, reflects it in the center glass of its facade, and allows it to stand alone with a greensward and garden between.

These two seem to have spawned a new series of imitators that incorporated facades into newer buildings. The trouble with most of them—Red Lion Row is typical, on I Street between 20th and 21st, completed in 1983 from designs by John Carl Warnecke and Helmut, Obata, and Kassabaum—is that the structures the high-rise overshadows do not still function as buildings on their own. With all of them it has become difficult to tell the replacement from the original, and all are dwarfed by the new buildings.

One recent example of the genre that does work, however, is the restoration of the 1940 Greyhound Bus Station, on New York Avenue, and the construction of a block-large new building behind it. In a streamlined Art Moderne style by William Arrasmith, the bus station stood alone in downtown Washington as an exemplar of its style. The 1991 building by Keyes Condon

Florance not only lets it continue to stand, but uses its own lines and decoration to call attention to the older station.

Internationally known architects have designed recent buildings in Washington. I. M. Pei's East Building of the National Gallery on the Mall is one of a number of Washington buildings by Pei. Philip Johnson's pre-Columbian museum of 1963 at Dumbarton Oaks in Georgetown is still worth seeing, as is Marcel Breuer's Housing and Urban Development Building at 451 7th Street, Southwest. Arthur Erickson is represented by the new Canadian Embassy on Pennsylvania Avenue at 5th, and Mitchell Giurgolo by the Marriott Hotel at Pennsylvania and 14th. A bit farther away, but well worth a visit, are Egon Eierman's German Embassy, at 4645 Reservoir Road, in Georgetown, and Eero Saarinen's Dulles Airport, in Chantilly, Virginia. Both are particularly pleasant at night, especially the Dulles terminal, which on approach seems to hover over the flat plain, as if ready itself to lift off.

We seem to have discovered recently something that the Victorians and the classicists certainly knew. There is a certain boredom in sameness and a certain liveliness in diversity. Washington buildings of today have rediscovered setbacks, advancing and retreating facades, variations in texture and material and color, complex and varied roof lines, towers, playful corners, and facades articulated as is the column, with base (first story), shaft (mass of the building), and capital (cornice and roofline). Even the clock is making a comeback, not only with time but also sound.

Washington is like that, forever changing but still maintaining its architectural identity. Though L'Enfant and the members of the McMillan commission would be aghast at some of the things we have done, and at other things we have failed to do, I suspect that overall they would be pleased at how well the city and their plans for it have worn these 200 years. ★

Washington on Foot

John P. Wiley Jr.

If ever a city was made for walking, Washington is it. Flat or gently rolling terrain, beautifully landscaped with parks seemingly at every turn, it has wild places and a river with complete access along both banks. Distances tend to be short, and a height limit on buildings means the seeing is better than in almost any other city in the country. It is the nation's capital, and there are too many monuments, museums, and historical

places for even the most ambitious visitor to see. Yet some of the most rewarding moments on any visit will come on walks away from the centers of attraction when the visitor can absorb the beauty of the city itself. Walking will rejuvenate legs aching from standing on marble floors and allow the mind to sort all that has been taken in.

★ ★ ★ ★ ★

Joggers ply the Chesapeake and Ohio—or C & O—Canal towpath, which stretches 180 miles from Washington to Cumberland, Maryland. Above right, glass panes of the National Cathedral's Herb House.

This chapter will suggest a few of the many possibilities, in deep woods and along the river. Most can be reached, appropriately, on foot. For some it will make sense to take the Tourmobile or the Metro to the starting point. And many of the Capital's great walking opportunities begin and end with the National Mall, truly the key to America's City.

Many of the walks can be combined with a visit to a major attraction. Suppose, for instance, you've gone to the Kennedy Center for a daytime tour. From the balcony, you look across the river at the woods of Theodore Roosevelt Island, an anomaly with office buildings rising in back of them. In a few short minutes you can go out the front entrance of the center, turn right, cross one driveway, and be on a paved path that takes you up to a pedestrian walkway on the Theodore Roosevelt Bridge. On the other side, the path curves down to the footbridge that takes you onto the island. Turn right, or downstream, and follow the path across the mouth of a marsh toward the river. Walk through the trees to the beach. You are standing in a place of beavers

214

and great blue herons that is not all that different from 500 years ago. And directly across the water is your starting point, the cultural center of the nation's capital.

All four bridges across the Potomac are worth walking over, because each gives a different perspective of the capital. An organized approach might be to start with Key Bridge, the farthest upriver, which connects Rosslyn, Virginia, to Georgetown. On the Metro, take a blue- or orange-line train to the Rosslyn station, and then walk the three blocks downhill to the river. Walk through a formal gateway park, then around a small park that forms a traffic circle. You want to get to the walkway on the right or downstream side of the bridge.

You will be standing at Lee Highway and North Lynn Street, looking across the river at Georgetown and D.C. A paved bicycle trail that starts here runs all the way past National Airport and through Alexandria, by Dyke Marsh and on to Mount Vernon. Across the park, at Lee Highway and Fort Myer Drive, the Custis bicycle trail

begins. This runs through Arlington and Fairfax counties, where it joins up with the Washington & Old Dominion trail, which takes you out to Loudoun County, 55 miles from where that trail begins in Alexandria.

Walking across the bridge to Georgetown, look upriver to see wooded banks and hills rising from the river; only the occasional flash of sunlight on a windshield betrays the presence of Canal Road and the George Washington

Parkway. On the other shore rise the buildings of Georgetown University, with its historical telescope dome on the left edge of the campus. To the right is the converted car barn, which you can recognize by the arched doors—big enough for buses—at each end. Above the houses and trees on the hill between appear the towers of the National Cathedral, rising in the east like some majestic constellation. Downstream past the car barn, past the converted buildings of what once was industrial waterfront, crowds promenade in good weather in front of the fanciful Washington Harbour building. During a crew regatta, the waterfront is packed. The racing lanes pass under the bridge, giving pedestrians a unique view of the rowers. Straight down the river from our vantage point on the bridge, the familiar Washington Monument shoots up over the trees of Roosevelt Island.

From the downstream end of the bridge, a path curves down to the towpaths of the Chesapeake and Ohio—or C & O—Canal. You can walk along either side, through a canyon of industrial buildings long since gentrified. In season you can watch mule-drawn ferroconcrete canal boats moving through the locks that lower them to the level of the Potomac. The canal passes under a number of north-south streets, and the walker has to decide between the canal or the river. If you have chosen the latter, walk out the exit from Thompson's Boat House and across Rock Creek, and then you can keep walking along the river toward the Kennedy Center. A triangle of land, held up by crumbling sea walls, gives you a vantage point here from which to watch airliners make torturous turns as they follow the river (to minimize noise) and fly over Key Bridge when landing to the south. Across the river you can see occasional hikers moving through the trees of Roosevelt Island. In back, once again, are the office buildings of Rosslyn, Virginia.

A frequent visitor to Washington before moving there in 1973, John P. Wiley jr. has been an editor at *Smithsonian* magazine for the last 18 years. He is a weekend birder and hiker.

The catch of the day awaits visitors to the Maine Avenue fish market, left, which borders Washington's marina, below, home to yachts, houseboats, and sightseeing excursion cruisers.

To learn the pleasures of the Potomac, consider following a stream through four miles of wooded ravines to get to the river. Rock Creek Park is justly famed, and dealt with elsewhere in this book. But there is another, less known park that parallels Rock Creek. This is Glover-Archbold, which follows a stream known as Foundry Branch.

Take the red line on the Metro toward Shady Grove and get off at Tenley Circle. Come out of the station on the west side of Wisconsin Avenue (you will be in front of the Sears building) and head south, back toward downtown. Turn right at Van Ness and walk down the left side of the street until, opposite the parking lot for a garden center, you can turn left into a landscaped area that leads to a grassy open space with trees beyond. While you are still walking between satellite dishes and transmitter towers you will begin to hear woodpeckers and other birds from the trees in front of you.

Foundry Branch comes out of a culvert on one side of the field. Now you walk along the sides of a ravine and then down to the bottom, crossing the stream and working along it. Silt traps on storm-sewer outlets and manhole covers along a real, live sewer line take away some of the wilderness effect, but otherwise you are in the woods, watching hermit thrushes and flickers. All too soon the path rises to another open grassy area and you have reached Massachusetts Avenue, a major artery. Keep to the right of the clearing, following the trees, and cross the avenue where you see a brown National Park Service sign prohibiting bicycles. (The trail is fairly well marked with blue blazes painted on trees, but the "No bikes" signs are the best bet for picking up the trail across a street.) Steps

carry you back down to the ravine. You will pass other human artifacts, including a small, square, stone building, long roofless. You will see ugly scars, where water cascading down from Massachusetts Avenue cut six-foot gullies into the bank on your left. This is a short stretch and not so satisfying, because you can see houses on top all the way. Now you come up to cross Cathedral Avenue, drop down, and come up again to cross New Mexico Avenue. There is something pleasurable about popping out of the woods, crossing a busy street, and then disappearing into the woods again. It reverses our role, giving us what is almost an animal's-eye view of the city. Descending from New Mexico Avenue, you come to the stretch you have been hoping for.

You cross Foundry Branch on a small wooden bridge, and walk along the bottom of a ravine that is much wider than anything before. By the time you pass a community garden on your left, the sound of traffic has just about died away. All that is left are the sounds of jet engines on days when planes are taking off upriver from National Airport.

You come to a trail going off to the right and a sign informing you that it will take you to Foxhall Road and thence to Battery Kemble Park, 0.8 miles away. A little farther still, you notice red numbers painted on the trees. Breeding birds have been censused here since 1959, one of the early studies to document the decline of migratory songbirds.

Next comes a real crossroads. Double signs inform you that you have come 4.3 kilometers from Van Ness and have 1.9 to go to reach the C & O Canal. The other sign tells you that the trail leading off to your left is the Whitehaven and that on it the distance is 1.9 kilometers to Wisconsin Avenue and 3.5 to Rock Creek Park.

Finally you come to Reservoir Road. The horizontal white layers of the French Chancery

With the graceful arches of Memorial Bridge spanning the Potomac in the background, a lone jogger heads south on the Virginia side of the river. Opposite, thrill seekers at Gravelly Point brave the noise to watch jets land at National Airport, also in Virginia.

are visible through the trees as you approach the street; Georgetown University Hospital is just down the street to your left. You cross over into another park area (here you will see the blue blaze before the no-bikes sign), this one complete with picnic tables, and plunge into the woods for the last time. On your right are slabs of concrete, demolition debris; farther down on your left the dome of the Georgetown Observatory is visible through the trees. You walk under an abandoned railroad trestle and come to the intersection of Canal and Foxhall roads. Walk slightly east on Canal and follow the path that loops back around under Canal Road and the canal itself. The first half (under the street) is well-lighted poured concrete; the second half—perhaps 150 years older—is an arched tunnel of sharp fieldstone, leaking slightly and, on a warm day, distinctly cooler, with lights along a suspended wire.

From the tunnel you can walk down to the

Potomac or climb a set of steps up to the canal towpath. At the river's edge you discover that you are a few hundred yards upstream from Key Bridge, approximately across from Spout Run. Water from the canal flows over a spillway into a rocky channel looking for all the world like a mountain stream. To get back to "civilization," you go up to the towpath and walk toward Georgetown. Where the Whitehurst Freeway curves into M Street there are stairs that carry you up to street level, on the upstream side of Key Bridge.

Closer to the center of things, the Smithsonian Castle is a good starting point for several walks. From the garden in back, one can cross Independence Avenue, walk south on L'Enfant Promenade, beneath the raised portion of the Forrestal Building, and up a slight grade to L'Enfant Plaza. Walk through the plaza to Banneker Circle at the end. From here you can look out over the fish market and restaurant row,

Washington Channel, East Potomac Park (known to everyone as Hains Point), the Potomac, and National Airport beyond. Circle around to the paved path that was on your left as you faced the river and walk down to Maine Avenue, Water Street, and between the restaurants until you are on the promenade above the marinas. You may want to stop at the fish markets, which sell not only fresh seafood to take home, but cooked treats to eat on the spot: spiced shrimp, steamed crabs, raw and fried oysters, crab cakes, and all the rest.

Then start walking down the channel with the restaurants just above you on your left, the boats on your right. Most of the boats are local (some are lived on year-round) but every now and then you will spot one from Europe. Yachts of the size of those once owned by Donald Trump and the late Malcolm Forbes may be tied up at the ends of the docks. Near the end of the marina section is a restaurant floating on a square hull, rising and falling with the tides and occasionally rocking just enough to let you know you are on the water. Next is the dock for the excursion boats *Spirit of Washington* and *Potomac Spirit,* which offer both cruises to Mount Vernon and lunch, dinner, and moonlight cruises on the river. Beyond is the pier where the police harbor patrol and the fireboat are stationed. It is a deep-water dock, and from time to time extraordinary visitors will be tied up there—a replica of the H.M.S. *Bounty,* for example.

At the end of the promenade is a memorial to the men who gave their lives on the *Titanic.* Behind the monument is Fort Lesley J. McNair; you look down the long row of generals' houses to where the channel meets the Anacostia River. Turn around for the walk back, orienting yourself to the city by the Jefferson Memorial and the Washington Monument.

For a longer walk, return to Banneker Circle and this time take the concrete path that runs across the top of a grassy hill to a pedestrian ramp leading up to the highway. There is a walkway protected by stout steel railings, and if you can mentally shut out the road noise it is liberating to walk high above the fish market and the water of Washington Channel before descending into East Potomac Park. You will walk by the covered tennis courts and then the sidewalk just ends. But 100 feet ahead is a pedestrian crossing that carries you into the parking lot for National Park Service headquarters, and then sidewalks appear that take you toward the river. Once at the river, there is a walk that circumnavigates the point. Turn left and begin. Across the way is Gravelly Point and National Airport and its constant show. The river is very wide here as it approaches its junction with the Anacostia; without Hains Point, on which we are walking, which has all been filled in, the river would be considerably wider. On windy days the wide expanse of water looks like a bay near the coast; gulls, cormorants, and diving ducks add to the feeling. To the left as we walk is a municipal golf course; this gives way near the end to an elaborate playground. The point has curved out into the river; if we look back from here we see the long, curving sea wall and, in the distance, the National Cathedral high upon Mount St. Albans, the loftiest point in the District. Downstream we can see the buildings of Alexandria on the right and just beyond them the Wilson Bridge, which carries I-95 across the river.

During lulls in the plane traffic there are moments of merciful quiet, and there are plenty of benches on which to relax. At the very tip of Hains Point, we can see the buoys that mark where the channels split. Behind us is a huge sculpture of a bearded man struggling to rise from the earth in which he has been buried. Titled "The Awakening," it marks the recovery of the river, once left for dead. (In April 1992 the head was hit by a drag-racing youngster and taken away for repairs costing $100,000.) The Anacostia, which turns north, was once deep enough for ocean-going vessels; now it has silted in. We come back on the Washington Channel side. Across the water is Fort Lesley J. McNair, with the imposing National War College facing the open water. Farther up is a row of generals' houses, with the Capitol dome rising behind them. Where Fort McNair ends and the promenade begins, we see the outstretched arms of the figure on the *Titanic* memorial, the apartment buildings put up after urban renewal, and the beginning of government: the HUD and DOT buildings. Back at the covered tennis courts, you can follow a well-worn path on the far side to get back to the bridge that will take you back across the channel. Or you can continue on, deciding after you pass under a railroad bridge whether to turn left to the Jefferson or right to 15th Street.

A third walk also begins at Banneker Circle (although this one also can be started by taking the Tourmobile to the Jefferson). Walk down the hill to the fish market, and this time turn right and walk under the highway bridges, past the Washington Marina and a small parking lot lined with good-sized trees, a forgotten nook that is almost a pocket park. Go under the railroad bridge and then turn left, leaving the Tidal Basin on your right. Use the crosswalk where you see the sign for Hains Point and then take the paved path that angles away from the road toward the Jefferson (but not the one that follows the water's edge). This path is a triumph for walkers; for years it was a well packed dirt track until the authorities gave in and paved it. Ignore the Jefferson for this trip and walk around the parking lot to the refreshment kiosk at the far corner. Across the street—joggers and cyclists will catch your eye—is the path that leads up onto the 14th Street Bridge, which carries traffic headed for Richmond and other points south. As you step up onto the bridge proper, take note of the formal gardens and fountain below you.

From the bridge you will see the Pentagon. About halfway between that and Memorial Bridge to the right, you can see the Lee Mansion high on a hill in Arlington National Cemetery. Jets will be landing or taking off right over your head: this bridge is the closest to National Airport. On the other side, where the bridge first begins to curve to the right, look back across the river. The National Cathedral will be directly above the Lincoln Memorial, with the Kennedy Center to its left.

As you come off the bridge, a dirt path descends steeply to the bicycle path along the river. This is the same path that goes all the way to Mount Vernon. Stay on the path you are on and it will join the bicycle path going upriver, alongside the George Washington Parkway. Soon you will cross the bridge over the channel into the marina; from the center you will have a full-on view of the Pentagon. Continue past the Navy and Marine Memorial and you will come to Lady Bird Johnson Park. There is a crosswalk that will take you into the park along the marina, but you have to choose your moment to cross four lanes of traffic. The prudent may prefer to stay on the river side. There are benches and picnic tables along the bank, a perfect place to contemplate our nation's capital. Here you realize the impact of the height limitation on Washington buildings: most of the city is hidden behind the trees

★ ★ ★ ★ ★

A couple stops to rest amid the ethereal beauty of the cherry blossoms, which celebrated the 80th anniversary of their planting around the Tidal Basin in April 1992. As with so much else in Washington, they are best enjoyed on foot.

of West Potomac Park. If you can shut out the noise of cars behind you and planes overhead, it is a surprisingly restful spot. Then it's back across the bridge, to take full advantage of the Tourmobile.

One of the best walks in Washington is right under the noses of nearly everyone who visits here. Most people who come to Washington find themselves walking on the Mall, rushing from one museum or memorial to the next. But the incomparable National Mall is an attraction in its own right. It is especially appealing in early-

morning haze and around sunset, but worth a look any time. This chapter is only a small sampling of a walker's guide to Washington. A book would not be enough. But perhaps something of the spirit of a walker of another generation has been conveyed. In a small park at the intersection of Wisconsin and Massachusetts avenues there is a plaque honoring Viscount Bryce of Dechmond, British ambassador to the United States from 1907 to 1913. It reads simply: "He delighted in the parks of Washington." We are invited to do the same. ★

Where the Wild Things Are

Amy Donovan

"The world is too much with us," wrote William Wordsworth in 1807 in pre-industrial England, lamenting the inevitable intrusions of human society, with all its attendant stresses and strains, in our lives. But

Wordsworth hadn't, as the saying goes, seen anything yet. Life has got nothing if not more complicated, and surely there is no city more caught up in the tumultuous whorl of modern-day politics and international affairs than Washington. As the nation's capital, the city has always been a magnet for those seeking fame, fortune, and power—or the company, at least, of those who have them. But if the

★ ★ ★ ★ ★

A lone cyclist enjoys the autumnal splendor of Rock Creek Park, a natural oasis in the nation's capital. Above right, a tiger swallowtail feeds on the blossoms of an aptly named butterfly bush.

rewards of these pursuits have been great, so, too, have the possible pitfalls; newspapers over the years are replete with stories of such downfalls.

And yet if Washington provides ample and well documented opportunities for personal and professional burn-out, it also offers refuges from the city's special brand of life in the fast lane where one can escape the pressures of society and seek solitude and renewal in another world, the natural. Chief among such places is Rock Creek Park, a 2,000-acre tract of woodland, streams, rocky glens, valleys, and meadows that

recently celebrated its 100th anniversary. The bill establishing the park passed both houses of Congress on September 25, 1890, and was signed into law two days later by President Benjamin Harrison. Crisscrossed by more than 12 miles of trails, many of which are open to horseback riders as well as hikers, the park offers scenic vistas and a chance to experience an abundant variety of native flora and fauna: at least 730 different kinds of flowering plants (as well as mosses, lichens, liverworts, and algae), 140 kinds of birds, and 27 mammals, not to men-

Amy Donovan, a native Washingtonian, is an editor at Smithsonian Books. An avid birder, she wrote on sandhill cranes in *Lords of the Air: The Smithsonian Book of Birds,* which she also edited.

tion several species of reptiles, amphibians, and fish, and the endemic Hayes Spring scud, a little-known, 1/4-inch invertebrate that is D.C.'s only endangered species.

To enter the park is to enter another world, thanks in great part to a study and master plan completed in 1918 by renowned Central Park planner Frederick Law Olmsted's two sons, Frederick Law Olmsted, Jr., and his step-brother, John C. Olmsted. They opened their report with a clear statement of priority: "The dominant consideration, never to be subordinate to any other purpose in dealing with Rock Creek Park, is the permanent preservation of its wonderful natural beauty, and the making of that beauty accessible to people without spoiling the natural scenery in the process." That mandate has been followed to a greater or lesser extent, and so today the park is not only one of the largest urban parks in the world, but surely the most pristine, a living tribute to the foresight of its earliest proponents.

Nestled against some of the park's wooded hillsides and bordered on the east by the creek itself is that celebrated home of many wild things, the National Zoo, which has occupied this site in Rock Creek Valley since 1891, or almost as long as the park has been in existence. Because of its stature as a national institution, the zoo has received numerous animals over the years as gifts to the American people from foreign governments. Today its collection includes the famous giant pandas Hsing-hsing and Ling-ling (surely the exotic-animal counterparts to what definitely is *not* an endangered animal in Washington, the VIP), which were received with great fanfare from the People's Republic of China in April 1972. The zoo's denizens certainly reflect Washington's international make-up: on certain mornings at certain times of the year,

people in neighborhoods surrounding the zoo are treated to the bugling unison calls of a pair of sarus cranes, native to India, or the wild, piercing hoots and cries of gibbons, indigenous to the forests of Vietnam.

Washington's relatively mild winters enable these and many other of the zoo's animals to spend much of the year outside. In the summer, as you stroll down Beaver Valley, you might look up and see beautiful, orange, squirrel-size monkeys disporting among the tulip poplars. These geographically incorrect woodland sprites are golden lion tamarins. Highly endangered in their native Brazilian coastal rain forest—only a small remnant of which remains, just north of Rio de Janeiro—they are in fine fettle here, oblivious to D.C.'s heat and humidity as they play about their nestbox.

The zoo offers visitors a superb variety of exotic animals—from reindeer to tapir, crocodile to cuttlefish—and of native American fauna—bison to prairie dog, brown bat to merganser. Perhaps in part because of the lure of this great congregation of wildlife, and in part because of its natural setting, the zoo also affords opportunities to see animals indigenous to the region. One of the most conspicuous of these is the black-crowned night heron, a chunky, medium-sized wading bird that nests in bustling colonies at the zoo each spring in trees located, appropriately, near the outdoor flight cage (in which a group of these birds were once on exhibit) and the Bird House. Not exactly endangered—it may be the world's most abundant heron species, and surely is the most cosmopolitan—the black-crowned night heron has been a welcome "wild" resident at the zoo for many years. The boisterous colonies, raucous with the birds' comings and goings, squabblings and squawkings, grow larger each year; in the

spring of 1991, zoo personnel counted some 130 night herons.

Many other kinds of birds, including the night heron's close cousin, the yellow-crowned night heron, and other members of the family—great blue herons, great egrets, and snowy egrets—also touch down at the zoo. Wood ducks and other kinds of waterfowl visit the ponds in the wetlands exhibit, and both red-tailed and red-shouldered hawks nest on zoo property. Because of their power of flight, birds have an easier time disregarding the boundary between zoo grounds and the surrounding wild environment. And recently, their colorful insect counterparts, butterflies, have been attracted to the zoo on a regular basis by special plantings of flowers and shrubs. Come July and August, one should look for monarchs, swallowtails, and others of these beautiful aerial insects.

★ ★ ★ ★ ★

Rock Creek Park's valleys, streams, meadows, rocky glens, and woodlands provide habitat for an abundant variety of plants and animals, including year-round resident rufous-sided towhees, above; wood thrushes, below, and other migratory birds; spring beauties, above right; and striking fungi, opposite bottom. Opposite, a winter woodland scene.

Without question, the animals at the zoo are fascinating and incredibly diverse, hailing from almost every habitat and every corner of the world imaginable. They are also on exhibit, and thus are generally quite easy to see. This is not the case for many of the denizens of Rock Creek Park and other natural areas in and around Washington. Often it is the mission of these wild animals to be neither seen nor heard, for to be either could bring injury or death. But this just heightens the challenge—and the rewards—for those who would find them. Mind that cavity high in the oak; lift your binoculars and there are two dark eyes behind a black mask staring back at you. Aren't those cloven-hoof marks in the path? There they go! White-tailed deer!

Doesn't that sapling's trunk look as though it had been chewed by a . . . ? Ah, but *that* one is really elusive!

Raccoons, deer, beaver—they all live in the park, along with opossums, both red and gray foxes, gray squirrels, chipmunks, and other mammals. Raccoons, of course, are scarcely a surprise, given their adaptability to urban and suburban life (their shrill, blood-curdling vocalizations no doubt have given many a D.C. resident a start). Further benefiting them locally is the fact that the age of Rock Creek's forest makes for ideal raccoon habitat. Some of the trees are 200 years old, and many are easily 100, having grown since the time of the Civil War when areas of the forest were clear-cut to allow a free line of cannon fire. These stately giants harbor numerous cavities that are seemingly custom-made for raccoons, and the abundant oaks produce a bounteous supply of acorns, upon which the raccoons rely heavily through the fall.

White-tailed deer became a permanent presence in the park only in the last three or four years; they are usually seen in groups of 10, becoming more solitary in the spring when the females go off to fawn. The beaver are also a recent arrival, and are also secretive. Because Rock Creek usually is fast flowing and floods easily, the large, flat-tailed rodents can't build dams as they would in other streams; instead, they den

in the creek's banks. They and the deer have few natural enemies here, but there is one particularly deadly one—the automobile. Park biologists are monitoring both white-tailed deer and beaver populations; so far as the latter are concerned, it is not much appreciated when one of them gets it into its buck-toothed head to gnaw into oblivion a newly planted, $300 tree in Lady Bird Johnson Park across the Potomac from the city.

Rock Creek's birds offer a clear indication of the park's importance as an urban refuge. By mid-May, the woods and valleys resound with birdsong: the ovenbird's "teacher, teacher, TEACHER" rings out from the understory; the loud, melodious notes of the northern waterthrush burble up from the edge of a rushing stream; the least flycatcher snaps his "wick-up" call from his perch beside the creek; the scarlet tanager dazzles the eye as well as the ear; and the wood thrush, "state" bird of the nation's capital, sends his haunting refrains, perhaps the most beautiful of all, floating through the evening stillness.

The songbirds bring the season to a climax,

and usher in the time of plenty. Many of them, like their human counterparts in the nation's capital, are ambassadors from other homelands, flying in from Mexico, the Caribbean, and other regions and countries in the Neotropics to represent their kind and then, inevitably, return to more southerly climes. But these birds' numbers are down. We know this from the data assembled by one of the country's oldest breeding-bird censuses. Each spring for some 40 years members of the local Audubon Naturalist Society recorded the migratory songbirds found in one particular

site in Rock Creek Park. The trend was disturbing: some species suffered what were called "terminal extinctions," disappearing from the plot altogether; others declined more or less drastically. Many biologists fear that the one-two punches of tropical deforestation in the birds' winter homes and ever increasing pressures on their nesting sites here—pressures in the form of real-estate development, forest fragmentation, vulnerability to greatly increased predation—

may be devastating these migrants. For now, biologists keep counting, but woe betide our fine city should it lose its wealth of birds.

Aside from nesting places, the park's beautiful trees provide shelter and food throughout the year for a variety of animals. And Rock Creek Park is home to much of the region's other original flora as well, including numerous wildflowers. Spring beauties open their delicate, pink-striped blossoms in early spring, followed in quick succession by the blooms of bloodroot, blue violet, jack-in-the-pulpit, toadshade, Dutchman's breeches, Virginia bluebells, and many others. To the consternation of park biologists, exotic pest plants are bringing increasing pressure to bear on the native flora, aggressively invading habitats and forcing out the locals. Efforts are underway to uproot and eradicate these introduced species, which include bittersweet, kudzu vine, porcelainberry, and rosa multiflora, all originally from Asia, but the time that park personnel can devote to this problem is limited, and new, potentially harmful exotic plants seem always to be threatening.

One place in the city where exotic plants are welcomed—where a place has literally been carved out for them—is Kenilworth Aquatic Gardens, home of the water lily. This 12-acre sanctuary is hidden away off the busy highways that traverse the city's far-northeast segment, and it borders the east bank of another of the capital's waterways, the Anacostia River. Back in 1880, Walter B. Shaw, who had lost his right arm fighting for Union forces in the Civil War, bought 37 acres here from his father-in-law, and took to farming the land. He missed the beauty of his native Maine, however—its ponds, and, especially, its water lilies—and the story has it that a few friends from his home state packed off

★　★　★　★　★

The oversize pads of the exotic Amazonian water lily *Victoria amazonica* dwarf those of other species, left, at Kenilworth Aquatic Gardens, whose first pools were dredged by founder W.B. Shaw, right, in the late-19th century. A 12-acre sanctuary on the east bank of the Anacostia River, this unique national park features hundreds of varieties of hardy and tropical water lilies, as well as lotuses and other water-loving plants, and is home to an array of wetland animals, too.

six water-lily tubers to him as reminders of the places and plants he loved.

The rest, as they say, is history. The Maine water lilies took, Shaw sought other species and cultivated them in specially dredged pools, and before long his hobby had become a business, selling the many varieties of plants he collected and developed to people near and far. W.B. Shaw Lily Ponds also became a popular Sunday retreat, its shining pools and blooming lilies attracting thousands of local admirers on sunny summer days.

Shaw was ably assisted in his work by his daughter, Helen Fowler, and it was she who transferred the land to the government for use as a park. Today it is administered by the National Park Service, and is the only national park devoted solely to these water-loving plants. And devoted it is, featuring hundreds of different species of tropical and hardy water lilies from around the world as well as exotic and native lotuses, whose showy flowers have long served as a symbol for Eastern religions.

The plants and their blooms may be the main attractions for people, but the park's overall mosaic of habitats attracts a wide variety of animals: muskrat, beaver, and even mink ply the river; foxes and raccoons ramble through the tidal marsh; crayfish and mole salamanders hide

★ ★ ★ ★ ★

Bromeliad above is one of a myriad botanical jewels to be seen at the U.S. Botanic Garden, a treasure trove of plants at the base of Capitol Hill. Herbs, annuals, shrubs, and such trees as European horse chestnut and jujube make their home across Independence Avenue in the company of sculptor Frédéric- Auguste Bartholdi's exquisite fountain, opposite.

in watery and damp niches, respectively; harmless (to humans) garter and water snakes slither about; red-winged blackbirds nest in the thickets; and, of course, frogs have a field day—bullfrogs, pickerel frogs, green frogs, spring peepers, and tiny cricket frogs. This is but a sampling of the park's rich offering of wetland animals, and there are many other kinds of plants to be seen as well.

The Aquatic Gardens' watery world of water lilies is wonderful indeed. And if plants are really what one wants to see, there are 450 acres of them just across the Anacostia at the National Arboretum. Here one finds botanical treats for all seasons, one of the most spectacular of which is the dazzling array of thousands of azaleas, the nation's most extensive collection of these flamboyant plants. For those who would seek out the native, or natural, one of the arboretum's most delightful spots is Fern Valley, a lovely, wooded area through which flows a small, spring-fed stream. Named for the initial gift of some 1,000 ferns in the spring of 1959, Fern Valley features plants of the eastern United States, with the different species planted to reflect the north-south, east-west succession of environments in which they grow naturally. Here are witch hazel and wild ginger, strawberry bush and mountain laurel, mayapples and partridgeberry, Canadian hemlocks and bald cypress, all sharing space beneath majestic stands of century-old beech, oak, and tulip-poplar trees. And in the meadow area near the valley's northern-forest section is a rare Franklin tree, discovered by naturalist John Bartram in Georgia in 1765 and named for Benjamin Franklin, and not found in the wild since 1803. Fern Valley is a beautiful living classroom (don't fail to get a copy of the

informative Fern Valley Trail Guide to accompany you on your tour), and, for those of us bordering on the botanically illiterate, one of the best things about it is that everything—as it is throughout the arboretum—is labeled.

Plants are labeled also in the conservatory of the U.S. Botanic Garden, a beautiful marble-and-glass structure from the last century that is located just down the hill from the Capitol. Even on the most frigid winter day one can enjoy a bit of the tropics here, reveling in such tropical vegetation as the aptly named sausage tree from Africa, the candle tree from Panama, the edible-fruit carambola from Malaysia, and several towering rubber and ficus trees. There is a profusion of orchids, of bromeliads, and of cactuses, and seasonal displays that showcase particular plant families, such as chrysanthemums and begonias. And, once again, native wildlife crops up amid the exotic, for the conservatory's charms are not lost on grackles (how tropical they make the place sound as they go about the business of nesting!), Carolina wrens, or, of course, the ubiquitous pigeons.

Come late summer, the herb garden just across Independence Avenue is in full bloom. The richly colored flowers, along with those of the aptly named butterfly bush, attract hordes of migrating monarch butterflies, their orange-and-black wings gleaming in the warm September sun. Other migrants turn up here, too—a common yellowthroat, searching for food beneath a viburnum; chimney swifts twittering overhead—as they do back across Independence on the Capitol grounds themselves, where the protection of so much of Washington's natural beauty was ensured. How fitting, then, that these grounds are so lovely and park-like, and that they offer some of the finest specimens of this nation's—and the world's—trees: American and European lindens, sugar maples, sycamores, bur oaks, white oaks, willow oaks, yellow buckeye, pecan, ash, Kentucky coffeetree, Osage orange, giant magnolia, sweetbay magnolia, saucer magnolia, cucumbertree magnolia, horse chestnut, and, of course, American elm. There are many others as well, all frequented regularly by the resident gray squirrels, mockingbirds, blue jays, crows, tufted titmice, song sparrows, cardinals, and Carolina chicadees.

Meanwhile, back in Rock Creek Park, the stars and planets are just coming into view. A pair of little brown bats makes its first foray out into the evening light. Nearby, a rufous-sided towhee sings the clean, clear notes of his even-song—"Drink your tea!"—and squirrels rustle about the leaves one more time before scampering up into the trees to their nests. Then, from a ridge, come the low, resonant hoots of a great horned owl, answered in short order by the call of its mate, and, as night finally falls, it seems that all might yet be well with the world. ★

INDEX

Illustrations and caption references appear in bold.

234

PICTURE CREDITS

Legend: B Bottom; C Center; L Left; R Right; T Top.

The following abbreviations are used to identify the Smithsonian Institution (SI) and other organizations.

KWC Kiplinger Washington Collection
LC Library of Congress
NA National Archives
NMAFA National Museum of African Art
NMAA National Museum of American Art
NMNH National Museum of Natural History
NPG National Portrait Gallery
NPS National Park Service
NZP National Zoological Park
WHHA White House Historical Association

Front Matter:
p.1 Duane Hincy, VA; 5 Steve Gottlieb, MD. pp. 8-9 Fred Ward/Black Star, NY.

A Tale of Two Rivers: 10 ©1992 CNES, provided by SPOT Image Corporation, VA; 11 Everett C. Johnson/Folio, Inc., DC; 12 Art by Eleanor M. Kish; 13 Reproduced from Stefan Lorrant, *The New World, The First Pictures of America,* NY: Duell Sloan & Pearce, 1946, photo by Ed Castle, MD; 14 KWC; 15T Virginia Polytechnic Institute & State University, Blacksburg, VA; 15B From Bruce Bustard, *Washington Behind the Monuments,* National Archives & Records Administration, 1990; 16 Kenneth Garrett/Woodfin Camp, Inc., DC; 16-17 C&O Canal, NPS, MD; 18 Ed Castle; 19 LC/Photo Researchers, Inc., NY.

Washington City: pp. 20-21 KWC; 21 Photo by Jack E. Boucher 1991, Historic American Buildings Survey, NPS; 22 KWC; 23 LC; 24 KWC; 24-25 LC; 26 NA; 27,28,29,31,32 LC; 33 NA; 34-35 Steve Gottlieb; 35 Walter P. Calahan/Folio, Inc.; 36 Jonathan Wallen, NY; 37T NA; 37B UPI/Bettmann Archive.

The City of Frederick Douglass: p.38 Hampton University Museum, Hampton, VA; 39 LC; 40T Architect of the Capitol, DC; 40B,41 LC; 42T

Scurlock Studio, DC; 42B Hilda Wilkinson Brown, *University Neighborhood,* courtesy of Lilian Thomas Burwell, photo by Gary Garrison, DC; 43T Bethune Museum and Archives, DC; 43B Scurlock Studio, DC; 44 Time-Life Picture Service, NY; 44-45 Scurlock Studio; 46T AP/Wide World Photos, NY; 46B LC; 47 AP/Wide World Photos; 48 From the exhibit and book *Songs of My People,* photo by Jason Miccolo Johnson, ©New African Visions, Inc., DC; 49T Chris Kleponis/Folio, Inc.; 49B Hampton University Museum, Hampton, VA.

The Rise of Imperial Washington: p.50 UPI/Bettmann Archive; 51 Painting by Frank Wright, MD; 52,53T NA; 53B AP/Wide World Photos; 54 LC; 55 Courtesy of NAACP Public Relations, MD; 56T UPI/Bettmann Archive; 56B Stacy Pick/Folio, Inc.; 56-57 Terry Ashe/Folio, Inc.; 58T Jesse Blackburn/Folio, Inc.; 58B Max Hirshfeld/Folio, Inc.; 59T,B Steve Gottlieb; 60-61 Ed Castle/Folio, Inc.; 62 AP/Wide World Photos; 63 Rick Buettner/Folio, Inc.; 64-65 Steve Gottlieb.

A Man with a Map: pp.66-67 KWC; 67 Painting by Bryan Leister, Historical Society of Washington, DC; 68 Line engraving by Tackara and Vallance, Philadelphia, 1792, restrike. John W. Reps, NY; 69

Pierre Patel, 1668, Giraudon/Art Resource, NY; 70 LC; 71 The George Washington University Permanent Collection. Courtesy of the Dimock Gallery, DC; 72 NA/Imagefinders, Inc., DC; 73 Carol Highsmith, DC.

The Capitol: p.74 Robert Shafer, DC; 75,76T LC; 76B C.B.J. Fevret de St. Memin, *Portrait of Dr. William Thornton,* Corcoran Gallery of Art, DC, gift of William Wilson Corcoran; 77,78 LC; 79 Samuel F.B. Morse, *Old House of Representatives,* 1822, Corcoran Gallery of Art; 80,81T Architect of the Capitol; 81BL LC; 81BR Architect of the Capitol; 82 Dennis Brack/Black Star; 83 Catherine Karnow/ Woodfin Camp, Inc.; 84 LC; 85 Bill Weems/Woodfin Camp, Inc.

Capitol Gallery: pp.86-91T Steve Gottlieb; 91B Architect of the Capitol; 92-93 Steve Gottlieb.

The White House: p.94 Robert Shafer; 95 Wally McNamee/Folio, Inc.; 96,97,98 WHHA; 99 Bill Weems/Woodfin Camp, Inc.; 100-101,101 WHHA; 102,103 Fred J. Maroon, DC; 104 Everett C. Johnson/Folio, Inc.; 105 Carol Powers/The White House.

At Home with the Presidents: pp.106-107,107 WHHA; 108L Ed Castle, MD; 108R Photo Researchers, Inc.; 109T WHHA; 109B Courtesy of the Pennsylvania Academy of Fine Arts, Philadelphia; 110 WHHA; 110-111,111T,112,113L Culver Pictures, NY; 113R WHHA; 114 Stanley Tretick/Sygma, NY; 115 UPI/Bettmann Archive; 117 WHHA. 118-119 Dennis Brack/Black Star.

Monuments and Memorials: pp.120-121 Steve Gottlieb; 121 Catherine Karnow/Woodfin Camp, Inc.; 122-123 Steve Gottlieb; 123,124 Robert Shafer; 125L Steve Gottlieb; 125R,126,127 Michael Richman, VA; 128T,C Steve Gottlieb; 128B Michael Richman; 128-129 Steve Gottlieb; 130 Michael Richman collection; 131T Fred Ward/Black Star;

131B Michael Richman collection; 132 Michael Richman; 133 Robert Shafer; 134T Steve Gottlieb; 134B Jonathan Wallen; 135 Steve Gottlieb; 136,137 Michael Richman; 138 Duane Hincy; 138-139 Everett C. Johnson/Folio, Inc.

The National Mall: p.140 Dennis Brack/Black Star; 141,142 William Clark/NPS; 143T Steve Gottlieb; 143B Fred Ward/Black Star; 144 William Clark/NPS; 144-145 John Hoke/NPS; 145,146 William Clark/NPS; 147 Steve Gottlieb.

Treasures of the Smithsonian: p.148 Jeff Zaruba/Folio, Inc.; 149 Steve Gottlieb; 150B,150-151 Lautman Photography, DC; 151 Laurie Minor/SI; 152T Everett C. Johnson/Folio, Inc.; 152B NMAFA/SI; 152-153 Freer Gallery of Art/SI; 153T Arthur M. Sackler Gallery/SI; 154 NPG/SI; 155T NMAA/SI, gift of Harmon Foundation; 155B Linda Bartlett, DC; 156B Chip Clark/SI; 156-157 Everett C. Johnson/Folio, Inc.; 157T NMNH/SI; 157B From Edwards Park, *Treasures of the Smithsonian* ©1983, SI, photo by Aldo Tutino; 158T Walter P. Calahan/Folio, Inc.; 158B NMAH/SI; 159 Eric Long/SI; 160-161 Bill Weems/Woodfin Camp, Inc.; 162 Fred Ward/Black Star; 163 Hirshhorn Museum & Sculpture Garden/SI.

Capital Arts: pp.164-165 Robert Llewellyn, VA; 165 Walter P. Calahan/Folio, Inc.; 166T Lelia Hendren/Folio, Inc.; 166B Fred J. Maroon/Folio, Inc.; 167 Everett C. Johnson/Folio, Inc.; 168 Medford Taylor/Woodfin Camp, Inc.; 168-169 Dennis Brack/Black Star; 170 Fred J. Maroon/Folio, Inc.; 170-171 James Sugar/Black Star; 171 Michael Ventura/Folio, Inc.; 172 Everett C. Johnson/Folio, Inc.; 173 Frida Kahlo, *Between the Curtains (Self Portrait Dedicated to Trotsky)*, 1937, The National Women's Museum, DC, gift of the Honorable Clare Boothe Luce; 174 Walter P. Calahan/Folio, Inc.; 175L Augustus Renoir, *The Luncheon of the Boating Party*, The Phillips Collection, DC; 175R,176T Catherine Karnow/Woodfin Camp, Inc.; 176B Steve Gottlieb; 176-177 Lelia Hendren/Folio, Inc.; 178 Linda Bartlett; 179 Robert Shafer.

The Nation's Reading Rooms: pp.180-181 Robert Llewellyn; 181 Edward Clark/Folio, Inc.; 182 Rick Buettner/Folio, Inc.; 183 Fred J. Maroon/Folio, Inc.; 184 LC; 185 Fred J. Maroon; 187 Linda Bartlett; 188 Robert Shafer; 189 Stephen R. Brown/Folio, Inc. 190-191 Lelia Hendren/Folio, Inc.

Hail to the Redskins: p.192 Steve Weber/Folio, Inc.; 193 Walter P. Calahan/Folio, Inc.; 194,194-95 National Football League/Hall of Fame, CA; 196 Bettmann Archive; 197T Al Messerschmidt/Folio, Inc.; 197B Richard Thompson, MD; 198T Al Messerschmidt/Folio, Inc.; 198B Greg Gibson/Wide World Photos; 199 Steve Gottlieb.

Washington Architecture: p.200 Patricia Fisher/Folio, Inc.; 201,202,203TR Robert Shafer; 203BL Mimi Levine/Folio, Inc.; 204 Roger Foley/Folio, Inc.; 205,206-207 Steve Gottlieb; 207 Robert Shafer; 208 Steve Gottlieb; 209T Michael Richman; 209B,210-211 Robert Shafer.

Washington on Foot: pp.212-213 Steve Gottlieb; 213 Walter P. Calahan/ Folio, Inc.; 214 Steve Gottlieb; 215T,B Sarah Hood, DC; 216 Ira Wexler/Folio, Inc.; 217 Rick Buettner/Folio, Inc.; 218-219 Dennis Brack/Black Star; 219 Steve Gottlieb; 221 Regis Lefebure/Folio, Inc.

Where the Wild Things Are: pp.222-223 Ed Castle/Folio, Inc.; 223,224T Milton H. Tierney, Jr., MD; 224B NZP/SI, photo by Jessie Cohen; 225T Lelia Hendren/Folio, Inc.; 225B Milton H. Tierney, Jr., MD; 226TR Milton H. Tierney, Jr., MD; 226TL,B John Trott, VA; 227T G. Frederick Stork/Folio, Inc.; 227B Sarah Hood; 228-229 Steve Gottlieb; 229 Courtesy J. Ethan Brent, Gloucester, VA.; 230 Lyle Rosbotham, MD; 231 Linda Bartlett/Folio, Inc.

ACKNOWLEDGMENTS

The Editors of Smithsonian Books would like to thank the following people for their assistance in the preparation of this book:

The staff of Smithsonian Institution Libraries; Lonnie G. Bunch III, Division of Political History, National Museum of American History (SI); Mary Ellen McCaffrey, Office of Printing & Photographic Services (SI); Steven C. Newsome, Lauri Hinksman, Harold Dorwin, Anacostia Museum (SI); J. Ethan Brent; Michael Cooper, Photo Duplication, and Sam Daniel, Prints & Photographs Division, Library of Congress; Michael Diamond, O'Toole, Rothwell, Nassau & Steinbach; Anne DuVivier; Robert Elwood; Timothy E. Foote; Bob Ford, Bill Yeaman, and Peggy Fleming, Rock Creek Park; James M. Goode; Steve Gottlieb; Lisa Hartjens, Imagefinders, Inc.; John Hedidian, Center for Urban Ecology; Jonathan Heller, National Archives; Carol M. Highsmith Photography; the staff of the Historical Society of Washington, D.C.; Sarah Hood; James O. Horton; Mary Lou Hultgren, Hampton University Museum; Kathy Kim, Smithsonian Collection of Recordings; Walter McDowell, Kenilworth Aquatic Gardens; the staff of the Washingtoniana Division and the *Washington Star* Collection, Martin Luther King Memorial Library; Mike Morgan, John Seidensticker, and Charlie Pickett, National Zoological Park; Michael Richman; Robin Richman; Cathy Sachs, Woodfin Camp, Inc.; Robert Scurlock, Scurlock Studio; Robert Shafer; Kathryn Schneider Smith, *Washington History;* Susan Soroko, Folio, Inc.; Frances Turgeon, Kiplinger Washington Collection.

Suppliers:
Jerry Benitez, Stanford Paper Company; Christopher P. Boehmcke, The Press, Inc.; Anthony Collins, Dale Fries, Simon Gore-Grimes, Colotone Graphics, Inc.; Stephanie Garber, Wetvaco; Bob Jillson, Holliston Mills, Inc.; Lynne and Don Komai, Marcelle Szurley, Don Wheeler, Watermark Design Office; William Liddell, Creative Automation Company; John McGough, TempoGraphics, Inc.; Cliff Mears, Shirley Schulz, R.R. Donnelley & Sons Company; Robert J. Muma, Allen Envelope Corporation; Robert Volkert, Calmark, Inc.

Washington D.C.: A Smithsonian Book of the Nation's Capital was designed and typeset by the Watermark Design Office, Alexandria, Virginia, with Quark XPress on an Apple Macintosh FX computer. The text type is 10.5 point ITC New Baskerville, with Helvetica Light Condensed for captions. Colotone Graphics, Branford, Connecticut, provided picture separation, type output, and film preparation. R.R. Donnelley & Sons Company printed the text on a four-color web press, printed the jackets on a sheet-fed press, and notch-bound the book at their manufacturing plant in Willard, Ohio. Text paper is 70-pound Somerset Web Gloss, the endsheets are Process Materials 80-pound Multicolor Antique, and the bookcloth is Holliston Kingston Natural Finish.